A Cool Brisk Walk
Through Discrete Mathematics

version 2.2

Stephen Davies, Ph.D.
Computer Science Department
University of Mary Washington

Copyright © 2023 Stephen Davies.

University of Mary Washington
Department of Computer Science
James Farmer Hall
1301 College Avenue
Fredericksburg, VA 22401

Permission is granted to copy, distribute, transmit and adapt this work under a Creative Commons Attribution-ShareAlike 4.0 International License:

http://creativecommons.org/licenses/by-sa/4.0/

The accompanying materials at www.allthemath.org are also under this license.

If you are interested in distributing a commercial version of this work, please contact the author at stephen@umw.edu.

The LaTeXsource for this book is available from: https://github.com/rockladyeagles/cool-brisk-walk.

Cover art copyright © 2014 Elizabeth M. Davies.

Contents at a glance

Contents at a glance   i

Preface   iii

Acknowledgements   v

1   Meetup at the trailhead   1

2   Sets   7

3   Relations   35

4   Probability   59

5   Structures   85

6   Counting   139

7   Numbers   163

8   Logic   195

9   Proof   221

Also be sure to check out the forever-free-and-open-source instructional videos that accompany this series, at `www.allthemath.org`!

Preface

Discrete math is a popular book topic — start Googling around and you'll find a zillion different textbooks about it. Take a closer look, and you'll discover that most of these are pretty thick, dense volumes packed with lots of equations and proofs. They're principled approaches, written by mathematicians and (seemingly) to mathematicians. I speak with complete frankness when I say I'm comforted to know that the human race is well covered in this area. We need smart people who can derive complex expressions and prove theorems from scratch, and I'm glad we have them.

Your average computer science practitioner, however, might be better served by a different approach. There are elements to the discrete math mindset that a budding software developer needs experience with. This is why discrete math is (properly, I believe) part of the mandatory curriculum for most computer science undergraduate programs. But for future programmers and engineers, the emphasis should be different than it is for mathematicians and researchers in computing theory. A practical computer scientist mostly needs to be able to *use* these tools, not to *derive* them. She needs familiarity, and practice, with the fundamental concepts and the thought processes they involve. The number of times the average software developer will need to construct a proof in graph theory is probably near zero. But the times she'll find it useful to reason about probability, logic, or the properties of collections are frequent.

I believe the majority of computer science students benefit most from simply gaining an appreciation for the richness and rigor of this material, what it means, and how it impacts their discipline. Becoming an expert theorem prover is not required, nor is deriving closed-form expressions for the sizes of trees with esoteric properties. Basic fluency with each topic area, and an intuition about when it can be applied, is the proper aim for most of those who would go forward and build tomorrow's technology.

To this end, the book in your hands is a quick guided tour of introductory-level discrete mathematics. It's like a cool, brisk walk through a pretty forest. I point out the notable features of the landscape and try to instill a sense of appreciation and even of awe. I want the reader to get a feel for the lay of the land, and a little exercise. If the student acquires the requisite vocabulary, gets some practice playing with the toys, and learns to start thinking in terms of the concepts here described, I will count it as a success.

Acknowledgements

A hearty thanks to Karen Anewalt, Crystal Burson, Prafulla Giri, Tayyar Hussain, Jennifer Magee, Veena Ravishankar, Jacob Shtabnoy, and a decade's worth of awesome UMW Computer Science students for their many suggestions and corrections to make this text better!

Chapter 1

Meetup at the trailhead

Before we set out on our "cool, brisk walk," let's get oriented. What *is* discrete mathematics, anyway? Why is it called that? What does it encompass? And what is it good for?

Let's take the two words of the subject, in reverse order. First, *math*. When most people hear "math," they think "numbers." After all, isn't math the study of quantity? And isn't that the class where we first learned to count, add, and multiply?

Mathematics certainly has its root in the study of numbers — specifically, the "natural numbers" (the integers from 1 on up) that fascinated the ancient Greeks. Yet math is broader than this, almost to the point where numbers can be considered a special case of something deeper. In this book, when we talk about trees, sets, or formal logic, there might not be a number in sight.

Math is about **abstract, conceptual objects that have properties, and the implications of those properties.** An "object" can be any kind of "thought material" that we can define and reason about precisely. Much of math deals with questions like, "suppose we defined a certain kind of thing that had certain attributes. What would be the implications of this, if we reasoned it all the way out?" The "thing" may or may not be numerical, whatever it turns out to be. Like a number, however, it will be crisply defined, have certain known aspects to it, and be capable of combining with other things in some way.

Fundamental to math is that it deals with the *abstract*. Abstract, which is the opposite of concrete, essentially means something that can't be perceived with the senses. A computer chip is concrete: you can touch it, you can see it. A number is not; nor is a function, a binary tree, or a logical implication. The only way to perceive these things is with the power of the mind. We will write expressions and draw pictures of many of our mathematical structures in order to help visualize them, and nearly everything we study will have practical applications whereby the abstractness gets grounded in concreteness for some useful purpose. But the underlying mathematical entity remains abstract and ethereal — only accessible to the mind's eye. We may use a pencil to form the figure "5" on a piece of paper, but that is only a concrete manifestation of the underlying concept of "five-ness." Don't mistake the picture or the symbol for the thing itself, which always transcends any mere physical representation.

The other word in the name of our subject is "discrete" (not to be confused with "discreet," which means something else entirely). The best way to appreciate what discrete means is to contrast it with its opposite, continuous. Consider the following list:

Discrete	Continuous
whole numbers ($\mathbb{Z}$)	real numbers ($\mathbb{R}$)
int	double
digital	analog
quantum	continuum
counting	measuring
number theory	analysis
Σ	$\int$
—	$\frac{d}{dx}$

What do the left-hand entries have in common? They describe things that are measured in crisp, distinct intervals, rather than varying smoothly over a range. Discrete things jump suddenly from position to position, with rigid precision. If you're 5 feet tall, you might some day grow to 5.3 feet; but though there might be 5 people in your family, there will never be 5.3 of them (although there could be 6 someday).

The last couple of entries on this list are worth a brief comment. They are math symbols, some of which you may be familiar with. On the right side — in the continuous realm — are $\int$ and $\frac{d}{dx}$, which you'll remember if you've taken calculus. They stand for the two fundamental operations of integration and differentiation. Integration, which can be thought of as finding "the area under a curve," is basically a way of adding up a whole infinite bunch of numbers over some range. When you "integrate the function x^2 from 3 to 5," you're really adding up all the tiny, tiny little vertical slivers that comprise the area from $x = 3$ on the left to $x = 5$ on the right. Its corresponding entry in the left-column of the table is Σ, which is just a short-hand for "sum up a bunch of things." Integration and summation are equivalent operations, it's just that when you integrate, you're adding up all the (infinitely many) slivers across the real-line continuum. When you sum, you're adding up a fixed sequence of entries, one at a time, like in a loop. Σ is just the discrete "version" of $\int$.

The same sort of relationship holds between ordinary subtraction ("−") and differentiation ($\frac{d}{dx}$). If you've plotted a bunch of discrete points on x-y axes, and you want to find the slope between two of them, you just subtract their y values and divide by the (x) distance between them. If you have a smooth continuous function, on the other hand, you use differentiation to find the slope at a point: this is essentially subtracting the tiny tiny difference between two supremely close points and then dividing by the distance between them. Thus subtraction is just the discrete "version" of $\frac{d}{dx}$.

Don't worry, you don't need to have fully understood any of the integration or differentiation stuff I just talked about, or even to have taken calculus yet. I'm just trying to give you some feel for what "discrete" means, and how the dichotomy between discrete and continuous really runs through all of math and computer science. In this book, we will mostly be focusing on discrete values and structures, which turn out to be of more use in computer science. That's partially because as you probably know, computers themselves are discrete, and can only store and compute discrete values. There can be many of them — megabytes, gigabytes, terabytes — but each value stored is fundamentally comprised of bits, each of which has a value of either 0 or 1. This is unlike the human brain, by the way, whose neuronal synapses communicate based on the *continuous* quantities of chemicals present in their axons. So I guess "computer" and "brain" are another pair of entries we could add to our discrete vs. continuous list.

There's another reason, though, why discrete math is of more use to computer scientists than continuous math is, beyond just the bits-and-bytes thing. Simply put, computers operate algorithmically. They carry out programs in step-by-step, iterative fashion. First do this, then do that, then move on to something else. This mechanical execution, like the ticking of a clock, permeates everything the computer can do, and everything we can tell it to do. At a given moment in time, the computer *has* completed step 7, but *not* step 8; it has accumulated 38 values, but not yet 39; its database has exactly 15 entries in it, no more and no less; it knows that after accepting this friend request, there will be exactly 553 people in your set of friends. The whole paradigm behind reasoning about computers and their programs is discrete, and that's why we computer scientists find different problems worth thinking about than most of the world did a hundred years ago.

But it's still math. It's just *discrete* math. There's a lot to come, so limber up and let me know when you're ready to hit the road.

1.1 Exercises

Use an index card or a piece of paper folded lengthwise, and cover up the right-hand column of the exercises below. Read each exercise in the left-hand column, answer it in your mind, then slide the index card down to reveal the answer and see if you're right! For every exercise you missed, figure out why you missed it before moving on.

1.1. EXERCISES

1. What's the opposite of concrete?	Abstract.
2. What's the opposite of discrete?	Continuous.
3. Consider a quantity of water in a glass. Would you call it abstract, or concrete? Discrete, or continuous?	Concrete, since it's a real entity you can experience with the senses. Continuous, since it could be any number of ounces (or liters, or tablespoons, or whatever). The amount of water certainly doesn't have to be an integer. (Food for thought: since all matter is ultimately comprised of atoms, are even substances like water discrete?)
4. Consider the number 27. Would you call it abstract, or concrete? Discrete, or continuous?	Abstract, since you can't see or touch or smell "twenty-seven." Probably discrete, since it's an integer, and when we think of whole numbers we think "discrete." (Food for thought: in real life, how would you know whether I meant the integer "27" or the decimal number "27.0?" And does it matter?)
5. Consider a bit in a computer's memory. Would you call it abstract, or concrete? Discrete, or continuous?	Clearly it's discrete. Abstract vs. concrete, though, is a little tricky. If we're talking about the actual transistor and capacitor that's physically present in the hardware, holding a tiny charge in some little chip, then it's concrete. But if we're talking about the value "1" that is conceptually part of the computer's currently executing state, then it's really abstract just like 27 was. In this book, we'll always be talking about bits in this second, abstract sense.
6. If math isn't just about numbers, what else is it about?	Any kind of abstract object that has properties we can reason about.

Chapter 2

Sets

The place from which we'll start our walk is a body of mathematics called "set theory." Set theory has an amazing property: it's so simple and applicable that almost all the rest of mathematics can be based on it! This is all the more remarkable because set theory itself came along pretty late in the game (as things go) — it was singlehandedly invented by one brilliant man, Georg Cantor, in the 1870's. That may seem like a long time ago, but consider that by the time Cantor was born, mankind had already accumulated an immense wealth of mathematical knowledge: everything from geometry to algebra to calculus to prime numbers. Set theory was so elegant and universal, though, that after it was invented, nearly everything in math was redefined from the ground up to be couched in the language of sets. It turns out that this simple tool is an amazingly powerful way to reason about mathematical concepts of all flavors. Thus everything else in this book stands on set theory as a foundation.

Cantor, by the way, went insane as he tried to extend set theory to fully encompass the concept of infinity. Don't let that happen to you.

2.1 The idea of a set

A **set** is a selection of certain things out of a (normally larger) group. When we talk about a set, we're declaring that certain specific items from that group are *in* the set, and certain items are *not* in the set. There's no shades of gray: every element is either in or out.

For instance, maybe the overall group I'm considering is my family, which consists of five people: Dad, Mom, Lizzy, T.J., and Johnny. We could define one set — call it A — that contains Dad and Lizzy, but not the other three. Another set B might have Lizzy, T.J., and Johnny in it, but not the two parents. The set C might have Dad and *only* Dad in it. The set D might have all five Davieses, and the set E might have nobody at all. *Etc.* You can see that every set is just a way of specifying which elements are in and which are out.

Normally a set will be based on some property of its members, rather than just being some random assortment of elements. That's what makes it worth thinking about. For example, the set P (for "parents") might be "all the Davieses who are parents": this set would contain Dad and Mom, and no one else. The set F (for "female") might be declared as the female members, and contain Mom and Lizzy. The set H (for "humans") would contain all five elements of the group. And so on.

As with most of math, it turns out to be useful to define symbols for these concepts, because then we can talk about them more precisely and concisely. We normally list the members of a set using curly braces, like this:

$$A = \{ \text{Dad}, \text{Lizzy} \}$$

or

$$B = \{ \text{Lizzy}, \text{T.J.}, \text{Johnny} \}$$

Note that it doesn't matter what order you list the members in. The set F of females contains Mom and Lizzy, but it's not like Mom is the "first" female or anything. That doesn't even make any sense. There is no "first." A set's members are all equally

2.1. THE IDEA OF A SET

members. So P is the same whether we write it like this:

$$P = \{ \text{ Dad}, \text{Mom } \}$$

or this:

$$P = \{ \text{ Mom}, \text{Dad } \}.$$

Those are just two different ways of writing the same thing.

The set E that had nobody in it can be written like this, of course:

$$E = \{ \, \}$$

but we sometimes use this special symbol instead:

$$E = \varnothing.$$

However you write it, this kind of set (one that has no elements) is referred to as an **empty set**.

The set H, above, contained *all* the members of the group under consideration. Sometimes we'll refer to "the group under consideration" as the "domain of discourse." It too is a set, and we usually use the symbol Ω to refer to it.[1] So in this case,

$$\Omega = \{ \text{ Mom}, \text{Johnny}, \text{T.J.}, \text{Dad}, \text{Lizzy } \}.$$

Another symbol we'll use a lot is "$\in$", which means "is a member of." Since Lizzy is a female, we can write:

$$\text{Lizzy} \in F$$

to show that Lizzy is a member of the F set. Conversely, we write:

$$\text{T.J.} \notin F$$

to show that T.J. is not.

As an aside, I mentioned that every item is either in, or not in, a set: there are no shades of gray. Interestingly, researchers have developed another body of mathematics called (I kid you not) "fuzzy

---

[1] Some authors use the symbol U for this, and call it the "universal set."

set theory." Fuzzy sets change this membership assumption: items can indeed be "partially in" a set. One could declare, for instance, that Dad is "10% female," which means he's only 10% in the F set. That might or might not make sense for gender, but you can imagine that if we defined a set T of "the tall people," such a notion might be useful. At any rate, this example illustrates a larger principle which is important to understand: in math, things are the way they are simply because we've decided it's useful to think of them that way. If we decide there's a different useful way to think about them, we can define new assumptions and proceed according to new rules. It doesn't make any sense to say "sets are (or aren't) *really* fuzzy": because there is no "really." All mathematics proceeds from whatever mathematicians have decided is useful to define, and any of it can be changed at any time if we see fit.

2.2 Defining sets

There are two ways to define a set: **extensionally** and **intensionally**[2]. I'm not saying there are two kinds of sets: rather, there are simply two *ways to specify* a set.

To define a set extensionally is to list its actual members. That's what we did when we said $P = \{$ Dad, Mom $\}$, above. In this case, we're not giving any "meaning" to the set; we're just mechanically spelling out what's in it. The elements Dad and Mom are called the *extension* of the set P.

The other way to specify a set is intensionally, which means to describe its meaning. Another way to think of this is specifying a rule by which it can be determined whether or not a given element is in the set. If I say "Let P be the set of all parents," I am defining P intensionally. I haven't explicitly said which specific elements of the set are in P. I've just given the meaning of the set, from which you can figure out the extension. We call "parent-ness" the *intension* of P.

---

[2]Spelling nit: "intensionally" has an 's' in it. "Intentionally," meaning "deliberately," is a completely different word.

2.2. DEFINING SETS

Note that two sets with different intensions might nevertheless have the same extension. Suppose O is "the set of all people over 25 years old" and R is "the set of all people who wear wedding rings." If our Ω is the Davies family, then O and R have the same extension (namely, Mom and Dad). They have different intensions, though: conceptually speaking, they're describing different things. One could imagine a world in which older people don't all wear wedding rings, or one in which some younger people do. Within the domain of discourse of the Davies family, however, the extensions happen to coincide.

Fact: we say two sets are equal *if they have the same extension.* This might seem unfair to intensionality, but that's the way it is. So it is totally legit to write:

$$O = R$$

since by the definition of set equality, they are in fact equal. I thought this was weird at first, but it's really no weirder than saying "the number of years the Civil War lasted = Brett Favre's jersey number when he played for the Packers." The things on the left and right side of that equals sign refer conceptually to two very different things, but that doesn't stop them from both having the value 4, and thus being equal.

By the way, we sometimes use the curly brace notation in combination with a colon to define a set intensionally. Consider this:

$$M = \{\, k : k \text{ is between 1 and 20, and a multiple of 3} \,\}.$$

When you reach a colon, pronounce it as "such that." So this says "M is the set of all numbers k such that k is between 1 and 20, and a multiple of 3." (There's nothing special about k, here; I could have picked any letter.) This is an intensional definition, since we haven't listed the specific numbers in the set, but rather given a rule for finding them. Another way to specify this set would be to write
$$M = \{\, 3, 6, 9, 12, 15, 18 \,\}$$

which is an extensional definition of the same set.

Interesting thought experiment: what happens if you enlarge the intension of a set by adding conditions to it? Answer: increasing the intension *decreases* the extension. For example, suppose M is initially defined as the set of all males (in the Davies family). Now suppose I decide to add to that intension by making it the set of all *adult* males. By adding to the intension, I have now reduced the extension from { Dad, T.J., Johnny } to just { Dad }. The reverse is true as well: trimming down the intension by removing conditions effectively increases the extension of the set. Changing "all male persons" to just "all persons" includes Mom and Lizzy in the mix.

2.3 Finite and infinite sets

Sets can have an infinite number of members. That doesn't make sense for the Davies family example, but for other things it does, of course, like:

$$I = \{\ k : k \text{ is a multiple of 3 }\}.$$

Obviously there are infinitely many multiples of 3, and so I has an unlimited number of members. Not surprisingly, we call I an **infinite set**. More surprisingly, it turns out that there are different *sizes* of infinite sets, and hence different *kinds* of infinity. For instance, even though there are infinitely many whole numbers, and also infinitely many real (decimal) numbers, there are nevertheless *more* real numbers than whole numbers. This is the thing that drove Cantor insane, so we won't discuss it more here. For now, just realize that every set is either finite or infinite.

You might think, by the way, that there's no way to define an infinite set extensionally, since that would require infinite paper. This isn't true, though, if we creatively use an ellipsis:

$$I = \{\ 3, 6, 9, 12, 15, \ldots\ \}$$

This is an extensional definition of I, since we're explicitly listing all the members. It could be argued, though, that it's really intensional, since the interpretation of "..." requires the reader to figure out the rule and mentally apply it to all remaining numbers. Perhaps in reality we are giving an intensional definition, cloaked in an extensional-looking list of members. I'm on the fence here.

2.4 Sets are not arrays

If you've done some computer programming, you might see a resemblance between sets and the collections of items often used in a program: arrays, perhaps, or linked lists. To be sure, there are some similarities. But there are also some very important differences, which must not be overlooked:

- **No order.** As previously mentioned, there is no order to the members of a set. "{Dad, Mom}" is the same set as "{Mom, Dad}". In a computer program, of course, most arrays or lists have first, second, and last elements, and an index number assigned to each.

- **No duplicates.** Suppose M is the set of all males. What would it possibly mean to say $M = \{$T.J., T.J., Johnny$\}$? Would that mean that "T.J. is twice the man that Johnny is"? This is obviously nonsensical. The set M is based on a property: maleness. Each element of Ω is either male, or it isn't. It can't be "male three times." Again, in an array or linked list, you could certainly have more than one copy of the same item in different positions.

- **Infinite sets.** 'Nuff said. I've never seen an array with infinitely many elements, and neither will you.

- **Untyped.** Most of the time, an array or other collection in a computer program contains elements of only a single *type*: it's an array of integers, or a linked list of `Customer` objects, for example. This is important because the program often needs to treat all elements in the collection the same way. Perhaps it needs to loop over the array to add up all the numbers, or iterate through a customer list and search for customers who have not placed an order in the last six months. The program would run into problems if it tried to add a string of text to its cumulative total, or encountered a `Product` object in the middle of its list of `Customer`s. Sets, though, can be **heterogeneous**, meaning they can contain different kinds of things. The Davies family example had all human beings, but nothing stops me from creating a set $X = \{$ Jack Nicholson, Kim Kardashian, Universal Studios, 5786, ★ $\}$.

I don't press this point too hard for a couple of reasons. First, most programming languages do allow heterogeneous collections of some sort, even if they're not the most natural thing to express. In Java, you can define an `ArrayList` as a non-generic so that it simply holds items of class "`Object`." In C, you can have an array of `void *`'s — pointers to some unspecified type — which allows your array to point to different kinds of things. Unless it's a loosely-typed language, though (like Perl or JavaScript), it sort of feels like you're bending over backwards to do this. The other reason I make this distinction lightly is that when we're dealing with sets, we often *do* find it useful to deal with things of only one type, and so our Ω ends up being **homogeneous** anyway.

Perhaps the biggest thing to remember here is that a set is a purely abstract concept, whereas an array is a concrete, tangible, explicit list. When we talk about sets, we're reasoning in general about large conceptual things, whereas when we deal with arrays, we're normally iterating through them for some specific purpose. You can't iterate through a set very easily because (1) there's no order to the members, and (2) there might well be infinitely many of them anyway.

2.5 Sets are not ordered pairs (or tuples)

You'll remember from high school algebra the notion of an **ordered pair** (x, y). We dealt with those when we wanted to specify a point to plot on a graph: the first coordinate gave the distance from the origin on the x-axis, and the second coordinate on the y-axis. Clearly an ordered pair is not a set, because as the name implies it is ordered: $(3, -4) \neq (-4, 3)$. For this reason, we'll be very careful to use curly braces to denote sets, and parentheses to denote ordered pairs.

By the way, although the word "coordinate" is often used to describe the elements of an ordered pair, that's really a geometry-centric word that implies a visual plot of some kind. Normally we won't be plotting elements like that, but we will still have use to deal with ordered pairs. I'll just call the constituent parts "elements" to make it more general.

Three-dimensional points need **ordered triple**s (x, y, z), and it doesn't take a rocket scientist to deduce that we could extend this to any number of elements. The question is what to call them, and you *do* sort of sound like a rocket scientist (or other generic nerd) when you say **tuple**. (Some people rhyme this word with "Drupal," and others with "couple," by the way, and there seems to be no consensus). If you have an ordered-pair-type thing with 5 elements, therefore, it's a 5-tuple (or a quintuple). If it has 117 elements, it's a 117-tuple, and there's really nothing else to call it. The general term (if we don't know or want to specify how many elements) is **n-tuple**. In any case, it's an ordered sequence of elements that may contain duplicates, so it's very different than a set.

2.6 Sets of sets

Sets are heterogeneous — a single set can contain four universities, seven integers, and an ahi tuna — and so it might occur to you that they can contain other *sets* as well. This is indeed true, but let me issue a stern warning: you can get in deep water very quickly when you start thinking about "sets of sets." In 1901, in fact, the philosopher Bertrand Russell pointed out that this idea can lead to unresolvable contradictions unless you put some constraints on it. What became known as "Russell's Paradox" famously goes as follows: consider the set R of all sets that do *not* have themselves as members[3]. Now is R a member of itself, or isn't it? Either way you answer turns out to be wrong (try it!) which means that this whole setup must be flawed at some level.

The good news is that as long as you don't deal with this kind of self-referential loop ("containing yourself as a member") then it's pretty safe to try at home. Consider this set:

$$V = \{\ 3, 5, \{\ 5, 4\ \}, 2\ \}.$$

This set has *four* (not five) members. Three of V's members are integers: 2, 3, and 5. The other one is a set (with no name given). That other set, by the way, has two members of its own: 4 and 5. If you were asked, "is $4 \in V$"? the answer would be *no*.

As a corollary to this, there's a difference between

$$\varnothing$$

and

$$\{\ \varnothing\ \}.$$

The former is a set with no elements. The latter is a set with *one* element: and that element just happens to be a set with nothing in it.

2.7 Cardinality

When we talk about the number of elements in a set, we use the word **cardinality**. You'd think we could just call it the "size" of the set, but mathematicians sometimes like words that sound cool. The cardinality of M (the set of males, where the Davies family is the domain of discourse) is 3, because there are three elements in it. The cardinality of the empty set $\varnothing$ is 0. The cardinality of the set of all integers is ∞. Simple as that.

---

[3]For instance, the set Z of all zebras is a member of R, since Z itself is a set (not a zebra) and so $Z \notin Z$. The set S, on the other hand, defined as "the set of all sets mentioned in this book," is *not* a member of R, since S contains itself as a member.

The notation we use for cardinality is vertical bars, like with absolute value. So we write: $|M| = 3$.

To restate the example immediately above, $|\varnothing| = 0$, but $|\{\varnothing\}| = 1$.

2.8 Some special sets

In addition to the empty set, there are symbols for some other common sets, including:

- $\mathbb{Z}$ — the integers (positive, negative, and zero)

- $\mathbb{N}$ — the natural numbers (positive integers and zero)

- $\mathbb{Q}$ — the rational numbers (all numbers that can be expressed as an integer divided by another integer)

- $\mathbb{R}$ — the real numbers (all numbers that aren't imaginary, even decimal numbers that aren't rational)

The cardinality of all these sets is infinity, although as I alluded to previously, $|\mathbb{R}|$ is in some sense "greater than" $|\mathbb{N}|$. For the curious, we say that $\mathbb{N}$ is a **countably infinite** set, whereas $|\mathbb{R}|$ is **uncountably infinite**. Speaking very loosely, this can be thought of this way: if we start counting up all the natural numbers 0, 1, 2, 3, 4, ..., we will never get to the end of them. But *at least we can start counting*. With the real numbers, we can't even get off the ground. Where do you begin? Starting with 0 is fine, but then what's the "next" real number? Choosing anything for your second number inevitably skips a lot in between. Once you've digested this, I'll spring another shocking truth on you: $|\mathbb{Q}|$ is actually *equal* to $|\mathbb{N}|$, not greater than it as $|\mathbb{R}|$ is. Cantor came up with an ingenious numbering scheme whereby all the rational numbers — including 3, -9, $\frac{4}{17}$, and $-\frac{1517}{29}$ — can be listed off regularly, in order, just like the integers can. And so $|\mathbb{Q}| = |\mathbb{N}| \neq |\mathbb{R}|$. This kind of stuff can blow your mind.

2.9 Combining sets

Okay, so we have sets. Now what can we do with them? When you first learn about numbers back before kindergarten, the next thing you learn is how to combine numbers using various operations to produce other numbers. These include $+, -, \times, \div$, exponents, roots, *etc.* Sets, too, have operations that are useful for combining to make other sets. These include:

- **Union** ($\cup$). The union of two sets is a set that includes the elements that *either (or both)* of them have as members. For instance, if $A = \{$ Dad, Lizzy $\}$, and $B = \{$ Lizzy, T.J., Johnny $\}$, then $A \cup B = \{$ Dad, Lizzy, T.J., Johnny $\}$. Note that an element is in the union if it is in A *or* B. For this reason, there is a strong relationship between the union operator of sets and the "or" ($\vee$) operator of boolean logic that we'll see later.

- **Intersection** ($\cap$). The intersection of two sets is a set that includes the elements that *both* of them have as members. In the above example, $A \cap B = \{$ Lizzy $\}$. There is a strong connection between intersection and the "and" ($\wedge$) boolean logic operator.

- **(Partial) complement** ($-$). Looks like subtraction, but significantly different. $A - B$ contains *the elements from A that are not also in B*. So you start with A, and then "subtract off" the contents of B, if they occur. In the above example, $A - B = \{$ Dad $\}$. (Note that T.J. and Johnny didn't really enter in to the calculation.) Unlike $\cup$ and $\cap$, $-$ is not **commutative**. This means it's not symmetrical: $A - B$ doesn't (normally) give the same answer as $B - A$. In this example, $B - A$ is $\{$ T.J., Johnny $\}$, whereas if you ever reverse the operands with union or intersection, you'll always get the same result as before.

- **(Total) complement** ($\overline{X}$). Same as the partial complement, above, except that the implied first operand is Ω. In other words, $A - B$ is "all the things in A that aren't in B," whereas

$\overline{B}$ is "all the things *period* that aren't in B." Of course, "all the things period" means "all the things that we're currently talking about." The domain of discourse Ω is very important here. If we're talking about the Davies family, we would say that $\overline{M} = \{$ Mom, Lizzy $\}$, because those are all the Davieses who aren't male. If, on the other hand, Ω is "the grand set of absolutely everything," then not only is Mom a member of $\overline{M}$, but so is the number 12, the French Revolution, and my nightmare last Tuesday about a rabid platypus.

- **Cartesian product** ($\times$). Looks like multiplication, but *very* different. When you take the Cartesian product of two sets A and B, you don't even get the elements from the sets in the result. Instead, you get *ordered pairs* of elements. These ordered pairs represent each combination of an element from A and an element from B. For instance, suppose $A = \{$ Bob, Dave $\}$ and $B = \{$ Jenny, Gabrielle, and Tiffany $\}$. Then:

    $A \times B = \{$ (Bob, Jenny), (Bob, Gabrielle), (Bob, Tiffany), (Dave, Jenny), (Dave, Gabrielle), (Dave, Tiffany) $\}$.

    Study that list. The first thing to realize is that it consists of neither guys nor girls, but of ordered pairs. (Clearly, for example, Jenny $\notin A \times B$.) Every guy appears exactly once with every girl, and the guy is always the first element of the ordered pair. Since we have two guys and three girls, there are six elements in the result, which is an easy way to remember the $\times$ sign that represents Cartesian product. (Do not, however, make the common mistake of thinking that $A \times B$ *is* 6. $A \times B$ is a set, not a number. The cardinality of the set, of course, is 6, so it's appropriate to write $|A \times B| = 6$.)

Laws of combining sets

There are a bunch of handy facts that arise when combining sets using the above operators. The important thing is that these are all easily seen just by thinking about them for a moment. Put another way, *these aren't facts to memorize; they're facts to look at and see for yourself.* They're just a few natural consequences of the way we've defined sets and operations, and there are many others.

- **Union and intersection are commutative.** As noted above, it's easy to see that $A \cup B$ will always give the same result as $B \cup A$. Same goes for $\cap$. (Not true for $-$, though.)

- **Union and intersection are associative.** "Associative" means that if you have an operator repeated several times, left to right, it doesn't matter which order you evaluate them in. $(A \cup B) \cup C$ will give the same result as $A \cup (B \cup C)$. This means we can freely write expressions like "$X \cup Y \cup Z$" and no one can accuse us of being ambiguous. This is also true if you have three (or more) intersections in a row. Be careful, though: associativity does *not* hold if you have unions and intersections mixed together. If I write $A \cup B \cap C$ it matters very much whether I do the union first or the intersection first. This is just how it works with numbers: $4 + 3 \times 2$ gives either 10 or 14 depending on the order of operations. In algebra, we learned that $\times$ has precedence over $+$, and you'll always do that one first in the absence of parentheses. We could establish a similar order for set operations, but we won't: we'll always make it explicit with parens.

- **Union and intersection are distributive.** You'll recall from basic algebra that $a \cdot (b + c) = ab + ac$. Similarly with sets,

$$X \cap (Y \cup Z) = (X \cap Y) \cup (X \cap Z).$$

It's important to work this out for yourself rather than just memorize it as a rule. Why does it work? Well, take a concrete example. Suppose X is the set of all female students, Y is the set of all computer science majors, and Z is the set of all math majors. (Some students, of course, double-major in both.) The left-hand side of the equals sign says "first take all the math and computer science majors and put them in a group. Then, intersect that group with the women to extract only the female students." The result is "women who are either computer science majors or math majors (or both)."

2.9. COMBINING SETS

Now look at the right-hand side. The first pair of parentheses encloses only female computer science majors. The right pair encloses female math majors. Then we take the union of the two, to get a group which contains only females, and specifically only the females who are computer science majors or math majors (or both). Clearly, the two sides of the equals sign have the same extension.

The distributive property in basic algebra doesn't work if you flip the times and plus signs (normally $a+b \cdot c \neq (a+b) \cdot (a+c)$), but remarkably it does here:

$$X \cup (Y \cap Z) = (X \cup Y) \cap (X \cup Z).$$

Using the same definitions of X, Y, and Z, work out the meaning of this one and convince yourself it's always true.

- **Identity laws.** Simplest thing you've learned all day: $X \cup \varnothing = X$ and $X \cap \Omega = X$. You don't change X by adding nothing to it, or taking nothing away from it.

- **Domination laws.** The flip side of the above is that $X \cup \Omega = \Omega$ and $X \cap \varnothing = \varnothing$. If you take X, and then add everything and the kitchen sink to it, you get everything and the kitchen sink. And if you restrict X to having nothing, it of course has nothing.

- **Complement laws.** $X \cup \overline{X} = \Omega$. This is another way of saying "everything (in the domain of discourse) is either in, or not in, a set." So if I take X, and then I take everything *not* in X, and smoosh the two together, I get everything. In a similar vein, $X \cap \overline{X} = \varnothing$, because there can't be any element that's both in X and not in X: that would be a contradiction. Interestingly, the first of these two laws has become controversial in modern philosophy. It's called "the law of the excluded middle," and is explicitly repudiated in many modern logic systems.

- **De Morgan's laws.** Now these are worth memorizing, if only because (1) they're incredibly important, and (2) they may not slip right off the tongue the way the previous properties do. The first one can be stated this way:

$$\overline{X \cup Y} = \overline{X} \cap \overline{Y}.$$

Again, it's best understood with a specific example. Let's say you're renting a house, and want to make sure you don't have any surly characters under the roof. Let X be the set of all known thieves. Let Y be the set of all known murderers. Now as a landlord, you don't want any thieves or murderers renting your property. So who are you willing to rent to? Answer: if Ω is the set of all people, you are willing to rent to $\overline{X \cup Y}$.

Why that? Because if you take $X \cup Y$, that gives you all the undesirables: people who are either murderers or thieves (or both). You don't want to rent to any of them. In fact, you want to rent to the *complement* of that set; namely, "anybody else." Putting an overbar on that expression gives you all the non-thieves and non-murderers.

Very well. But now look at the right hand side of the equation. $\overline{X}$ gives you the non-thieves. $\overline{Y}$ gives you the non-murderers. Now in order to get acceptable people, you want to rent only to someone who's *in both groups*. Put another way, they have to be both a non-thief and a non-murderer in order for you to rent to them. Therefore, they must be in the intersection of the non-thief group and the non-murderer group. Therefore, the two sides of this equation are the same.

The other form of De Morgan's law is stated by flipping the intersections and unions:

$$\overline{X \cap Y} = \overline{X} \cup \overline{Y}.$$

Work this one out for yourself using a similar example, and convince yourself it's always true.

Augustus De Morgan, by the way, was a brilliant 19th century mathematician with a wide range of interests. His name will come up again when we study logic and mathematical induction.

2.10 Subsets

We learned that the "$\in$" symbol is used to indicate set membership: the element on the left is a member of the set on the right. A related but distinct notion is the idea of a **subset**. When we say $X \subseteq Y$ (pronounced "X is a subset of Y"), it means that *every member of X is also a member of Y*. The reverse is not necessarily true, of course, otherwise "$\subseteq$" would just mean "=". So if $A = \{$ Dad, Lizzy $\}$ and $K = \{$ Dad, Mom, Lizzy $\}$, then we can say $A \subseteq K$.

Be careful about the distinction between "$\in$" and "$\subseteq$", which are often confused. With $\in$, the thing on the left is an *element*, whereas with $\subseteq$, the thing on the left is a set. This is further complicated by the fact that the element on the left-hand side of $\in$ might well *be* a set.

Let's give some examples. Suppose that Q is the set $\{$ 4, $\{$ 9, 4 $\}$, 2 $\}$. Q has three elements here, one of which is itself a set. Now suppose that we let P be the set $\{$ 4, 9 $\}$. Question: is $P \in Q$? The answer is yes: the set $\{$ 4, 9 $\}$ (which is the same as the set $\{$ 9, 4 $\}$, just written a different way) is in fact an element of the set Q. Next question: is $P \subseteq Q$? The answer is no, $P \nsubseteq Q$. If P were a subset of Q, that would imply that every member of P (there are two of them: 9 and 4) is also an element of Q, whereas in fact, only 4 is a member of Q, not 9. Last question: if R is defined to be $\{$ 2, 4 $\}$, is $R \subseteq Q$? The answer is yes, since both 2 and 4 are also members of Q.

Notice that by the definition, every set is a subset of itself. Sometimes, though, it's useful to talk about whether a set is really a *sub*set of another, and you don't want it to "count" if the two sets are actually equal. This is called a **proper subset**, and the symbol for it is $\subset$. You can see the rationale for the choice of symbol, because "$\subseteq$" is kind of like "$\leq$" for numbers, and "$\subset$" is like "$<$".

Every set is a subset (not necessarily a proper one) of Ω, because our domain of discourse by definition contains everything that can come up in conversation. Somewhat less obviously, the empty set is a subset of every set. It's weird to think that $\varnothing \subseteq Q$ when Q has several things in it, but the definition does hold. "Every" member of $\varnothing$ (there are none) is in fact also a member of Q.

One note about reading this notation that I found confusing at first. Sometimes the expression "$a \in X$" is pronounced "a is an element of X," but other times it is read "a, *which is* an element of X". This may seem like a subtle point, and I guess it is, but if you're not ready for it it can be a extra stumbling block to understanding the math (which is the last thing we need). Take this hypothetical (but quite typical) excerpt from a mathematical proof:

$$\text{"Suppose } k \in \mathbb{N} < 10 \ldots \text{"}$$

If you read this as "Suppose k *is* a natural number *is* less than 10," it's ungrammatical. It really should be understood as "Suppose k (which is a natural number) is less than 10." This is sometimes true of additional clauses as well. For instance, the phrase "Suppose $k \in \mathbb{R} > 0$ is the x-coordinate of the first point" should be read "Suppose k, *which is a real number greater than zero*, is the x-coordinate of the first point."

I'll leave you with a statement about numbers worth pondering and understanding:

$$\varnothing \subset \mathbb{N} \subset \mathbb{Z} \subset \mathbb{Q} \subset \mathbb{R} \subset \Omega.$$

2.11 Power sets

Power set is a curious name for a simple concept. We talk about the power set "of" another set, which is *the set of all subsets of that other set*. Example: suppose $A = \{$ Dad, Lizzy $\}$. Then the power set of A, which is written as "$\mathbb{P}(A)$" is: $\{$ $\{$ Dad, Lizzy $\}$, $\{$ Dad $\}$, $\{$ Lizzy $\}$, $\varnothing$ $\}$. Take a good look at all those curly braces, and

2.11. POWER SETS

don't lose any. There are four elements to the power set of A, each of which is one of the possible subsets. It might seem strange to talk about "*all* of the possible subsets" — when I first learned this stuff, I remember thinking at first that there would be no limit to the number of subsets you could make from a set. But of course there is. To create a subset, you can either include, or exclude, each one of the original set's members. In A's case, you can either (1) include both Dad and Lizzy, or (2) include Dad but not Lizzy, or (3) include Lizzy but not Dad, or (4) exclude both, in which case your subset is $\varnothing$. Therefore, $\mathbb{P}(A)$ includes all four of those subsets.

Now what's the cardinality of $\mathbb{P}(X)$ for some set X? That's an interesting question, and one well worth pondering. The answer ripples through the heart of a lot of combinatorics and the binary number system, topics we'll cover later. And the answer is right at our fingertips, if we just extrapolate from the previous example. To form a subset of X, we have a choice to either *in*clude, or else *ex*clude, each of its elements. So there's two choices for the first element[4], and then whether we choose to include or exclude that first element, there are two choices for the second. Regardless of what we choose for those first two, there are two choices for the third, *etc.* So if $|X| = 2$ (recall that this notation means "X has two elements" or "X has a cardinality of 2"), then its power set has 2×2 members. If $|X| = 3$, then its power set has $2 \times 2 \times 2$ members. In general:

$$|\mathbb{P}(X)| = 2^{|X|}.$$

As a limiting case (and a brain-bender) notice that if X is the empty set, then $\mathbb{P}(X)$ has *one* (not zero) members, because there is in fact *one* subset of the empty set: namely, the empty set itself. So $|X| = 0$, and $|\mathbb{P}(X)| = 1$. And that jives with the above formula.

---

[4] I know there's really no "first" element, but work with me here.

2.12 Partitions

Finally, there's a special variation on the subset concept called a **partition**. A partition is a group of subsets of another set that together are both **collectively exhaustive** and **mutually exclusive**. This means that every element of the original set is in *one and only one* of the sets in the partition. Formally, a partition of X is a group of sets $X_1, X_2, \ldots, X_n$ such that:

$$X_1 \cup X_2 \cup \cdots \cup X_n = X,$$

and

$$X_i \cap X_j = \varnothing \quad \text{for all } i, j.$$

So let's say we've got a group of subsets that are supposedly a partition of X. The first line, above, says that if we combine the contents of all of them, we get everything that's in X (and nothing more). This is called being collectively exhaustive. The second line says that no two of the sets have anything in common: they are mutually exclusive.

As usual, an example is worth a thousand words. Suppose the set D is { Dad, Mom, Lizzy, T.J., Johnny. } A partition is any way of dividing D up into subsets that meet the above conditions. One such partition is:

{ Lizzy, T.J. }, { Mom, Dad }, and { Johnny }.

Another one is:

{ Lizzy }, { T.J. }, { Mom }, and { Johnny, Dad }.

Yet another is:

$\varnothing$, $\varnothing$, { Lizzy, T.J., Johnny, Mom, Dad }, and $\varnothing$.

2.12. PARTITIONS

All of these are ways of dividing up the Davies family into groups so that no one is in more than one group, and everyone is in some group. The following is *not* a partition:

{ Mom, Lizzy, T.J. }, and { Dad }

because it leaves out Johnny. This, too, is *not* a partition:

{ Dad }, { Mom, T.J. }, and { Johnny, Lizzy, Dad }

because Dad appears in two of the subsets.

By the way, realize that every set (S) together with its (total) complement ($\overline{S}$) forms a partition of the entire domain of discourse Ω. This is because every element either is, or is not, in any given set. The set of males and non-males are a partition of Ω because everything is either a male or a non-male, and never both (inanimate objects and other nouns are non-males, just as women are). The set of prime numbers and the set of everything-except-prime-numbers are a partition. The set of underdone cheeseburgers and the set of everything-except-underdone-cheeseburgers form a partition of Ω. By pure logic, this is true no matter what the set is.

You might wonder why partitions are an important concept. The answer is that they come up quite a bit, and when they do, we can make some important simplifications. Take S, the set of all students at UMW. We can partition it in several different ways. If we divide S into the set of freshmen, sophomores, juniors, and seniors, we have a partition: every student is one of those grade levels, and no student is more than one.[5] If we group them into in-state and out-of-state students, we again have a partition. And if we divide them into those who live on-campus and those who live off, we again have a partition.

Note that dividing S into computer science majors and English majors does *not* give us a partition. For one thing, not everyone is majoring in one of those two subjects. For another, some students

---

[5]Apologies to fifth-year (or sixth-year, or...) "super seniors."

might be double-majoring in both. Hence this group of subsets is neither mutually exclusive nor collectively exhaustive. It's interesting to think about gender and partitions: when I grew up, I was taught that males and females were a partition of the human race. But now I've come to realize that there are non-binary persons who do not identify with either of those genders, and so it's not a partition after all.

Question: is the number of students $|S|$ equal to the number of off-campus students plus the number of on-campus students? Obviously yes. But why? The answer: because the off-campus and on-campus students form a partition. If we added up the number of freshmen, sophomores, juniors, and seniors, we would also get $|S|$. But adding up the number of computer science majors and English majors would almost certainly *not* be equal to $|S|$, because some students would be double-counted and others counted not at all. This is an example of the kind of beautiful simplicity that partitions provide.

2.13 Exercises

Use an index card or a piece of paper folded lengthwise, and cover up the right-hand column of the exercises below. Read each exercise in the left-hand column, answer it in your mind, then slide the index card down to reveal the answer and see if you're right! For every exercise you missed, figure out why you missed it before moving on.

1. Is the set { Will, Smith } the same as the set { Smith, Will }?	Yes indeed.
2. Is the ordered pair (Will, Smith) the same as (Smith, Will)?	No. Order matters with ordered pairs (hence the name), and with any size tuple for that matter.
3. Is the set { { Luke, Leia }, Han } the same as the set { Luke, { Leia, Han } }?	No. For instance, the first set has Han as a member but the second set does not. (Instead, it has another set as a member, and that inner set happens to include Han.)
4. What's the first element of the set { Cowboys, Redskins, Steelers }?	The question doesn't make sense. There is no "first element" of a set. All three teams are equally members of the set, and could be listed in any order.
5. Let G be { Matthew, Mark, Luke, John }, J be { Luke, Obi-wan, Yoda }, S be the set of all Star Wars characters, and F be the four gospels from the New Testament. Now then. Is $J \subseteq G$?	No.
6. Is $J \subseteq S$?	Yes.
7. Is Yoda $\in J$?	Yes.

8. Is Yoda $\subseteq J$?	No. Yoda isn't even a set, so it can't be a subset of anything.
9. Is { Yoda } $\subseteq J$?	Yes. The (unnamed) set that contains only Yoda is in fact a subset of J.
10. Is { Yoda } $\in J$?	No. Yoda is one of the elements of J, but { Yoda } is not. In other words, J contains Yoda, but J does not contain a set which contains Yoda (nor does it contain any sets at all, in fact).
11. Is $S \subseteq J$?	No.
12. Is $G \subseteq F$?	Yes, since the two sets are equal.
13. Is $G \subset F$?	No, since the two sets are equal, so neither is a *proper* subset of the other.
14. Is $\varnothing \subseteq S$?	Yes, since the empty set is a subset of *every* set.
15. Is $\varnothing \subseteq \varnothing$?	Yes, since the empty set is a subset of *every* set.
16. Is $F \subseteq \Omega$?	Yes, since every set is a subset of Ω.
17. Is $F \subset \Omega$?	Yes, since every set is a subset of Ω, and F is certainly not equal to Ω.
18. Suppose $X = \{$ Q, $\varnothing$, { Z } $\}$. Is $\varnothing \in X$? Is $\varnothing \subseteq X$?	Yes and yes. The empty set is an element of X because it's one of the elements, and it's also a subset of X because it's a subset of every set. Hmmm.
19. Let A be { Macbeth, Hamlet, Othello }, B be { Scrabble, Monopoly, Othello }, and T be { Hamlet, Village, Town }. What's $A \cup B$?	{ Macbeth, Hamlet, Othello, Scrabble, Monopoly }. (The elements can be listed in any order.)
20. What's $A \cap B$?	{ Othello }.

2.13. EXERCISES

21. What's $A \cap \overline{B}$?	{ Macbeth, Hamlet }.
22. What's $B \cap T$?	$\varnothing$.
23. What's $B \cap \overline{T}$?	B. (which is { Scrabble, Monopoly, Othello }.)
24. What's $A \cup (B \cap T)$?	{ Hamlet, Othello, Macbeth }.
25. What's $(A \cup B) \cap T$?	{ Hamlet }. (Note: not the same answer as in item 24 now that the parens are placed differently.)
26. What's $A - B$?	{ Macbeth, Hamlet }.
27. What's $T - B$?	Simply T, since the two sets have nothing in common.
28. What's $T \times A$?	{ (Hamlet, Macbeth), (Hamlet, Hamlet), (Hamlet, Othello), (Village, Macbeth), (Village, Hamlet), (Village, Othello), (Town, Macbeth), (Town, Hamlet), (Town, Othello) }. The order of the ordered pairs within the set is not important; the order of the elements within each ordered pair *is* important.
29. What's $(B \cap B) \times (A \cap T)$?	{ (Scrabble, Hamlet), (Monopoly, Hamlet), (Othello, Hamlet) }.
30. What's $\lvert A \cup B \cup T \rvert$?	7.
31. What's $\lvert A \cap B \cap T \rvert$?	0.
32. What's $\lvert (A \cup B \cup T) \times (B \cup B \cup B) \rvert$?	21. (The first parenthesized expression gives rise to a set with 7 elements, and the second to a set with three elements (B itself). Each element from the first set gets paired with an element from the second, so there are 21 such pairings.)

33. Is A an extensional set, or an intensional set?	The question doesn't make sense. Sets aren't "extensional" or "intensional"; rather, a given set can be *described* extensionally or intensionally. The description given in item 19 is an extensional one; an intensional description of the same set would be "The Shakespeare tragedies Stephen studied in high school."
34. Recall that G was defined as { Matthew, Mark, Luke, John }. Is this a partition of G? • { Luke, Matthew } • { John }	No, because the sets are not collectively exhaustive (Mark is missing).
35. Is this a partition of G? • { Mark, Luke } • { Matthew, Luke }	No, because the sets are neither collectively exhaustive (John is missing) nor mutually exclusive (Luke appears in two of them).
36. Is this a partition of G? • { Matthew, Mark, Luke } • { John }	Yes. (Trivia: this partitions the elements into the synoptic gospels and the non-synoptic gospels).
37. Is this a partition of G? • { Matthew, Luke } • { John, Mark }	Yes. (This partitions the elements into the gospels which feature a Christmas story and those that don't).

38. Is this a partition of G? • { Matthew, John } • { Luke } • { Mark } • ∅	Yes. (This partitions the elements into the gospels that were written by Jews, those that were written by Greeks, those that were written by Romans, and those that were written by Americans).
39. What's the power set of { Rihanna }?	{ { Rihanna }, ∅ }.
40. Is { peanut, jelly } ∈ $\mathbb{P}$({ peanut, butter, jelly })?	Yes, since { peanut, jelly } is one of the eight subsets of { peanut, butter, jelly }. (Can you name the other seven?)
41. Is it true for *every* set S that $S \in \mathbb{P}(S)$?	Yep.

Chapter 3

Relations

Sets are fundamental to discrete math, both for what they represent in themselves and for how they can be combined to produce other sets. In this chapter, we're going to learn a new way of combining sets, called relations.

3.1 The idea of a relation

A **relation** between a set X and Y is *a subset of the Cartesian product*. That one sentence packs in a whole heck of a lot, so spend a moment thinking deeply about it. Recall that $X \times Y$ yields a set of ordered pairs, one for each combination of an element from X and an element from Y. If X has 5 elements and Y has 4, then $X \times Y$ is a set of 20 ordered pairs. To make it concrete, if X is the set { Harry, Ron, Hermione }, and Y is the set { Dr. Pepper, Mt. Dew }, then $X \times Y$ is { (Harry, Dr. Pepper), (Harry, Mt. Dew), (Ron, Dr. Pepper), (Ron, Mt. Dew), (Hermione, Dr. Pepper), (Hermione, Mt. Dew) }. Convince yourself that every possible combination is in there. I listed them out methodically to make sure I didn't miss any (all the Harry's first, with each drink in order, then all the Ron's, *etc.*) but of course there's no order to the members of a set, so I could have listed them in any order.

Now if I define a relation between X and Y, I'm simply specifying that certain of these ordered pairs are in the relation, and certain ones are not. For example, I could define a relation R that contains only { (Harry, Mt. Dew), (Ron, Mt. Dew) }. I could define another relation S that contains { (Hermione, Mt. Dew), (Hermione, Dr. Pepper), (Harry, Dr. Pepper) }. I could define another relation T that has *none* of the ordered pairs; in other words, $T = \varnothing$.

A question that should occur to you is: how many different relations are there between two sets X and Y? Think it out: every one of the ordered pairs in $X \times Y$ either is, or is not, in a particular relation between X and Y. Very well. Since there are a total of $|X| \cdot |Y|$ ordered pairs, and each one of them can be either present or absent from each relation, there must be a total of

$$2^{|X| \cdot |Y|}$$

different relations between them. Put another way, the set of all relations between X and Y is the power set of $X \times Y$. I told you that would come up a lot.

In the example above, then, there are a whopping 2^6, or 64 different relations between those two teensey little sets. One of those relations is the empty set. Another one has all six ordered pairs in it. The rest fall somewhere in the middle. (Food for thought: how many of these relations have exactly one ordered pair? How many have exactly five?)

Notation

I find the notation for expressing relations somewhat awkward. But here it is. When we defined the relation S, above, we had the ordered pair (Harry, Dr. Pepper) in it. To explicitly state this fact, we could simply say

$$\text{(Harry, Dr. Pepper)} \in S$$

and in fact we can do so. More often, though, mathematicians write:

$$\text{Harry } S \text{ Dr. Pepper.}$$

which is pronounced "Harry is S-related-to Dr. Pepper." Told you it was awkward.

If we want to draw attention to the fact that (Harry, Mt. Dew) is *not* in the relation S, we could strike it through to write

$$\text{Harry } \cancel{S} \text{ Mt. Dew}$$

3.2 Defining relations

Just as with sets, we can define a relation extensionally or intensionally. To do it extensionally, it's just like the examples above — we simply list the ordered pairs: { (Hermione, Mt. Dew), (Hermione, Dr. Pepper), (Harry, Dr. Pepper) }.

Most of the time, however, we want a relation to *mean* something. In other words, it's not just some arbitrary selection of the possible ordered pairs, but rather reflects some larger notion of how the elements of the two sets are related. For example, suppose I wanted to define a relation called "hasTasted" between the sets X and Y, above. This relation might have the five of the possible six ordered pairs in it:

(Harry, Dr. Pepper)
(Ron, Dr. Pepper)
(Ron, Mt. Dew)
(Hermione, Dr. Pepper)
(Hermione, Mt. Dew)

Another way of expressing the same information would be to write:

Harry hasTasted Dr. Pepper
Harry ~~hasTasted~~ Mt. Dew
Ron hasTasted Dr. Pepper
Ron hasTasted Mt. Dew
Hermione hasTasted Dr. Pepper
Hermione hasTasted Mt. Dew

Both of these are extensional definitions. But of course the *meaning* behind the relation "hasTasted" is that if x hasTasted y, then in real life, the person x has given a can of y a try. We're using this relation to state that although Ron and Hermione have sampled both drinks, Harry (perhaps because of his persecuted childhood at the Dursleys) has not.

We can of course define other relations on the same two sets. Let's define a relation "likes" to contain { (Harry, Dr. Pepper), (Ron, Dr. Pepper), (Hermione, Dr. Pepper), (Hermione, Mt. Dew) }. This states that while everybody likes Dr. Pepper, Hermione herself has broad tastes and also likes Mt. Dew.

Another relation, "hasFaveDrink," might indicate which drink is each person's *favorite*. Maybe the extension is { (Harry, Dr. Pepper), (Ron, Dr. Pepper) }. There's no ordered pair with Hermione in it, perhaps because she actually prefers iced tea.

Yet another relation, "ownsStockIn," represents which people own stock in which beverage companies. In this case, ownsStockIn = ∅ since all of the members of X are too busy studying potions to be stock owners in anything.

Bottom line is: when we talk about a relation, we're simply designating certain elements of one set to "go with" or "be associated with" certain elements of another set. Normally this corresponds to something interesting in the real world — like which people have tasted which drinks, or which people own stock in which companies. Even if it doesn't, though, it still "counts" as a relation, and we can simply list the ordered pairs it contains, one for each association.

3.3 Relations between a set and itself

In the above example, the two sets contained different kinds of things: people, and drinks. But many relations are defined in which the left and right elements are actually drawn from the same set. Such a relation is called (don't laugh) an **endorelation**.

Consider the relation "hasACrushOn" between X and X, whose intensional meaning is that if $(x,y) \in$ hasACrushOn, then in real life x is romantically attracted to y. The extension is probably only { (Ron, Hermione), (Hermione, Ron) }, although who knows what goes through teenagers' minds.

Another example would be the relation "hasMoreCaloriesThan" between Y and Y: this relation's extension is { (Mt. Dew, Dr. Pepper) }. (Fun fact: Dr. Pepper has only 150 calories per can, whereas Mt. Dew has 170.)

Note that just because a relation's two sets are the same, that doesn't necessarily imply that the two *elements* are the same for any of its ordered pairs. Harry clearly doesn't have a crush on himself, nor does anyone else have a self-crush. And no soda has more calories than itself, either — that's impossible. That being said, though, an ordered pair *can* have the same two elements. Consider the relation "hasSeen" between X and X. Surely all three wizards have looked in a mirror at some point in their lives, so in addition to ordered pairs like (Ron, Harry) the hasSeen relation also contains ordered pairs like (Ron, Ron) and (Hermione, Hermione).

3.4 Finite and infinite relations

Sets can be infinite, and relations can be too. An **infinite relation** is simply a relation with infinitely many ordered pairs in it. This might seem strange at first, since how could we ever hope to specify all the ordered pairs? But it's really no different than with sets: we either have to do it intensionally, or else have a rule for systematically computing the extension.

As an example of the first, consider the relation "isGreaterThan" between $\mathbb{Z}$ and $\mathbb{Z}$. (Recall that "$\mathbb{Z}$" is just a way of writing "the set of integers.") This relation contains ordered pairs like (5, 2) and (17, –13), since 5 isGreaterThan 2 and 17 isGreaterThan –13, but not (7, 9) or (11, 11). Clearly it's an infinite relation. We couldn't list all the pairs, but we don't need to, since the name implies the underlying meaning of the relation.

As an example of the second, consider the relation "isLuckierThan" between $\mathbb{N}$ and $\mathbb{N}$. (The "$\mathbb{N}$" means "the natural numbers.") We specify it extensionally as follows:

{ (1, 13), (2, 13), (3, 13), ... (12, 13), (14, 13), (15, 13), (16, 13), ... }

Here we're just saying "every number is luckier than 13 (except for 13 itself, of course)."

3.5 Properties of endorelations

As I mentioned, lots of the relations we care about are endorelations (relations between a set and itself). Some endorelations have one or more of the following simple properties which are useful to talk about. Throughout this section, assume that R is the relation in question, and it's defined from set A to set A.

- **Reflexivity**. A relation R is reflexive if xRx for every $x \in A$. Other ordered pairs can also be in the relation, of course, but if we say it's reflexive we're guaranteeing that every element is in there with itself. "hasSeen" is almost certainly a reflexive relation, presuming that mirrors are relatively widespread in the world. "thinksIsBeautiful" is not reflexive, however: some people think themselves beautiful, and others do not.

- **Symmetry**. A relation is symmetric if xRy whenever yRx and vice versa. This doesn't mean that (x, y) is in the relation for every x and y — only that *if* (x, y) is in the relation, then (y, x) is guaranteed to also be in the relation. An example would be "hasShakenHandsWith." If I've shaken hands with you, then you've shaken hands with me, period. It doesn't make sense otherwise.

- ***Anti*symmetry**. A relation is *anti*symmetric if $x\cancel{R}y$ whenever yRx and vice versa (unless x and y are the same.) Put another way, if (x, y) is in the relation, fine, but then (y, x) *can't* be. An example would be "isTallerThan." If I'm taller than you, then you can't be taller than me. We could in fact be the same height, in which case neither the pair (you, me)

3.5. PROPERTIES OF ENDORELATIONS

nor (me, you) would be in the relation, but in any event the two cannot co-exist.

Note that *anti*symmetric is very different from *a*symmetric. An *a*symmetric relation is simply one that's not symmetric: in other words, there's some (x, y) in there without a matching (y, x). An *anti*symmetric relation, on the other hand, is one in which there are guaranteed to be *no* matching (y, x)'s for *any* (x, y).

If you have trouble visualizing this, here's another way to think about it: realize that most relations are *neither* symmetric *nor antisymmetric*. It's kind of a coincidence for a relation to be symmetric: that would mean for every single (x, y) it contains, it also contains a (y, x). (What are the chances?) Similarly, it's kind of a coincidence for a relation to be *anti*symmetric: that would mean for every single (x, y) it contains, it *doesn't* contain a (y, x). (Again, what are the chances?) Your average Joe relation is going to contain some (x, y) pairs that have matching (y, x) pairs, and some that don't have matches. Such relations (the vast majority) are simply *a*symmetric: that is, neither symmetric nor antisymmetric.

Shockingly, it's actually possible for a relation to be *both* symmetric *and* antisymmetric! (but not asymmetric.) For instance, the empty relation (with no ordered pairs) is both symmetric and antisymmetric. It's symmetric because for every ordered pair (x, y) in it (of which there are zero), there's also the corresponding (y, x).[1] And similarly, for every ordered pair (x, y), the corresponding (y, x) is *not* present. Another example is a relation with only "doubles" in it — say, { (3,3), (7,7), (Fred, Fred) }. This, too, is both symmetric and antisymmetric (work it out!)

---

[1] Wait — how can I say that? How can there be "the corresponding" ordered pair in a relation that has *no* ordered pairs?! The answer has to do with the first clause: *for every ordered pair (x, y) in it*. There are none of these, therefore, no (y, x)'s are required. The condition is trivially satisfied. This is common in mathematics: we say that A requires B, but this means that if A is *not* true, then B is not forced.

- **Transitivity**. A relation is transitive if whenever xRy and yRz, then it's guaranteed that xRz. The "isTallerThan" relation we defined is transitive: if you tell me that Bob is taller than Jane, and Jane is taller than Sue, then I *know* Bob must be taller than Sue, without you even having to tell me that. That's just how "taller than" works. An example of a *non*-transitive relation would be "hasBeaten" with NFL teams. Just because the Patriots beat the Steelers this year, and the Steelers beat the Giants, that does not imply that the Patriots necessarily beat the Giants. The Giants might have actually beaten the-team-who-beat-the-team-who-beat-them (such things happen), or heck, the two teams might not even have played each other this year.

All of the above examples were defined intensionally. Just for practice, let's look at some extensionally defined relations as well. Using our familiar Harry Potter set as A, consider the following relation:

(Harry, Ron)
(Ron, Hermione)
(Ron, Ron)
(Hermione, Ron)
(Ron, Harry)
(Hermione, Hermione)

Consider: is this relation reflexive? **No.** It has (Ron, Ron) and (Hermione, Hermione), but it's missing (Harry, Harry), so it's not reflexive. Is it symmetric? **Yes.** Look carefully at the ordered pairs. We have a (Harry, Ron), but also a matching (Ron, Harry). We have a (Hermione, Ron), but also a matching (Ron, Hermione). So every time we have a (x, y) we also have the matching (y, x), which is the definition of symmetry. Is it antisymmetric? **No,** because (among other things) both (Harry, Ron) and (Ron, Harry) are present. Finally, is it transitive? **No.** We have (Harry, Ron) and (Ron, Hermione), which means that if it's transitive we would have to also have (Harry, Hermione) in there, which we don't. So it's not transitive. Remember: to meet any of these properties, they have to *fully* apply. "Almost" only counts in horseshoes.

Let's try another example:

(Ron, Harry)
(Ron, Ron)
(Harry, Harry)
(Hermione, Hermione)
(Harry, Hermione)
(Hermione, Harry)

Is this one reflexive? **Yes.** We've got all three wizards appearing with themselves. Is it symmetric? **No,** since (Ron, Harry) has no match. Is it antisymmetric? **No,** since (Harry, Hermione) *does* have a match. Is it transitive? **No,** since the presence of (Ron, Harry) and (Harry, Hermione) implies the necessity of (Ron, Hermione), which doesn't appear, so no dice.

Partial orders and posets

A couple of other fun terms: an endorelation which is (1) reflexive, (2) *anti*symmetric, and (3) transitive is called a **partial order**. And a set together with a partial order is called a **partially ordered set**, or "**poset**" for short. The name "partial order" makes sense once you think through an example.

You may have noticed that when dogs meet each other (especially male dogs) they often circle each other and take stock of each other and try to establish dominance as the so-called "alpha dog." This is a pecking order of sorts that many different species establish. Now suppose I have the set D of all dogs, and a relation "isAtLeastAsToughAs" between them. The relation starts off with every reflexive pair in it: (Rex, Rex), (Fido, Fido), *etc.* This is because obviously every dog is at least as tough as itself. Now every time two dogs x and y encounter each other, they establish dominance through eye contact or physical intimidation, and then one of the following ordered pairs is added to the relation: either (x, y) or (y, x), but never both.

I contend that in this toy example, "isAtLeastAsToughAs" is a partial order, and D along with isAtLeastAsToughAs together form a poset. I reason as follows. It's reflexive, since we started off by adding every dog with itself. It's antisymmetric, since we never add both (x, y) and (y, x) to the relation. And it's transitive, because if Rex is tougher than Fido, and Fido is tougher than Cuddles, this means that if Rex and Cuddles ever met, Rex would quickly establish dominance. (I'm no zoologist, and am not sure if the last condition truly applies with real dogs. But let's pretend it does.)

It's called a "*partial* order" because it establishes a partial, but incomplete, hierarchy among dogs. If we ask, "is dog X tougher than dog Y?" the answer is never ambiguous. We're never going to say, "well, dog X was superior to dog A, who was superior to dog Y ... but then again, dog Y was superior to dog B, who was superior to dog X, so there's no telling which of X and Y is truly toughest." No. A partial order, because of its transitivity and antisymmetry, guarantees we never have such an unreconcilable conflict.

However, we could have a lack of information. Suppose Rex has never met Killer, and nobody Rex has met has ever met anyone Killer has met. There's no chain between them. They're in two separate universes as far as we're concerned, and we'd have no way of knowing which was toughest. It doesn't have to be that extreme, though: Suppose Rex established dominance over Cuddles, and Killer *also* established dominance over Cuddles, but those are the only ordered pairs in the relation. Again, there's no way to tell whether Rex or Killer is the tougher dog. They'd either need to encounter a common opponent that only one of them can beat, or else get together for a throw-down.

So a partial order gives us some semblance of structure — the relation establishes a directionality, and we're guaranteed not to get wrapped up in contradictions — but it doesn't *completely* order all the elements. If it does, it's called a **total order**.

3.6 Functions

One very, very important type of relation is called a **function**. Some mathematicians treat functions totally separately from relations, but I think it's more useful to think of a function as a special *kind* of relation. Many of the ideas are the same, as you'll see.

Think back to the relations between wizards and soft drinks. One such relation (we called it R) had (Harry, Mt. Dew) and (Ron, Mt. Dew) in it. Another one (S) contained (Hermione, Mt. Dew), (Hermione, Dr. Pepper), and (Harry, Dr. Pepper). Since there were three wizards and two soft drinks, we calculated that there were 2^6 such relations.

Now some of those relations have *exactly one ordered pair for each wizard*. For instance, the relation F which contains { (Harry, Dr. Pepper), (Ron, Mt. Dew), (Hermione, Mt. Dew) }. This kind of relation is a **function**. It associates each element of the first set with *exactly one* element of the second set. Obviously not all relations are functions: R, for example, is not (there's no pair with Hermione) and neither is S (there's more than one pair with Hermione). But those that do form a very special class of interest, and warrant a whole new terminology.

When we have a function F between a set X and Y, we write $F : X \to Y$ to indicate this. The set X is called the **domain** of the function, and the set Y is called the **codomain**. The colon and the arrow are just there to complete the syntax. The rule with functions is very simple: every element of the domain is related to *exactly one* element of the codomain. Sometimes we say that a domain element is "**mapped**" to its corresponding codomain element. Note very carefully that the reverse is not necessarily true. In fact, with the wizards-and-drinks example, it *can't* possibly be true: there are fewer drinks than wizards, so some drink is bound to be related to more than one wizard. (Think about it.) It's also perfectly legit to have a function like { (Harry, Dr. Pepper), (Ron, Dr. Pepper), (Hermione, Dr. Pepper) }, where some element(s) of the codomain are left out altogether.

One of the things that makes functions useful is that we can ask "*which* element of Y goes with X?" and we will always get back a well-defined answer. We can't really do that with relations in general, because the answer might be "none" or "several." Take a look back at the R and S examples, above: what answer would we get if we asked "which drink goes Hermione map to?" for either relation? Answer: there is no answer.

But with functions, I can freely ask that question because I know I'll get a kosher answer. With F, I can ask, "which drink does Hermione map to?" and the answer is "Mt. Dew." In symbols, we write this as follows:

$$F(\text{Hermione}) = \text{Mt. Dew}$$

This will look familiar to computer programmers, since it resembles a function call. In fact, it *is* a function call. That's exactly what it is. "Functions" in languages like C++ and Java were in fact named after this discrete math notion. And if you know anything about programming, you know that in a program I can "call the F() function" and "pass it the argument 'Hermione'" and "get the return value 'Mt.Dew.'" I never have to worry about getting more than one value back, or getting none at all.

You might also remember discussing functions in high school math, and the so-called "vertical line test." When you plotted the values of a numerical function on a graph, and there was no vertical (up-and-down) line that intersected more than one point, you could safely call the plot a "function." That's really exactly the same thing as the condition I just gave for functions, stated graphically. If a plot passes the vertical line test, then there is no x value for which there's more than one y value. This means it makes sense to ask "which is *the* value of y for a particular value of x?" You'll always get one and only one answer. (There's no such thing, of course, as a "horizontal line test," since functions are free to map more than one x value to the same y value. They just can't do the reverse.)

The difference between the functions of high school math and the functions we're talking about here, by the way, is simply that our

3.6. FUNCTIONS

functions aren't necessarily numeric. Sometimes we do draw "plots" of sorts, though, like this one:

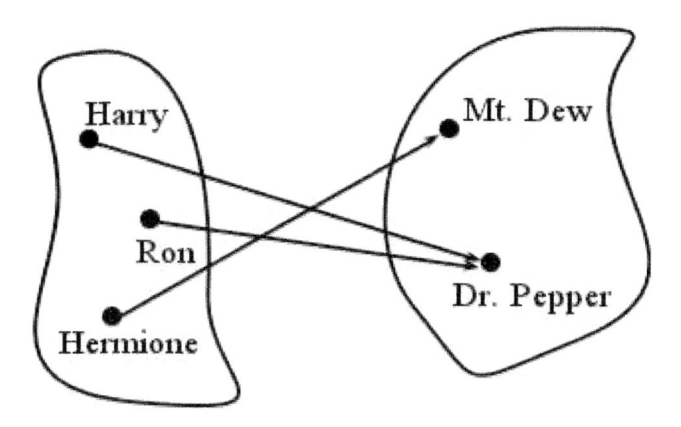

Figure 3.1: A function represented graphically.

This simply shows which elements of the domain map to which elements of the codomain. The left blob is the domain, the right blob is the codomain, and there's an arrow representing each mapping.

Now as with relations, functions normally have "meaning." We could define a function called "firstTasted" that associates each wizard with the soft drink he or she *first* sampled as a child. We could define another called "faveDrink" that maps each wizard to his or her favorite — presuming that every wizard has a favorite drink in the set (Hermione will have to overlook her iced tea and choose among the options provided). A third function called "wouldChooseWithMexicanFood" provides information about which drink each wizard provides with that type of cuisine. Here are Ron's values for each of the three functions:

$$\text{firstTasted(Ron)} = \text{Mt. Dew}$$
$$\text{faveDrink(Ron)} = \text{Mt. Dew}$$
$$\text{wouldChooseWithMexicanFood(Ron)} = \text{Dr. Pepper}$$

These values indicate that Mt. Dew was the soda pop that Ron first sipped, and it has been his favorite ever since, although at *La Estrellita* he prefers a Pepper.

Functions can be defined intensionally or extensionally, just as with relations. Intensionally, we provide the conceptual meaning of what the function represents. Extensionally, we list the values for each element of the domain.

One other term that applies to every function is its **range**. A function's range is the subset of the codomain that at least one element the domain actually maps to. It's the part of the codomain that's "reachable." For instance, if the function $G : X \to Y$ is { (Harry, Dr. Pepper), (Ron, Dr. Pepper), (Hermione, Dr. Pepper) }, then even though the codomain is { Dr. Pepper, Mt. Dew } the *range* is merely { Dr. Pepper }. That's because there isn't any ordered pair that contains Mt. Dew, so it's left out of the range. You can't "reach" Mt. Dew via the G function by starting with any of its inputs, so it's left out in the cold.

By the way, a function's range is sometimes called its **image**. These terms are synonymous.

3.7 Properties of functions

As with relations, there are certain simple properties that some (not all) functions have, and it's useful to reason about them. A function can be:

- **Injective**. An injective function is not only a function, but also kind of a "function in reverse": *i.e.*, not only does no x map to two different y's (which is the case for all functions), but no two x's map to the same y. In graphical terms, it *does* pass a "horizontal line test" in addition to the vertical. Note that this can't happen if the domain is larger than the codomain (as with wizards & soft drinks), since there aren't enough y values to accommodate all the x values uniquely. So there is no injective function between wizards and soft drinks to be found, no matter how hard we try.

The function phoneExtension — with employees as the domain and four-digit numbers as the codomain — is an example of an injective function. One mapping of this function would be "phoneExtension(Sally) = 1317", indicating that Sally can be reached at x1317. Some of the available extensions may be currently unused, but every employee does have one (and only one) which makes it a function. But since no two employees have the *same* extension, it is also an injective function.

Injective functions are sometimes called **one-to-one** functions. (One-to-one and injective are exact synonyms.)

- **Surjective**. A surjective function is one that reaches all the elements of its codomain: some x does in fact reach every y. Another way of saying this is: for a surjective function, the range equals the entire codomain. You can see that this is impossible if the domain is smaller than the codomain, since there wouldn't be enough x values to reach all the y values. If we added Pepsi and Barq's Root Beer to our Y set, we would thereby eliminate the possibility of any surjective functions from X to Y (unless we also added wizards, of course).

  The function worksIn — with employees as the domain and departments as the codomain — is an example of an surjective function. One mapping of this function would be "worksIn(Sid) = Marketing", indicating that Sid works in the Marketing department. Each employee works for one department, which makes it a function. But at least *one* employee works in *every* department (*i.e.*, there are no empty departments with no people in them) which makes it surjective.

  Surjective functions are sometimes called "**onto**" functions. (Onto and surjective are exact synonyms.)

- **Bijective**. Finally, a bijective function is simply one that is both injective and surjective. With an injective function, every y is mapped to by *at most* one x; with a surjective function, every y is mapped to by *at least* one x; so with a bijective function, every y is mapped to by *exactly* one x.

Needless to say, the domain and the codomain must have the same cardinality for this to be possible.

The function employeeNumber — with employees as the domain and employee numbers as the codomain — is a bijective function. Every employee has an employee number, and every employee number goes with exactly one employee. As a corollary of this, there are the same number of employees as employee numbers.

Finally, a few extensionally-defined examples. With $X = \{$ Harry, Ron, Hermione $\}$ and $Y = \{$ Dr. Pepper, Mt. Dew $\}$, consider the function f_1:

$$f_1(\text{Harry}) = \text{Mt. Dew}$$
$$f_1(\text{Ron}) = \text{Mt. Dew}$$
$$f_1(\text{Hermione}) = \text{Mt. Dew}$$

Is f_1 injective? **No**, since more than one wizard (all of them, in fact) map to Mt. Dew. Is it surjective? **No**, since *no* wizard maps to Dr. Pepper. Is it bijective? **No**, duh, since to be bijective it must be both injective and surjective.

Now for f_2, change Ron to map to Dr. Pepper instead:

$$f_2(\text{Harry}) = \text{Mt. Dew}$$
$$f_2(\text{Ron}) = \text{Dr. Pepper}$$
$$f_2(\text{Hermione}) = \text{Mt. Dew}$$

Is f_2 injective? Still **no**, since more than one wizard maps to Mt. Dew. (And of course *no* function between these two sets can be injective, since there aren't enough soft drinks for each wizard to have his/her own.) But is it surjective? **Yes**, it is now surjective, since *every* soft drink has at least one wizard mapping to it. (Still not bijective for obvious reasons.)

Now let's add Pepsi and Barqs Root Beer to our set of soft drinks Y, so that it now has four elements: $\{$ Dr. Pepper, Mt. Dew, Pepsi, Barqs Root Beer $\}$. Consider the function f_3:

3.7. PROPERTIES OF FUNCTIONS

$$f_3(\text{Harry}) = \text{Pepsi}$$
$$f_3(\text{Ron}) = \text{Pepsi}$$
$$f_3(\text{Hermione}) = \text{Mt. Dew}$$

Is f_3 injective? **No**, since more than one wizard maps to Pepsi. Is it surjective? **No**, since *no* wizard maps to Dr. Pepper or Barqs. (And of course *no* function between these two sets can be surjective, since there aren't enough wizards for each drink to have one.) And of course not bijective.

Now for f_4, change Ron to map to Dr. Pepper instead:

$$f_4(\text{Harry}) = \text{Pepsi}$$
$$f_4(\text{Ron}) = \text{Dr. Pepper}$$
$$f_4(\text{Hermione}) = \text{Mt. Dew}$$

Still not surjective, of course, but now it *is* injective, since no drink has more than one wizard. (Still of course not bijective.)

Finally, let's add one more wizard (Neville) to the mix for two more examples. Let f_5 be:

$$f_5(\text{Harry}) = \text{Barqs Root Beer}$$
$$f_5(\text{Ron}) = \text{Dr. Pepper}$$
$$f_5(\text{Hermione}) = \text{Mt. Dew}$$
$$f_5(\text{Neville}) = \text{Dr. Pepper}$$

Is f_5 injective? **No**, since Dr. Pepper has two wizards. Is it surjective? **No**, since Pepsi has none. Struck out on all counts. However, one small change and everything falls into place:

$$f_6(\text{Harry}) = \text{Barqs Root Beer}$$
$$f_6(\text{Ron}) = \text{Pepsi}$$
$$f_6(\text{Hermione}) = \text{Mt. Dew}$$
$$f_6(\text{Neville}) = \text{Dr. Pepper}$$

Is this last function injective, surjective, bijective? **Yes** to all three! Every wizard gets his/her own soft drink, every soft drink gets its own wizard, and no soft drinks (or wizards) are left out. How exciting. This is a perfectly bijective function, also called a **bijection**. Again, the only way to get a bijection is for the domain and codomain to be the same size (although that alone does not *guarantee* a bijection; witness f_5, above). Also observe that if they *are* the same size, then injectivity and surjectivity go hand-in-hand. Violate one, and you're bound to violate the other. Uphold the one, and you're bound to uphold the other. There's a nice, pleasing, symmetrical elegance to the whole idea.

3.8 Exercises

1. Let A be the set { Chuck, Julie, Sam } and S be the set { basketball, volleyball }. Is { (Julie, basketball), (Sam, basketball), (Julie, volleyball) } a relation between A and S?	Yes it is, since it is a subset of $A \times S$.
2. Is the above relation an endorelation?	No, because an endorelation involves one set with itself, not two different sets (like A and S are.)
3. Is { (Chuck, basketball), (basketball, volleyball) } a relation between A and S?	No, since the first element of one of the ordered pairs is not from the set A.
4. Is $\varnothing$ a relation between A and S?	Yes it is, since it is a subset of $A \times S$.
5. How large could a relation between A and S be?	The maximum cardinality is 6, if all three athletes played all three sports. (I'm assuming that the meaning of the relation is "*plays*" instead of "*isAFanOf*" or "*knowsTheRulesFor*" or something else. In any case, the maximum cardinality is 6.)
6. Let T be the set { Spock, Kirk, McCoy, Scotty, Uhura }. Let O be an endorelation on T, defined as follows: { (Kirk, Scotty), (Spock, Scotty), (Kirk, Spock), (Scotty, Spock) }. Is T reflexive?	No, since it doesn't have any of the elements of T appearing with themselves.

7. Is T symmetric?	No, since it contains (Kirk, Scotty) but not (Scotty, Kirk).
8. Is T antisymmetric?	No, since it contains (Spock, Scotty) and also (Scotty, Spock).
9. Is T transitive?	Yes, since for every (x,y) and (y,z) present, the corresponding (x,z) is also present. (The only example that fits this is x=Kirk, y=Spock, z=Scotty, and the required ordered pair is indeed present.)
10. Let H be an endorelation on T, defined as follows: { (Kirk, Kirk), (Spock, Spock), (Uhura, Scotty), (Scotty, Uhura), (Spock, McCoy), (McCoy, Spock), (Scotty, Scotty), (Uhura, Uhura) }. Is H reflexive?	No, since it's missing (McCoy, McCoy).
11. Is H symmetric?	Yes, since for every (x,y) it contains, the corresponding (y,x) is also present.
12. Is H antisymmetric?	No, since it contains (Uhura, Scotty) and also (Scotty, Uhura).
13. Is H transitive?	Yes, since there aren't any examples of (x,y) and (y,z) pairs both being present.
14. Let *outranks* be an endorelation on the set of all crew members of the Enterprise, where $(x,y) \in$ *outranks* if character x has a higher Star Fleet rank than y. Is *outranks* reflexive?	No, since no officer outranks him/herself.

3.8. EXERCISES

15. Is *outranks* symmetric?	No, since an officer cannot outrank an officer who in turn outranks him/her.
16. Is *outranks* antisymmetric?	Yes, since if one officer outranks a second, the second one *cannot* also outrank the first.
17. Is *outranks* transitive?	Yes, since if one officer outranks a second, and that officer outranks a third, the first obviously also outranks the third.
18. Is *outranks* a partial order?	No, but close. It satisfies antisymmetry and transitivity, which are crucial. The only thing it doesn't satisfy is reflexivity, since none of the members appear with themselves. If we changed this relation to *ranksAtLeastAsHighAs*, then we could include these "double" pairs and have ourselves a partial order.
19. Let *sameShirtColor* be an endorelation on the set of all crew members of the Enterprise, where $(x, y) \in$ *sameShirtColor* if character x ordinarily wears the same shirt color as character y. Is *sameShirtColor* reflexive?	Yes, since you can't but help wear the same shirt color as you're wearing.
20. Is *sameShirtColor* symmetric?	Yes, since if a crew member wears the same shirt color as another, then that second crew member also wears the same shirt color as the first. If Scotty and Uhura both wear red, then Uhura and Scotty both wear red, duh.
21. Is *sameShirtColor* antisymmetric?	No, for probably obvious reasons.

22. Is *sameShirtColor* transitive?	Yes. If Kirk and Sulu wear the same color (yellow), and Sulu and Chekov wear the same color (yellow), then Kirk and Chekov most certainly will wear the same color (yellow).
23. Above, we defined A as the set { Chuck, Julie, Sam } and S as the set { basketball, volleyball }. Then we defined the relation { (Julie, basketball), (Sam, basketball), (Julie, volleyball) }. Is this relation a function?	No, because it's missing Chuck entirely.
24. Suppose we added the ordered pair (Chuck, basketball) to it. Now is it a function?	No, because Julie appears twice, mapping to two different values.
25. Okay. Suppose we then remove (Julie, volleyball). We now have { (Julie, basketball), (Sam, basketball), (Chuck, basketball) }. Is *this* a function?	Yes. Congratulations.
26. Let's call this function "*faveSport*," which suggests that its meaning is to indicate which sport is each athlete's favorite. What's the domain of faveSport?	{ Julie, Chuck, Sam }.
27. What's the codomain of faveSport?	{ basketball, volleyball }.
28. What's the range of faveSport?	{ basketball }.

3.8. EXERCISES

29. Is faveSport injective?	No, because Julie and Sam (and Chuck) all map to the same value (basketball). For a function to be injective, there must be no two domain elements that map to the same codomain element.
30. Is there any way to make it injective?	Not without altering the underlying sets. There are three athletes and two sports, so we can't help but map multiple athletes to the same sport.
31. Fine. Is faveSport surjective?	No, because no one maps to volleyball.
32. Is there any way to make it surjective?	Sure, for instance change Sam from basketball to volleyball. Now both of the codomain elements are "reachable" by some domain element, so it's surjective.
33. Is faveSport now also bijective?	No, because it's still not injective.
34. How can we alter things so that it's bijective?	One way is to add a third sport — say, kickboxing — and move either Julie or Chuck over to kickboxing. If we have Julie map to kickboxing, Sam map to volleyball, and Chuck map to basketball, we have a bijection.
35. How do we normally write the fact that "Julie maps to kickboxing"?	faveSport(Julie) = kickboxing.
36. What's another name for "injective?"	one-to-one.
37. What's another name for "surjective?"	onto.
38. What's another name for "range?"	image.

Chapter 4

Probability

Probability is the study of *uncertainty*. This may seem like a hopeless endeavor, sort of like knowing the unknowable, but it's not. The study of probability gives us tools for taming the uncertain world we live and program in, and for reasoning about it in a precise and helpful way.

We may not know exactly how long a particular visitor is willing to wait for our webpage to load in their browser, but we can use probability to estimate how much traffic we'll lose if this takes longer than a certain average duration. We may not know which specific passwords a hacker will try as he attempts to break our security protocol, but we can use probability to estimate how feasible this approach will be for him. We may not know exactly when a certain program will run out of RAM and have to swap its data out to virtual memory, but we can predict how often this is likely to occur — and how painful it will be for us — given a certain system load and user behavior.

The trick is to use the tools we've already built — sets, relations, functions — to characterize and structure our notions of the relative likelihood of various outcomes. Once those underpinnings are secured, a layer of deductive reasoning will help us make good use of that information to begin to predict the future.

4.1 Outcomes and events

Since life is uncertain, we don't know for sure what is going to happen. But let's start by assuming we know what things *might* happen. Something that might happen is called an **outcome**. You can think of this as the result of an experiment if you want to, although normally we won't be talking about outcomes that we have explicitly manipulated and measured via scientific means. It's more like we're just curious how some particular happening is going to turn out, and we've identified the different ways it can turn out and called them outcomes.

Now we've been using the symbol Ω to refer to "the domain of discourse" or "the universal set" or "all the stuff we're talking about." We're going to give it yet another name now: the **sample space**. Ω, the sample space, is simply *the set of all possible outcomes.* Any particular outcome — call it O — is an element of this set, just like in chapter 1 every conceivable element was a member of the domain of discourse.

If a woman is about to have a baby, we might define Ω as { boy, girl }. Any particular outcome o is either boy or girl (not both), but both outcomes are in the sample space, because both are possible. If we roll a die, we'd define Ω as { 1, 2, 3, 4, 5, 6 }. If we're interested in motor vehicle safety, we might define Ω for a particular road trip as { safe, accident }. The outcomes don't have to be equally likely, an important point we'll return to soon.

In probability, we define an **event** as *a subset of the sample space.* In other words, an event is a *group* of related outcomes (though an event might contain just one outcome, or even zero). I always thought this was a funny definition for the word "event": it's not the first thing that word brings to mind. But it turns out to be a useful concept, because sometimes we're not interested in any *particular* outcome necessarily, but rather in whether the outcome — whatever it is — has a certain property. For instance, suppose at the start of some game, my opponent and I each roll the die, agreeing that the highest roller gets to go first. Suppose he rolls a 2. Now it's my turn. The Ω for my die roll is of course { 1, 2, 3,

4, 5, 6 }. But in this case, it doesn't necessarily matter what my specific outcome is; only whether I beat a 2. So I could define the *event M* (for "me first") to be the set { 3, 4, 5, 6 }. I could define the event *H* ("him first") to be the set { 1 } (notice *H* is still a set, even though it has only one element.) Then I could define the event *T* ("tie") as the set { 2 }. I've now effectively collapsed a larger set of outcomes into only the groups of outcomes I'm interested in. Now I'm all ready to reason about the likelihood that each of these events actually occurs.

By the way, "the set of all outcomes" is simply Ω, since an outcome is an element of Ω. But an event is a *subset* of Ω, not a single element. What, then, is "the set of all events?" If you think it through, you'll realize that it's $\mathbb{P}(\Omega)$ (the *power set* of the sample space). Put another way, when defining an event, I can choose any subset of the possible outcomes, and so I can choose any set from $\mathbb{P}(\Omega)$.

4.2 Probability measures

Okay, we've defined sample spaces and events, but when do quantitative notions like "the odds of" and "percent chance" come into play? They enter the scene when we define a **probability measure**. A probability measure is simply *a function from the domain of events to the codomain of real numbers.* We'll normally use the letters "Pr" for our probability measure. In symbols, $\text{Pr} : \mathbb{P}(\Omega) \to \mathbb{R}$ (since the set of all events is the power set of the sample space, as per above). There's actually another constraint, though, which is that Pr's values must be in the range 0 to 1, inclusive. So it's more correct to write: $\text{Pr} : \mathbb{P}(\Omega) \to [0, 1]$. (You may recall from a previous math course that '[' and ']' are used to describe a closed interval in which the endpoints are included in the interval.)

The "meaning" of the probability measure is intuitive enough: it indicates how likely we think each event is to occur. In the baby example, if we say $\text{Pr}(\{\text{boy}\}) = .5$, it means there's a .5 probability (a.k.a., a 50% chance) that a male child will be born. In the game example, if we say $\text{Pr}(M) = .667$, if means there's a two-thirds chance of me winning the right to go first. In all cases, a probability of 0 means "impossible to occur" and a probability of 1 means "absolutely certain to occur." In colloquial English, we most often use percentages to talk about these things: we'll say "there's a 60% chance Biden will win the election" rather than "there's a .6 probability of Biden winning." The math's a bit clumsier if we deal with percentages, though, so from now on we'll get in the habit of using probabilities rather than 'percent chances,' and we'll use values in the 0 to 1 range rather than 0 to 100.

I find the easiest way to think about probability measures is to start with the probabilities of the *outcomes*, not events. Each outcome has a specific probability of occuring. The probabilities of events logically flow from that just by using addition, as we'll see in a moment.

For example, let's imagine that Fox Broadcasting is producing a worldwide television event called *All-time Idol*, in which the yearly winners of *American Idol* throughout its history all compete against each other to be crowned the "All-time American Idol champion." The four contestants chosen for this competition, along with their musical genres, and age when originally appearing on the show, are as follows:

Kelly Clarkson (20): pop, rock, R&B
Fantasia Barrino (20): pop, R&B
Carrie Underwood (22): country
David Cook (26): rock

Entertainment shows, gossip columns, and *People* magazine are all abuzz in the weeks preceding the competition, to the point where a shrewd analyst can estimate the probabilities of each contestant winning. Our current best estimates are: Kelly .2, Fantasia .2, Carrie .1, and David .5.

Computing the probability for a specific event is just a matter of adding up the probabilities of its outcomes. Define F as the event that a woman wins the competition. Clearly $\Pr(F) = .5$, since $\Pr(\{\text{Kelly}\}) = .2$, $\Pr(\{\text{Fantasia}\}) = .2$, and $\Pr(\{\text{Carrie}\}) = .1$. If P is the event that a rock singer wins, $\Pr(P) = .7$, since this is the sum of Kelly's and David's probabilities.

4.2. PROBABILITY MEASURES

Now it turns out that not just *any* function will do as a probability measure, even if the domain (events) and codomain (real numbers in the range[0,1]) are correct. In order for a function to be a "valid" probability measure, it must satisfy several other rules:

1. $\Pr(\Omega) = 1$

2. $\Pr(A) \geq 0$ for all $A \subseteq \Omega$

3. $\Pr(A \cup B) = \Pr(A) + \Pr(B) - \Pr(A \cap B)$

Rule 1 basically means "*something* has to happen." If we create an event that includes every possible outcome, then there's a probability of 1 (100% chance) the event will occur, because after all *some* outcome has got to occur. (And of course $\Pr(\Omega)$ can't be *greater* than 1, either, because it doesn't make sense to have any probability over 1.) Rule 2 says there's no negative probabilities: you can't define any event, no matter how remote, that has a less than zero chance of happening.

Rule 3 is called the "additivity property," and is a bit more difficult to get your head around. A diagram works wonders. Consider Figure 4.1, called a "Venn diagram," which visually depicts sets and their contents. Here we have defined three events: F (as above) is the event that the winner is a woman; R is the event that the winner is a rock musician (perhaps in addition to other musical genres); and U is the event that the winner is underage (*i.e.*, becomes a multimillionare before they can legally drink). Each of these events is depicted as a closed curve which encloses the outcomes that belong to it. There is obviously a great deal of overlap.

Now back to rule 3. Suppose I ask "what's the probability that the All-time Idol winner is underage or a rock star?" Right away we face an irritating ambiguity in the English language: does "or" mean "*either* underage *or* a rock star, but not both?" Or does it mean "underage *and/or* rock star?" The former interpretation is called an **exclusive or** and the latter an **inclusive or**. In computer science, we will almost always be assuming an *inclusive* or, unless explicitly noted otherwise.

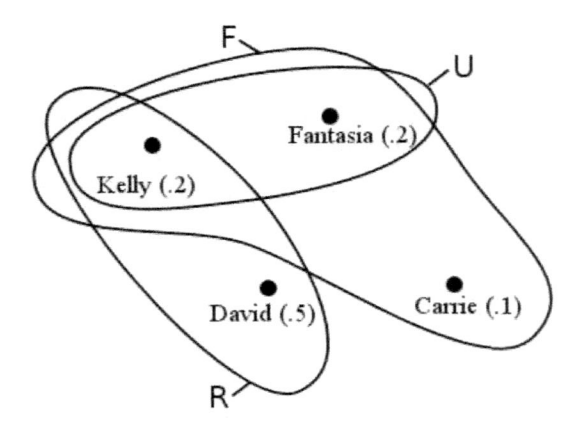

Figure 4.1: Various events, and their overlap.

Very well then. What we're really asking here is "what's $\Pr(U \cup R)$?" We want the union of the two events, since we're asking for the probability that *either* (or both) of them occurs. You might first think that we'd add the two probabilities for the two events and be done with it, but a glance at the diagram tells you this means trouble. $\Pr(U)$ is .4, and $\Pr(R)$ is .7. Even if we weren't very smart, we'd know something was wrong as soon as we added $.4 + .7 = 1.1$ to get a probability of over 1 and violate rule 1. But we are smart, and looking at the diagram it's easy to see what happened: *we double-counted Kelly's probability.* Kelly was a member of both groups, so her .2 got counted in there twice. Now you can see the rationale for rule 3. To get $\Pr(U \cup R)$ we add $\Pr(U)$ and $\Pr(R)$, but then we have to subtract back out the part we double-counted. And what did we double-count? Precisely the intersection $U \cap R$.

As a second example, suppose we want the probability of an underage or female winner? $\Pr(U) = .4$, and $\Pr(F) = .5$, so the first step is to just add these. Then we subtract out the intersection, which we double counted. In this case, the intersection $U \cap F$ is just U (check the diagram), and so subtract out the whole .4. The answer is .5, as it should be.

By the way, you'll notice that if the two sets in question are mutu-

4.2. PROBABILITY MEASURES

ally exclusive, then there is no intersection to subtract out. That's a special case of rule 3. For example, suppose I defined the event C as a country singer winning the competition. In this case, C contains only one outcome: Carrie. Therefore U and C are mutually exclusive. So if I asked "what's the probability of an underage or country winner?" we'd compute $\Pr(U \cup C)$ as

$$\begin{aligned} \Pr(U \cup C) &= \Pr(U) + \Pr(C) - \Pr(U \cap C) \\ &= .4 + .1 - 0 \\ &= .5. \end{aligned}$$

We didn't double-count anything, so there was no correction to make.

Here are a few more pretty obvious rules for probability measures, which follow logically from the first 3:

4. $\Pr(\emptyset) = 0$

5. $\Pr(\overline{A}) = 1 - \Pr(A)$ (recall the "total complement" operator from p. 18.)

6. $\Pr(A) \leq \Pr(B)$ if $A \subseteq B$

Finally, let me draw attention to a common special case of the above rules, which is the situation in which all outcomes are equally likely. This usually happens when we roll dice, flip coins, deal cards, *etc.* since the probability of rolling a 3 is (normally) the same as rolling a 6, and the probability of being dealt the 10♠ is the same as the Q♢. It may also happen when we generate encryption keys, choose between alternate network routing paths, or determine the initial positions of baddies in a first-person shooter level.

In this case, if there are N possible outcomes (note $N = |\Omega|$) then the probability of any event A is:

$$\Pr(A) = \frac{|A|}{N}.$$

It's the size (cardinality) of the event set that matters, and the ratio of this number to the total number of events is the probability. For example, if we deal a card from a fair deck, the probability of drawing a face card is

$$\Pr(F) = \frac{|F|}{N}$$
$$= \frac{|\{K\spadesuit, K\heartsuit, K\diamondsuit, \cdots, J\clubsuit\}|}{52}$$
$$= \frac{12}{52} = .231.$$

Please realize that this shortcut *only* applies when the probability of each outcome is the same. We certainly couldn't say, for example, that the probability of a user's password starting with the letter q is just $\frac{1}{26}$, because passwords surely don't contain all letters with equal frequency. (At least, I'd be very surprised if that were the case.) The only way to solve a problem like this is to know how often each letter of the alphabet occurs.

4.3 Philosophical interlude

Which brings me to an important question. How do we get these probability numbers, anyway? Everything so far has assumed that the numbers have been dropped into our lap.

The answer depends somewhat on your interpretation of what probability *means*. If we say "the probability of getting heads on a coin flip is .5," what are we really saying? There have traditionally been two opposing answers to this question, called the **frequentist** view and the **Bayesian** view. It's interesting to compare their claims.

The frequentist view is that we derive probabilities by simply running many trials, and counting the results. The proportions of various outcomes yield a good idea of their probabilities, particularly if the sample size is large. Consider flipping a coin. If we flip a coin ten times and count three heads, we might not have a great idea of how often heads will occur in the long run. But if we flip it a million times and get 500,372 heads, we can confidently say that the probability of getting a head on a single flip is approximately .500.

This much isn't controversial: it's more like common sense. But the frequentist philosophy states that this is really the *only* way that probability can be defined. It's what probability *is*: the frequency with which we can expect certain outcomes to occur, based on our observations of their past behavior. Probabilities only make sense for things that are repeatable, and reflect a known, reliable trend in how often they produce certain results. Historical proponents of this philosophy include John Venn, the inventor of the aforementioned Venn diagram, and Ronald Fisher, one of the greatest biologists and statisticians of all time.

If frequentism is thus on a quest for experimental objectivity, Bayesianism might be called "subjective." This isn't to say it's arbitrary or sloppy. It simply has a different notion of what probability ultimately means. Bayesians interpret probability as a quantitative personal assessment of the likelihood of something happening. They point out that for many (most) events of interest, trials are neither possible nor sensible. Suppose I'm considering asking a girl out to the prom, and I'm trying to estimate how likely it is she'll go with me. It's not like I'm going to ask her a hundred times and count how many times she says yes, then divide by 100 to get a probability. There is in fact no way to perform a trial or use past data to guide me, and at any rate she's only going to say yes or no once. So based on my background knowledge and my assumptions about her, myself, and the world, I form an opinion which could be quantified as a "percent chance."

Once I've formed this opinion (which of course involves guesswork and subjectivity) I can then reason about it mathematically, using all the tools we've been developing. Of special interest to Bayesians is the notion of *updating* probabilities when new information comes to light, a topic we'll return to in a moment. For the Bayesian, the probability of some hypothesis being true is between 0 and 1, and when an agent (a human, or a bot) makes decisions, he/she/it does so on the most up-to-date information he/she/it has, always revising beliefs in various hypotheses when confirming or refuting evidence is encountered. Famous Bayesians include Pierre-Simon Laplace, sometimes called "the French Isaac Newton" for his scientific brilliance, and 18th century theologian Thomas Bayes, for whom the theory is named.

I won't try to conceal that my own thinking on this topic is pretty Bayesian. But I find this whole topic fascinating because it shows how brilliant people, who unanimously agree on the rules and equations, can have such radically different interpretations of what it all means.

4.4 Conditional probability

I mentioned that Bayesians are especially concerned with the idea of revising estimates about probability based on new information that may come to light. This notion can be crystallized in the idea of **conditional probability**. When we talk about the conditional probability of an event A, we mean "what's the probability that A occurs, *given* that I know some other event K has also occurred?" Think of K as "background knowledge": it's additional information which, when known, may influence how likely we think A is to have occurred. It can be mathematically computed as follows:

$$\Pr(A|K) = \frac{\Pr(A \cap K)}{\Pr(K)}$$

We pronounce $\Pr(A|K)$ as "the probability of A given K." It is the conditional probability of A, or "the probability of A conditioned on K." We'll sometimes call plain old $\Pr(A)$ the ***a priori*** **probability**, or the **prior** probability if we don't want to sound Latin. The prior is simply the original unadjusted probability, if we aren't privy to the background information K.

Let's go back to *American Idol*. We know that the probability of an underage winner is only .4, because $U = \{$ Kelly, Fantasia $\}$, and we estimate that each of them has a .2 probability of winning. So it seems more likely than not that our winner will be over 21. But

4.4. CONDITIONAL PROBABILITY

wait: suppose we had some additional information. Just before the outcome is announced, news is leaked through a Rupert Murdoch news source that the winner is a *woman*! If we believe this reporter, does that change our expectation about how old the winner is likely to be?

Indeed it does. Knowing that the winner is female eliminates Dave from consideration. Looking back at Figure 4.1, we can see that once we know Dave is out of the running, the remaining pool consists of just F, which includes Kelly, Fantasia, and Carrie. The question is, how do we update our probability from .4 to reflect the fact that only these three ladies are left?

In this case F is the background knowledge: we know that the event F has occurred. And we want to know how likely U is to also have occurred. This is found easily:

$$\begin{aligned} \Pr(U|F) &= \frac{\Pr(U \cap F)}{\Pr(F)} \\ &= \frac{\Pr(\{\text{Kelly,Fantasia}\})}{\Pr(\{\text{Kelly,Fantasia,Carrie}\})} \\ &= \frac{.4}{.5} = .8. \end{aligned}$$

Our estimated chance of an underage winner doubled once we found out she was female (even though we don't yet know *which* female).

If you stare at the equation and diagram, you'll see the rationale for this formula. Kelly and Fantasia originally had only .4 of the entire probability between them. But once David was axed, the question became: "what percentage of the *remaining* probability do Kelly and Fantasia have?" The answer was no longer .4 out of 1, but .4 out of .5, since only .5 of the whole was left post-David. This is why we divided by $\Pr(F)$: that's what we know remains given our background fact.

Now in this case, the conditional probability was higher than the original probability. Could it ever be lower? Easily. Consider the probability of a rock-star winner, $\Pr(R)$. *A priori*, it's .7. But again, let's say we had information leaked to us that the winner, whoever she may be, is female. We can now update our estimate:

$$\Pr(R|F) = \frac{\Pr(R \cap F)}{\Pr(F)}$$
$$= \frac{\Pr(\{\text{Kelly}\})}{\Pr(\{\text{Kelly,Fantasia,Carrie}\})}$$
$$= \frac{.2}{.5} = .4.$$

You see, once we find out that David is no longer a possibility, our only remaining hope for a rock star is Kelly. And she has only 40% of the probability that's left over. Note that this is a higher chance for her personally — she's got to be excited by the press leak — but it's lower for *rock stars*, of which she is only one (and evidently, not the predicted strongest).

Background knowledge can even peg our probability estimate to an extreme: all the way to 0, or to 1. What's $\Pr(U|C)$, the probability of an underage winner, given that he/she is a country singer? The intersection of U and C is zero, so this makes $\Pr(U|C) = 0$. In words: a country winner eliminates any possibility of an underage winner. And what's $\Pr(F|U)$, the probability that a woman wins, given that we know the winner to be underage? Well, $F \cap U$ and U are the same (check me), so $\frac{\Pr(F \cap U)}{\Pr(U)} = \frac{.4}{.4} = 1$. Therefore, an underage winner guarantees a female winner.

The way I think about conditional probability is this: look at the diagram, consider the events known to have occurred, and then *mentally block out everything except that*. Once we know the background fact(s), we're essentially dealing with a restricted world. Take the example of the known female winner. Once we know that event F in fact occurred, we can visually filter out David, and look at the F blob as though that were our entire world. In this restricted female-only view, the underage elements comprise a greater percentage of the total than they did before. And half of the rock-star elements have now been obscured, leaving only Kelly as the one-of-the-remaining-three.

4.5. TOTAL PROBABILITY

Many psychologists, by the way, claim that we're constantly doing this sort of thing in our minds: gathering facts, then revising our beliefs about the world in light of those facts. We start by believing that $\Pr(X)$ is approximately some value. Then we learn K_1 has occurred, and we update this to $\Pr(X|K_1)$. Then we learn that K_2 has also occurred, and so now we have $\Pr(X|K_1 \cap K_2)$. (Can you see why it's the intersection?) The more we learn, the more we revise our estimate up or down, presumably getting more accurate as we go. Another way of looking at it is that every time we learn something new is true, we also learn that its opposite is *not* true, and therefore we can eliminate some parts of the theoretically-possible universe that we have now ruled out. The denominator gets smaller and smaller as we eliminate possibilities.

Keep in mind, by the way, that unlike union and intersection, conditional probability is not commutative. In other words, $\Pr(X|Y) \neq \Pr(Y|X)$ in general. To take just one example, look again at the F and U sets from *All-time Idol*. $\Pr(F|U)$, as we already computed, is equal to 1 since if U has occurred, we automatically know that F has also occurred (there aren't any underage contestants *except* females). But the reverse is certainly not true: just because we have a female winner doesn't mean we have an underage winner, since the winner might be Carrie. Working it out, $\Pr(U|F) = \frac{\Pr(U \cap F)}{\Pr(F)} = \frac{.4}{.5} = .8$. Higher than $\Pr(U)$, but not 1.

4.5 Total probability

There's a very useful fact that goes by the grandiose name "The Law of Total Probability." It goes like this. If there's an event whose probability we'd like to know, we can split it up into pieces and add up their probabilities, as long as we do it in the right way.

"The right way" bit is the key, of course. And it has to do with partitions. Recall from section 2.12 that a partition of a set is a mutually exclusive and collectively exhaustive group of subsets. One example is that *every* set and its complement together form a partition of Ω. By the same token, for any sets A and B, these two sets together form a partition of A:

$$A \cap B$$
$$A \cap \overline{B}$$

This is worth taking a moment to understand completely. Suppose A is the set of all WWE professional wrestling fans, and B is the set of all people born in southern states. The first set listed above, $A \cap B$ contains professional wrestling fans born in southern states, and the second set, $A \cap \overline{B}$, the wrestling fans not born in southern states. Clearly, every wrestling fan is in one of these two sets, and no fan is in both. So it's a partition of A. This works for *any* two sets A and B: $A \cap B$ and $A \cap \overline{B}$ are a partition of A. We're just dividing up the A's into the A's that are also B's, and the A's that are not B's. Every A is in one (and just one) of those groups.

This idea can be extended to more than two sets. Let C_1 be the set of all people born in southern states, C_2 the set of people born in western states, and C_3 those not born in either region. (The set C_3 includes lots of things: people born in Ohio, people born in Taiwan, and ham sandwiches, among others.) The following three sets, then, together form another partition of A: $A \cap C_1$, $A \cap C_2$, and $A \cap C_3$. This is because every professional wrestling fan is either born in the south, or born in the west, or neither one.

Okay, now back to probability. In the two-set case, no matter what the event A is, we can divide up its probability like this:

$$\Pr(A) = \Pr(A \cap B) + \Pr(A \cap \overline{B})$$
$$= \Pr(A|B)\Pr(B) + \Pr(A|\overline{B})\Pr(\overline{B})$$

where B is any other event. The last step makes use of the conditional probability definition from above. We're dividing up A into the B's and the non-B's, in a strategy to determine A's probability. In the general case, if N sets named C_k (where k is a number from 1 to N) make up a partition of Ω, then:

4.5. TOTAL PROBABILITY

$$\begin{aligned}\Pr(A) &= \Pr(A \cap C_1) + \Pr(A \cap C_2) + \cdots + \Pr(A \cap C_N) \\ &= \Pr(A|C_1)\Pr(C_1) + \Pr(A|C_2)\Pr(C_2) + \cdots + \Pr(A|C_N)\Pr(C_N) \\ &= \sum_{k=1}^{N} \Pr(A|C_k)\Pr(C_k)\end{aligned}$$

is the formula.[1]

Let's take an example of this approach. Suppose that as part of a promotion for Muvico Cinemas movie theatre, we're planning to give a door prize to the 1000th customer this Saturday afternoon. We want to know, though, the probability that this person will be a minor. Figuring out how many patrons overall will be under 18 might be difficult. But suppose we're showing these three films on Saturday: *Spiderman: No Way Home*, *Here Before*, and *Sonic the Hedgehog 2*. We can estimate the fraction of each movie's viewers that will be minors: .6, .01, and .95, respectively. We can also predict how many tickets will be sold for each film: 2,000 for the Spiderman, 500 for Here Before, and 1,000 for Sonic.

Applying frequentist principles, we can compute the probability that a particular visitor will be seeing each of the movies:

$$\Pr(\text{Spiderman}) = \tfrac{2000}{2000+500+1000} = .571$$

$$\Pr(\text{Here Before}) = \tfrac{500}{2000+500+1000} = .143$$

$$\Pr(\text{Sonic}) = \tfrac{1500}{2000+500+1000} = .286$$

---

[1] If you're not familiar with the notation in that last line, realize that Σ (a capital Greek "sigma") just represents a sort of loop with a counter. The "$k = 1$" under the sign means that the counter is k and starts at 1; the "N" above the sign means the counter goes up to N, which is its last value. And what does the loop do? It adds up a cumulative sum. The thing being added to the total each time through the loop is the expression to the right of the sign. The last line with the Σ is just a more compact way of expressing the preceding line.

To be clear: this is saying that if we select a visitor at random on Saturday, the probability that they will be seeing Spiderman is .571.

But (and this is the trick) we can also compute the *conditional* probability that an attendee of each of these films will be a minor:

$$\Pr(\text{minor}|\text{Spiderman}) = .6$$
$$\Pr(\text{minor}|\text{Here Before}) = .01$$
$$\Pr(\text{minor}|\text{Sonic}) = .95$$

In words: "If we know that a visitor is coming to see Spiderman, there's a .6 probability that they'll be a minor." We're using the background knowledge to determine the conditional probability. It might be hard to figure out the probability of minors in general, but easier to figure out the probability of minors watching a specific movie.

Now, it's just a matter of stitching together the parts:

$$\begin{aligned}\Pr(\text{minor}) &= \Pr(\text{minor}|\text{Spiderman})\Pr(\text{Spiderman}) + \\ &\quad \Pr(\text{minor}|\text{Here Before})\Pr(\text{Here Before}) + \\ &\quad \Pr(\text{minor}|\text{Sonic})\Pr(\text{Sonic}) \\ &= .6 \cdot .571 + .01 \cdot .143 + .95 \cdot .286 \\ &= .343 + .00143 + .272 \approx .616 \end{aligned}$$

In words, there are three different ways for a visitor to be a minor: they could be a Spiderman fan and a minor (pretty likely, since there's lots of Spiderman fans), or a Here Before fan and a minor (not likely), or a Sonic fan and a minor (fairly likely, since although there's not a ton of Sonic fans overall, most of them are minors). Adding up these probabilities is legit only *because* the three movies form a partition of the visitors (*i.e.*, every visitor is there to see one and only one movie).

The Law of Total Probability comes in handy in scenarios where there's more than one "way" for an event to occur. It lets you break that event apart into the different ways, then apply your knowledge of the likelihood of each of those ways in order to compute the grand, overall probability of the event.

4.6 Bayes' Theorem

Another trick that helps compute probabilities in practice is **Bayes' Theorem**. We've defined $\Pr(A|K)$ as $\frac{\Pr(A \cap K)}{\Pr(K)}$, and by swapping the letters we get $\Pr(K|A) = \frac{\Pr(K \cap A)}{\Pr(A)}$. Combining these with a little bit of algebra yields:

$$\Pr(A|K) = \frac{\Pr(K|A) \Pr(A)}{\Pr(K)}$$

Now this is a very, very powerful equation that has a multitude of uses throughout computer science and statistics. What makes it powerful is that it allows us to express $\Pr(A|K)$, a quantity often very difficult to estimate, in terms of $\Pr(K|A)$, which is often much easier.

A simple and commonly cited example is that of interpreting medical exam results for the presence of a disease. If your doctor recommends that you undergo a blood test to see if you have some rare condition, you might test positive or negative. But suppose you do indeed test positive. What's the probability that you actually have the disease? That, of course, is the key point.

In symbols, we're looking for $\Pr(D|T)$, where D is the event that you actually have the disease in question, and T is the event that you test positive for it. But this is hard to approximate with available data. For one thing, most people who undergo this test *don't* test positive, so we don't have a ton of examples of event T occurring whereby we could count the times D also occurred. But worse, it's hard to tell whether a patient *has* the disease, at least before advanced symptoms develop — that, after all, is the purpose of our test!

Bayes' Theorem, however, lets us rewrite this as:

$$\Pr(D|T) = \frac{\Pr(T|D)\, \Pr(D)}{\Pr(T)}.$$

Now we have $\Pr(D|T)$, the hard quantity to compute, in terms of three things we *can* get data for. To estimate $\Pr(T|D)$, the probability of a person who has the disease testing positive, we can administer the test to unfortunate patients with advanced symptoms and count how many of them test positive. To estimate $\Pr(D)$, the prior probability of having the disease, we can divide the number of known cases by the population as a whole to find how prevalent it is. And getting $\Pr(T)$, the probability of testing positive, is easy since we know the results of the tests we've administered.

In numbers, suppose our test is 99% accurate — *i.e.*, if someone actually has the disease, there's a .99 probability they'll test positive for it, and if they don't have it, there's a .99 probability they'll test negative. Let's also assume that this is a very rare disease: only one in a thousand people contracts it.

When we interpret those numbers in light of the formula we're seeking to populate, we realize that $\Pr(T|D) = .99$, and $\Pr(D) = \frac{1}{1000}$. The other quantity we need is $\Pr(T)$, and we're all set. But how do we figure out $\Pr(T)$, the probability of testing positive?

Answer: use the Law of Total Probability. There are two different "ways" to test positive: (1) to actually have the disease, and (correctly) test positive for it, or (2) to *not* have the disease, but incorrectly test positive for it anyway because the test was wrong. Let's compute this:

$$\begin{aligned}
\Pr(T) &= \Pr(T|D)\, \Pr(D) + \Pr(T|\overline{D})\, \Pr(\overline{D}) \\
&= .99 \cdot \frac{1}{1000} + .01 \cdot \frac{999}{1000} \\
&= .00099 + .00999 = .01098
\end{aligned} \tag{4.1}$$

4.6. BAYES' THEOREM

See how that works? If I *do* have the disease (and there's a 1 in 1,000 chance of that), there's a .99 probability of me testing positive. On the other hand, if I *don't* have the disease (a 999 in 1,000 chance of that), there's a .01 probability of me testing positive anyway. The sum of those two mutually exclusive probabilities is .01098.

Now we can use our Bayes' Theorem formula to deduce:

$$\Pr(D|T) = \frac{\Pr(T|D)\Pr(D)}{\Pr(T)}$$
$$= \frac{.99 \cdot \frac{1}{1000}}{.01098} \approx .0902$$

Wow. We tested positive on a 99% accurate medical exam, yet we only have about a 9% chance of actually having the disease! Great news for the patient, but a head-scratcher for the math student. How can we understand this? Well, the key is to look back at that Total Probability calculation in equation 4.1. Remember that there were two ways to test positive: one where you had the disease, and one where you didn't. Look at the contribution to the whole that each of those two probabilities produced. The first was .00099, and the second was .00999, over ten times higher. Why? Simply because the disease is so rare. Think about it: the test fails once every hundred times, but a random person only has the disease once every *thousand* times. If you test positive, it's far more likely that the test screwed up than that you actually have the disease, which is rarer than blue moons.

Anyway, all the stuff about diseases and tests is a side note. The main point is that Bayes' Theorem allows us to recast a search for $\Pr(X|Y)$ into a search for $\Pr(Y|X)$, which is often far easier to find numbers for.

One of many computer science applications of Bayes' Theorem is in text mining. In this field, we computationally analyze the words in documents in order to automatically classify them or form summaries or conclusions about their contents. One goal might be to identify the true author of a document, given samples of the writing of various suspected authors. Consider the *Federalist Papers*, the group of highly influential 18th century essays that argued for ratifying the Constitution. These essays were jointly authored by Alexander Hamilton, James Madison, and John Jay, but it was uncertain for many years which of these authors wrote which specific essays.

Suppose we're interested in determining which of these three Founding Fathers actually wrote essay #84 in the collection. To do this, the logical approach is to find Pr(Hamilton|essay84), Pr(Madison|essay84), and Pr(Jay|essay84), and then choose the author with the highest probability. But how can we possibly find out Pr(Hamilton|essay84)? "Given that essay #84 has these words in this order, what's the probability that Hamilton wrote it?" Impossible to know.

But with Bayes' Theorem, we can restructure this in terms of Pr(essay84|Hamilton) instead. That's a horse of a different color. We have lots of known samples of Hamilton's writing (and Madison's, and Jay's), so we can ask, "given that Hamilton wrote an essay, what's the probability that he would have chosen the words that appear in essay #84?" Perhaps essay #84 has a turn of phrase that is very characteristic of Hamilton, and contains certain vocabulary words that Madison never used elsewhere, and has fewer sentences per paragraph than is typical of Jay's writing. If we can identify the relevant features of the essay and compare them to the writing styles of the candidates, we can use Bayes' Theorem to estimate the relative probabilities that each of them would have produced that kind of essay. I'm glossing over a lot of details here, but this trick of exchanging one conditional probability for the other is the backbone of this whole technique.

4.7 Independence

We've seen that a particular problem can involve multiple different events. In the *All-time Idol* example, we considered the probability of a female winner, a country singer winner, and an underage winner, among other things.

Now one question that often arises concerns the *independence* of events. Two events A and B are called **independent** if the prior

4.7. INDEPENDENCE

probability is the same as the conditional probability; that is, if $\Pr(A|B) = \Pr(A)$.

If you reflect on what this means, you'll see that with independent events, knowing that one of them occurred tells you *nothing* (either for or against) about whether the other one also occurred.

For example, let S be the event that Strike For Gold wins the Kentucky Derby next May. Let R be the event that it rains that day. If I say that S and R are independent, I'm claiming that rain (or the absence thereof) would have no impact either way on the horse's chances. If you were able to see the future, and reveal to me the weather on Derby Day, that's fine but it wouldn't help me in my betting. Knowing $\Pr(R)$ wouldn't give me any helpful information, because $\Pr(S|R)$ is the same as just plain old $\Pr(S)$ anyway.

That's a conceptual explanation. In the end, it boils down to numbers. Suppose we have the following **contingency table** that shows the results of a survey we conducted at UMW on dominant handedness:

	Male	Female
Left-handed	20	26
Right-handed	160	208

The data is self-explanatory. Obviously there were a lot more right-handers who took our survey than left, and slightly more women than men. Now consider: if this data is reflective of the population as a whole, what's $\Pr(L)$, where L is the event that a randomly chosen person is left-handed? We surveyed 160+208=368 right-handers and only 20+26=46 southpaws, so we'll estimate that $\Pr(L) = \frac{46}{368+46} \approx .111$. If you pick a random person on campus, our best guess is that there's a .111 probability of them being left-handed.

Suppose I told you, however, before you knew anything about the randomly chosen person's handedness, that she was a woman. Would that influence your guess? In this case, you'd have extra information that the F event had occurred (F being the event of a female selection), and so you want to revise your estimate as

$\Pr(L|F)$. Considering only the women, then, you compute $\Pr(L|F)$ = $\frac{26}{234} \approx .111$ from the data in the table.

Wait a minute. That's exactly what we had before. Learning that we had chosen a woman told us *nothing* useful about her handedness. That's what we mean by saying that the L and F events are independent of each other.

The shrewd reader may object that this was a startling coincidence: the numbers worked out exactly perfectly to produce this result. The proportion of left-handed females was precisely the same as that of left-handed males, down to the penny. Is this really likely to occur in practice? And if not, isn't independence so theoretical as to be irrelevant?

There are two ways of answering that question. The first is to admit that in real life, of course, we're bound to get some noise in our data, just because the sample is finite and there are random fluctuations in who we happened to survey. For the same reason, if we flipped an ordinary coin 1,000 times, we aren't likely to get *exactly* 500 heads. But that doesn't mean we should rush to the conclusion that the coin is biased. Statisticians have sophisticated ways of answering this question by computing *how much* the experimental data needs to deviate from what we'd expect before we raise a red flag. Suffice to say here that even if the contingency table we collect isn't picture perfect, we may still conclude that two events are independent if they're "close enough" to independence.

The other response, though, is that yes, the burden of proof is indeed on independence, rather than on non-independence. In other words, we shouldn't start by cavalierly assuming all the events we're considering are in fact independent, and only changing our mind if we see unexpected correlations between them. Instead, we should always be suspicious that two events will affect each other in some way, and only conclude they're independent if the data we collect works out more or less "evenly" as in the example above. To say that $\Pr(A|B)$ is the same as $\Pr(A)$ is an aggressive statement, outside the norm, and we shouldn't assume it without strong evidence.

4.7. INDEPENDENCE

Whoops!

One last point on the topic of independence: please don't make the mistake of thinking that *mutually exclusive* events are *independent*! This is by no means the case, and in fact, the opposite is true. If two events are mutually exclusive, they are extremely *de*pendent on each other!

Consider the most trivial case: I choose a random person on campus, and define I as the event that they're an in-state student, and O as the event that they're out-of-state. Clearly these events are mutually exclusive. But are they *independent*? Of course not! Think about it: if I told you a person was in-state, would that tell you anything about whether they were out-of-state? Duh. In a mutual exclusive case like this, event I completely rules out O (and vice versa), which means that although $\Pr(I)$ might be .635, $\Pr(I|O)$ is a big fat zero. More generally, $\Pr(A|B)$ is most certainly not going to be equal to $\Pr(A)$ if the two events are mutually exclusive, because learning about one event tells you *everything* about the other.

4.8 Exercises

1. At a swim meet, the competitors in the 100-m freestyle are Ben, Chad, Grover, and Tim. These four swimmers make up our sample space Ω for the winner of this heat. Is Chad $\in \Omega$?	Yes.
2. Is Tim an outcome?	Yes.
3. Is Ben an event?	No, since outcomes are *elements* of the sample space, while events are *subsets* of the sample space.
4. Is { Chad, Grover } an event?	Yes.
5. Is { Ben } an event?	Yes.
6. Suppose I told you that Pr({Ben})=.1, Pr({Chad})=.2, Pr({Grover})=.3, and Pr({Tim})=.3. Would you believe me?	Better not. This is not a valid probability measure, since the sum of the probabilities of all the outcomes, $Pr(\Omega)$, is not equal to 1.
7. Suppose I told you that Pr({Ben, Chad})=.3, and Pr({Ben, Tim})=.4, and Pr({Grover})=.4. Could you tell me the probability that Ben wins the heat?	Yes. If Pr({Ben, Chad})=.3 and Pr({Grover})=.4, that leaves .3 probability left over for Tim. And if Pr({Ben, Tim})=.4, this implies that Pr({Ben})=.1.
8. And what's the probability that someone besides Chad wins?	$Pr(\overline{\{Chad\}}) = 1 - Pr(\{Chad\})$, so we just need to figure out the probability that Chad wins, and take one minus that. Clearly if Pr({Ben, Chad})=.3 (as we were told), and Pr({Ben})=.1 (as we computed), then Pr({Chad})=.2, and the probability of a non-Chad winner is .8.

4.8. EXERCISES

9. Okay, so we have the probabilities of our four swimmers Ben, Chad, Grover, and Tim each winning the heat at .1, .2, .4, and .3, respectively. Now suppose Ben, Chad, and Grover are UMW athletes, Tim is from Marymount, Ben and Tim are juniors, and Chad and Grover are sophomores. We'll define $U=\{$Ben,Chad,Grover$\}$, $M=\{$Tim$\}$, $J=\{$Ben,Tim$\}$, and $S=\{$Chad,Grover$\}$. What's $\Pr(U)$?	.7.
10. What's $\Pr(J)$?	.4.
11. What's $\Pr(\overline{U})$?	.3. (1 - $\Pr(U)$, of course.)
12. What's $\Pr(J \cup S)$?	Exactly 1. All of the outcomes are represented in the two sets J and S. (Put another way, all competitors are juniors or seniors.)
13. What's $\Pr(J \cap S)$?	Zero. Sets J and S have no elements in common, therefore their intersection is a set with no outcomes, and the probability of a non-existent outcome happening is 0. (Put another way, nobody is both a junior and a senior.)
14. What's the probability of a UMW junior winning the heat?	This is $\Pr(U \cap J)$, which is the probability that the winner is a junior *and* a UMW student. Since $U \cap J = \{$ Ben $\}$, the answer is .1.

15. What's the probability that the winner is from UMW or a junior (or both)?	This is $\Pr(U \cup J)$, which is the probability that the winner is a junior *or* a UMW student (or both). This calls for computing $\Pr(U)$ plus $\Pr(J)$, but don't forget to then subtract $\Pr(U \cap J)$ so we don't double-count Ben! The correct answer is .7 + .4 - .1, which is equal to **1**. If this surprises you, look again at the data and realize that *every* swimmer is either a UMW student (Chad and Grover), a junior (Tim), or both (Ben).
16. What's $\Pr(J\|U)$?	By the definition of conditional probability, $\Pr(J\|U) = \frac{\Pr(J \cap U)}{\Pr(U)}$ or $\frac{.1}{.7} = \frac{1}{7} \approx \mathbf{.143}$. This is quite a bit lower than the .4 we computed for $\Pr(J)$ in item 10. So if you knew nothing about the winner other than the swimmers' baseline probabilities, you'd estimate a 40% chance of a junior winning...but if you learned the winner was a UMW student, your estimate of a junior winner would drop down to nearly 14%.
17. What's $\Pr(\overline{U}\|J)$?	$\Pr(\overline{U}\|J) = \frac{\Pr(\overline{U} \cap J)}{\Pr(J)}$ or $\frac{.3}{.4} = \frac{3}{4} = \mathbf{.75}$, way higher than the .3 from item 11. Learning that the swimmer is a junior makes the likelihood of a non-UMW winner leap sky high.
18. Suppose 75% of Twitter users vote, whereas only about half of people in general vote. Now say that about one out of every three people are on Twitter. If you see someone emerge from a voting booth, what's the probability they have a Twitter account?	The relevant probabilities here are $\Pr(\text{vote}\|\text{Twitter}) = .75$, $\Pr(\text{vote}) = .5$, and $\Pr(\text{Twitter}) = \frac{1}{3}$. By Bayes' Theorem, $\Pr(\text{Twitter}\|\text{vote}) = \frac{\Pr(\text{vote}\|\text{Twitter}) \cdot \Pr(\text{Twitter})}{\Pr(\text{vote})} = \frac{.75 \cdot .333}{.5} = \mathbf{.5}$. So although only a third of people tweet, the chances are 50-50 that someone tweets once you see them coming out of a voting booth.

Chapter 5

Structures

Much of computer science deals with representing and manipulating information. To do this, people have devised various **structures** for organizing chunks of data in a way that makes it easy to store, search, and retrieve. There's a whole course in most computer science curricula called "data structures" which covers how to implement these structures in code. In this book, we won't be talking about the code, but rather the abstract structures themselves. This chapter has a lot of pictures in it, which depict examples of the various structures in a very general way. The concepts here map directly to code when you need to put them into practice.

There are all kinds of data structures — arrays, linked lists, queues, stacks, hashtables, and heaps, to name a few — but they almost all boil down to one of two fundamental kinds of things: graphs, and trees. These are the two structures we'll focus on in this chapter. A graph is just about the most general structure you can envision: a bunch of scattered data elements that are related to each other in some way. Almost every data structure imaginable can be recast as a type of graph. Trees are sort of a special case of graphs, but also sort of a topic in their own right, kind of like functions were a special type of relation, but also kind of different. A tree can be seen as a type of graph that imposes extra special conditions which give some navigational benefit.

5.1 Graphs

In many ways, the most elegant, simple, and powerful way of representing knowledge is by means of a **graph**. A graph is composed of a bunch of little bits of data, each of which may (or may not) be attached to each of the others. An example is in Figure 5.1. Each of the labeled ovals is called a **vertex** (plural: *vertices*), and the lines between them are called **edges**. Each vertex does, or does not, contain an edge connecting it to each other vertex. One could imagine each of the vertices containing various descriptive attributes — perhaps the *John Wilkes Booth* oval would have information about Booth's birthdate, and *Washington, DC* information about its longitude, latitude, and population — but these are typically not shown on the diagram. All that really matters, graph-wise, is what vertices it contains, and which ones are joined to which others.

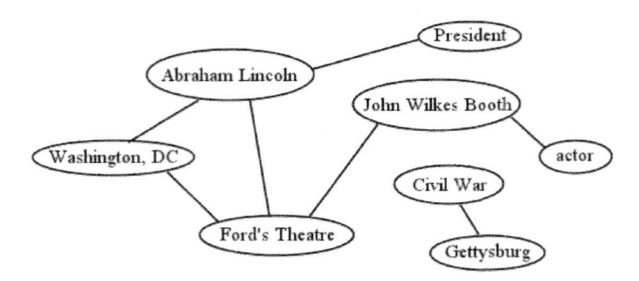

Figure 5.1: A graph (undirected).

Cognitive psychologists, who study the internal mental processes of the mind, have long identified this sort of structure as the principal way that people mentally store and work with information. After all, if you step back a moment and ask "what is the 'stuff' that's in my memory?" a reasonable answer is "well I know about a bunch of things, and the properties of those things, and the relationships between those things." If the "things" are vertices, and the "properties" are attributes of those vertices, and the "relationships" are the edges, we have precisely the structure of a graph. Psychologists have given this another name: a *semantic network*. It is thought that the myriad of concepts you have committed to memory —

5.1. GRAPHS

Abraham Lincoln, and *bar of soap*, and *my fall schedule*, and perhaps millions of others — are all associated in your mind in a vast semantic network that links the related concepts together. When your mind recalls information, or deduces facts, or even drifts randomly in idle moments, it's essentially traversing this graph along the various edges that exist between vertices.

That's deep. But you don't have to go near that deep to see the appearance of graph structures all throughout computer science. What's MapQuest, if not a giant graph where the vertices are travelable locations and the edges are routes between them? What's Facebook, if not a giant graph where the vertices are people and the edges are friendships? What's the World Wide Web, if not a giant graph where the vertices are pages and the edges are hyperlinks? What's the Internet, if not a giant graph where the vertices are computers or routers and the edges are communication links between them? This simple scheme of linked vertices is powerful enough to accommodate a whole host of applications, which is why it's worth studying.

Graph terms

The study of graphs brings with it a whole bevy of new terms which are important to use precisely:

vertex. Every graph contains zero or more vertices.[1] (These are also sometimes called nodes, concepts, or objects.)

edge. Every graph contains zero or more edges. (These are also sometimes called links, connections, associations, or relationships.) Each edge connects exactly two vertices, unless the edge connects a vertex to itself, which is possible, believe it or not. An edge that connects a vertex to itself is called a **loop**.

---

[1]The phrase "zero or more" is common in discrete math. In this case, it indicates that the **empty graph**, which contains no vertices at all, is still a legitimate graph.

path. A path is a sequence of consecutive edges that takes you from one vertex to the other. In Figure 5.1, there is a path between *Washington, DC* and *John Wilkes Booth* (by means of *Ford's Theatre*) even though there is no direct edge between the two. By contrast, no path exists between *President* and *Civil War*. Don't confuse the two terms edge and path: the former is a single link between two nodes, while the second can be a whole step-by-step traversal. (A single edge does count as a path, though.)

directed/undirected. In some graphs, relationships between nodes are inherently bidirectional: if A is linked to B, then B is linked to A, and it doesn't make sense otherwise. Think of Facebook: friendship always goes both ways. This kind of graph is called an **undirected** graph, and like the Abraham Lincoln example in Figure 5.1, the edges are shown as straight lines. In other situations, an edge from A to B doesn't necessarily imply one in the reverse direction as well. In the World Wide Web, for instance, just because webpage A has a link on it to webpage B doesn't mean the reverse is true (it usually isn't). In this kind of **directed** graph, we draw arrowheads on the lines to indicate which way the link goes. An example is Figure 5.2: the vertices represent famous boxers, and the directed edges indicate which boxer defeated which other(s). It is possible for a pair of vertices to have edges in both directions — Muhammad Ali and Joe Frazier each defeated the other (in separate bouts, of course) — but this is not the norm, and certainly not the rule, with a directed graph.

weighted. Some graphs, in addition to merely containing the *presence* (or absence) of an edge between each pair of vertices, also have a number on each edge, called the edge's **weight**. Depending on the graph, this can indicate the distance, or cost, between vertices. An example is in Figure 5.3: in true MapQuest fashion, this graph contains locations, and the mileage between them. A graph can be both directed and weighted, by the way. If a pair of vertices in such a graph is attached "both ways," then each of the two edges will have

5.1. GRAPHS

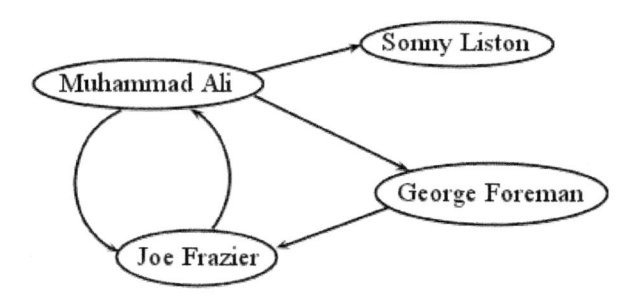

Figure 5.2: A directed graph.

its own weight.

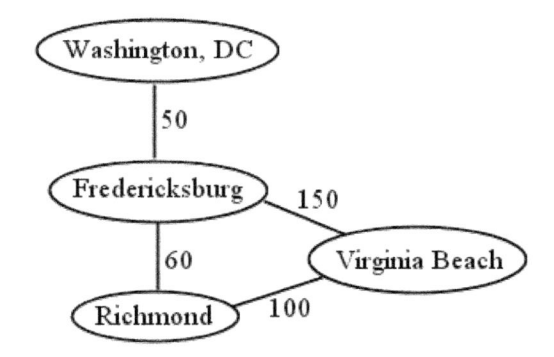

Figure 5.3: A weighted (and undirected) graph.

adjacent. If two vertices have an edge between them, they are said to be adjacent.

connected. The word **connected** has two meanings: it applies both to pairs of vertices and to entire graphs.

We say that two vertices are connected if there is at least one path between them. Each vertex is therefore "reachable" from the other. In Figure 5.1, *President* and *actor* are connected, but *Ford's Theatre* and *Civil War* are not.

"Connected" is also used to describe entire graphs, if *every* node can be reached from all others. It's easy to see that Figure 5.3 is a connected graph, whereas Figure 5.1 is not (because *Civil War* and *Gettysburg* are isolated from the other nodes). It's not always trivial to determine whether a graph is connected, however: imagine a tangled morass of a million vertices, with ten million edges, and having to figure out whether or not every vertex is reachable from every other. (And if that seems unrealistically large, consider Facebook, which has over a billion nodes.)

degree. A vertex's degree is simply the number of edges that connect to it. *Virginia Beach* has degree 2, and *Fredericksburg* 3. In the case of a directed graph, we sometimes distinguish between the number of incoming arrows a vertex has (called its **in-degree**) and the number of outgoing arrows (the **out-degree**). *Muhammad Ali* had a higher out-degree (3) than in-degree (1) since he won most of the time.

cycle. A cycle is a path that begins and ends at the same vertex.[2] In Figure 5.3, *Richmond–to–Virginia Beach–to–Fredericksburg–to–Richmond* is a cycle. Any loop is a cycle all by itself. For directed graphs, the entire loop must comprise edges in the "forward" direction: no fair going backwards. In Figure 5.2, *Frazier–to–Ali–to–Foreman–to–Frazier* is a cycle, as is the simpler *Ali–to–Frazier–to–Ali*.

DAG (directed, acyclic graph). One common use of graphs is to represent flows of dependencies, for instance the prerequisites that different college courses have for one another. Another example is project management workflows: the tasks needed to complete a project become vertices, and then the dependencies they have on one another become edges. The graph in Figure 5.4 shows the steps in making a batch of brownies, and how these steps depend on each other. The eggs have to be cracked before the ingredients can be mixed,

---

[2]We'll also say that a cycle can't repeat any edges or vertices along the way, so that it can't go back and forth repeatedly and pointlessly between two adjacent nodes. Some mathematicians call this a **simple cycle** to distinguish it from the more general **cycle**, but we'll just say that no cycles can repeat like this.

5.1. GRAPHS

and the oven has to be preheated before baking, but the pan can be greased any old time, provided that it's done before pouring the brown goop into it.

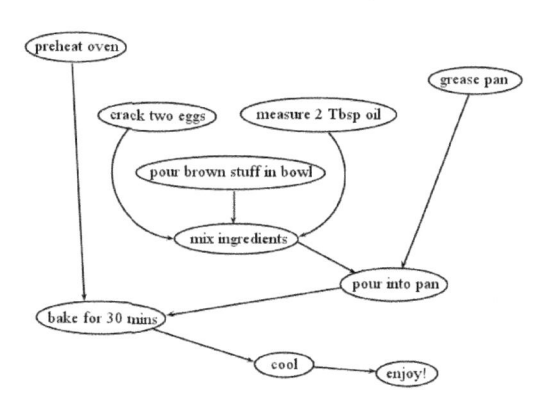

Figure 5.4: A DAG.

A graph of dependencies like this must be both **directed** and **acyclic**, or it wouldn't make sense. Directed, of course, means that task X can require task Y to be completed before it, without the reverse also being true. If they both depended on each other, we'd have an infinite loop, and no brownies could ever get baked! Acyclic means that *no* kind of cycle can exist in the graph, even one that goes through multiple vertices. Such a cycle would again result in an infinite loop, making the project hopeless. Imagine if there were an arrow from *bake for 30 mins* back to *grease pan* in Figure 5.4. Then, we'd have to grease the pan before pouring the goop into it, and we'd have to pour the goop before baking, but we'd also have to bake before greasing the pan! We'd be stuck right off the bat: there'd be no way to complete any of those tasks since they'd all indirectly depend on each other. A graph that is both directed and acyclic (and therefore free of these problems) is sometimes called a **DAG** for short.

Spatial positioning

One important thing to understand about graphs is which aspects of a diagram are relevant. Specifically, *the spatial positioning of the vertices doesn't matter*. In Figure 5.2 we drew *Muhammad Ali* in the mid-upper left, and *Sonny Liston* in the extreme upper right. But this was an arbitrary choice, and irrelevant. More specifically, this isn't part of the information the diagram claims to represent. We could have positioned the vertices differently, as in Figure 5.5, and had *the same graph*. In both diagrams, there are the same vertices, and the same edges between them (check me). Therefore, these are mathematically the same graph.

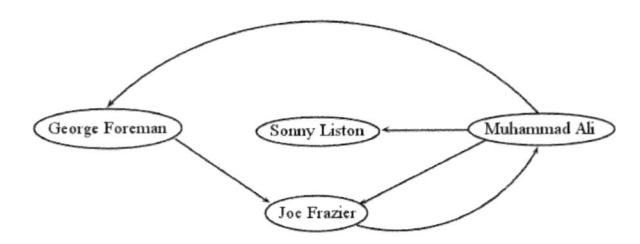

Figure 5.5: A different look to **the same graph as Figure 5.2**.

This might not seem surprising for the prize fighter graph, but for graphs like the MapQuest graph, which actually represent physical locations, it can seem jarring. In Figure 5.3 we could have drawn *Richmond* north of *Fredericksburg*, and *Virginia Beach* on the far west side of the diagram, and still had the same graph, provided that all the nodes and links were the same. Just remember that the spatial positioning is designed for human convenience, and isn't part of the mathematical information. It's similar to how there's no order to the elements of a set, even though when we specify a set extensionally, we have to list them in *some* order to avoid writing all the element names on top of each other. On a graph diagram, we have to draw each vertex *somewhere*, but where we put it is simply aesthetic.

5.1. GRAPHS

Relationship to sets

We seem to have strayed far afield from sets with all this graph stuff. But actually, there are some important connections to be made to those original concepts. Recall the wizards set A from chapter 3 that we extended to contain { Harry, Ron, Hermione, Neville }. Now consider the following endorelation on A:

(Harry, Ron)
(Ron, Harry)
(Ron, Hermione)
(Ron, Neville)
(Hermione, Hermione)
(Neville, Harry)

This relation, and all it contains, is represented faithfully by the graph in Figure 5.6. The elements of A are the vertices of course, and each ordered pair of the relation is reflected in an edge of the graph. Can you see how *exactly* the same information is represented by both forms?

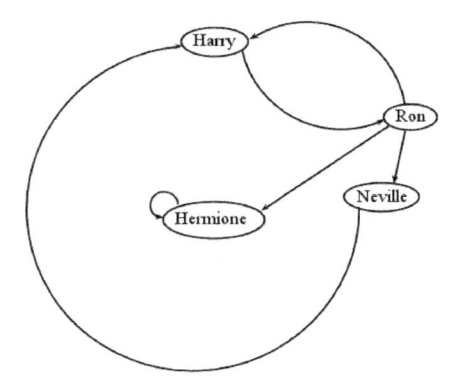

Figure 5.6: A graph depicting a endorelation.

Figure 5.6 is a directed graph, of course. What if it were an undirected graph? The answer is that the corresponding relation would be *symmetric*. An undirected graph implies that if there's an edge between two vertices, it goes "both ways." This is really identical to saying a relation is symmetric: if an (x, y) is in the relation, then the corresponding (y, x) must also be. An example is Figure 5.7, which depicts the following symmetric relation:

(Harry, Ron)
(Ron, Harry)
(Ron, Hermione)
(Hermione, Ron)
(Harry, Harry)
(Neville, Neville)

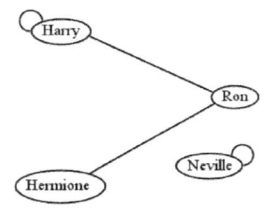

Figure 5.7: A graph depicting a symmetric endorelation.

Notice how the loops (edges from a node back to itself) in these diagrams represent ordered pairs in which both elements are the same.

Another connection between graphs and sets has to do with partitions. Figure 5.7 was not a connected graph: Neville couldn't be reached from any of the other nodes. Now consider: isn't a graph like this similar in some ways to a *partition* of A — namely, this one?

{ Harry, Ron, Hermione } and { Neville }.

We've simply partitioned the elements of A into the groups that are connected. If you remove the edge between Harry and Ron in that graph, you have:

{ Harry }, { Ron, Hermione }, and { Neville }.

5.1. GRAPHS

Then add one between Hermione and Neville, and now you have:

{ Harry } and { Ron, Hermione, Neville }.

In other words, the "connectedness" of a graph can be represented precisely as a partition of the set of vertices. Each connected subset is in its own group, and every vertex is in one and only one group: therefore, these isolated groups are mutually exclusive and collectively exhaustive. Cool.

Graph traversal

If you had a long list — perhaps of phone numbers, names, or purchase orders — and you needed to go through and do something to each element of the list — dial all the numbers, scan the list for a certain name, add up all the orders — it'd be pretty obvious how to do it. You just start at the top and work your way down. It might be tedious, but it's not confusing.

Iterating through the elements like this is called **traversing** the data structure. You want to make sure you encounter each element once (and only once) so you can do whatever needs to be done with it. It's clear how to traverse a list. But how to traverse a graph? There is no obvious "first" or "last" node, and each one is linked to potentially many others. And as we've seen, the vertices might not even *be* fully connected, so a traversal path through all the nodes might not even exist.

There are two different ways of traversing a graph: breadth-first, and depth-first. They provide different ways of exploring the nodes, and as a side effect, each is able to discover whether the graph is connected or not. Let's look at each in turn.

Breadth-first traversal

With **breadth-first traversal**, we begin at a starting vertex (it doesn't matter which one) and explore the graph cautiously and delicately. We probe equally deep in all directions, making sure we've looked a little ways down each possible path before exploring each of those paths a little further.

To do this, we use a very simple data structure called a **queue**. A queue is simply a list of nodes that are waiting in line. (In Britain, I'm told, instead of saying "line up" at the sandwich shop, they say "queue up.") When we enter a node into the queue at the tail end, we call it **enqueueing** the node, and when we remove one from the front, we call it **dequeueing** the node. The nodes in the middle patiently wait their turn to be dealt with, getting closer to the front every time the front node is dequeued.

An example of this data structure in action is shown in Figure 5.8. Note carefully that we always insert nodes at one end (on the right) and remove them from the *other* end (the left). This means that the first item to be enqueued (in this case, the triangle) will be the first to be dequeued. "Calls will be answered in the order they were received." This fact has given rise to another name for a queue: a "**FIFO**," which stands for "first-in-first-out."

Start with an empty queue:	|
Enqueue a triangle, and we have:	|△
Enqueue a star, and we have:	|△★
Enqueue a heart, and we have:	|△★♡
Dequeue the triangle, and we have:	|★♡
Enqueue a club, and we have:	|★♡♣
Dequeue the star, and we have:	|♡♣
Dequeue the heart, and we have:	|♣
Dequeue the club. We're empty again:	|

Figure 5.8: A queue in action. The vertical bar marks the "front of the line," and the elements are waiting to be dequeued in order from left to right.

Now here's how we use a queue to traverse a graph breadth-first. We're going to start at a particular node, and put all of its adjacent nodes into a queue. This makes them all safely "wait in line" until we get around to exploring them. Then, we repeatedly take the first node in line, do whatever we need to do with it, and then put

5.1. GRAPHS

all of *its* adjacent nodes in line. We keep doing this until the queue is empty.

Now it might have occurred to you that we can run into trouble if we encounter the same node multiple times while we're traversing. This can happen if the graph has a cycle: there will be more than one path to reach some nodes, and we could get stuck in an infinite loop if we're not careful. For this reason, we introduce the concept of **marking** nodes. This is kind of like leaving a trail of breadcrumbs: if we're ever about to explore a node, but find out it's marked, then we know we've already been there, and it's pointless to search it again.

So there are two things we're going to do to nodes as we search:

- To **mark** a node means to remember that we've already encountered it in the process of our search.

- To **visit** a node means to actually do whatever it is we need to do to the node (call the phone number, examine its name for a pattern match, add the number to our total, whatever.)

Now then. Breadth-first traversal (BFT) is an **algorithm**, which is just a step-by-step, reliable procedure that's guaranteed to produce a result. In this case, it's guaranteed to visit every node in the graph that's reachable from the starting node, and not get stuck in any infinite loops in the process. Here it is:

Breadth-first traversal (BFT)

1. Choose a starting node.
2. Mark it and enqueue it on an empty queue.
3. While the queue is not empty, do these steps:
    a) Dequeue the front node of the queue.
    b) Visit it.
    c) Mark and enqueue all of its *unmarked* adjacent nodes (in any order).

Let's run this algorithm in action on a set of Facebook users. Figure 5.9 depicts eleven users, and the friendships between them. First, we choose Greg as the starting node (not for any particular reason, just that we have to start somewhere). We mark him (in grey on the diagram) and put him in the queue (the queue contents are listed at the bottom of each frame, with the front of the queue on the left). Then, we begin our loop. When we take Greg off the queue, we visit him (which means we "do whatever we need to do to Greg") and then mark and enqueue his adjacent nodes Chuck and Izzy. It does not matter which order we put them into the queue, just as it did not matter what node we started with. In pane 3, Chuck has been dequeued, visited, and *his* adjacent nodes put on the queue. Only one node gets enqueued here — Adrian — because obviously Greg has already been marked (and even visited, no less) and this marking allows us to be smart and not re-enqueue him.

It's at this point that the "breadth-first" feature becomes apparent. We've just finished with Chuck, but instead of exploring Adrian next, *we resume with Izzy.* This is because she has been waiting patiently on the queue, and her turn has come up. So we lay Adrian aside (in the queue, of course) and visit Izzy, enqueueing her neighbor Elaine in the process. *Then*, we go back to Adrian. The process continues, in "one step on the top path, one step on the bottom path" fashion, until our two exploration paths actually meet each other on the back end. Visiting Jackie causes us to enqueue Brittany, and then when we take Kim off the queue, we do not re-enqueue Brittany because she has been marked and so we know she's already being taken care of.

For space considerations, Figure 5.9 leaves off at this point, but of course we would continue visiting nodes in the queue until the queue was empty. As you can see, Hank and Danielle will not be visited at all in this process: this is because apparently nobody they know knows anybody in the Greg crowd, and so there's no way to reach them from Greg. This is what I meant earlier by saying that as a side effect, the BFT algorithm tells us whether the graph is connected or not. All we have to do is start somewhere, run BFT, and then see whether any nodes have not been marked and visited. If there are any, we can continue with another starting point, and

5.1. GRAPHS

then repeat the process.

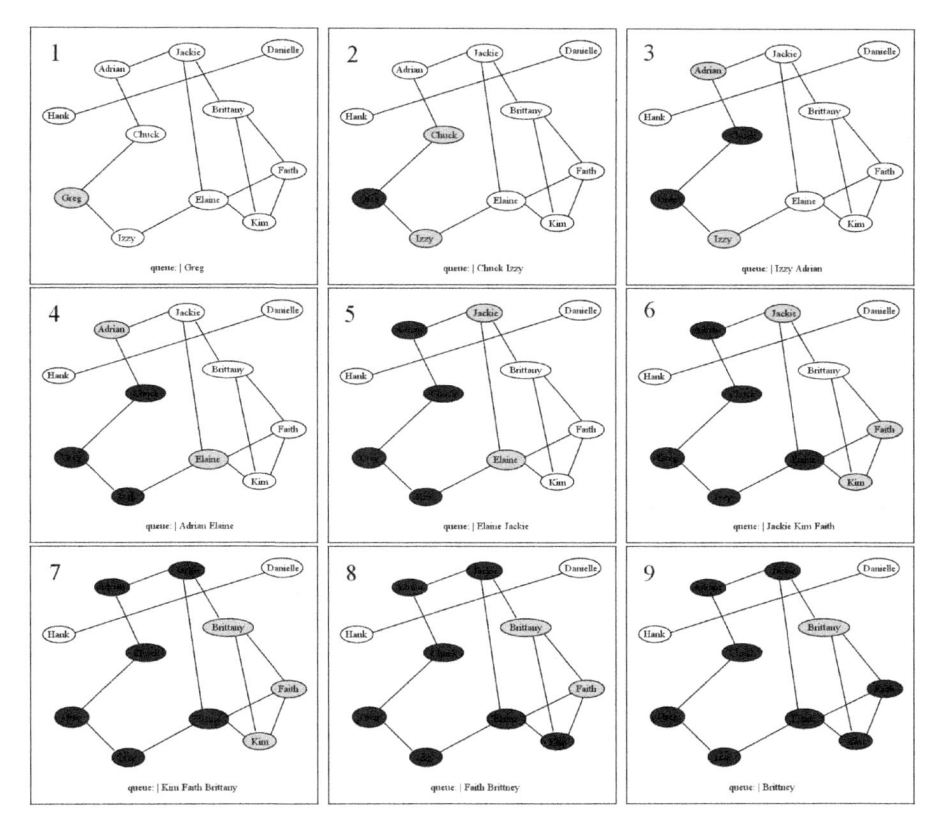

Figure 5.9: The stages of breadth-first traversal. Marked nodes are grey, and visited nodes are black. The order of visitation is: G, C, I, A, E, J, K, F, B.

Depth-first traversal (DFT)

With **depth-first traversal**, we explore the graph boldly and recklessly. We choose the first direction we see, and plunge down it all the way to its depths, before reluctantly backing out and trying the other paths from the start.

The algorithm is almost identical to BFT, except that instead of a queue, we use a **stack**. A stack is the same as a queue except

Start with an empty stack:	▁
Push a triangle, and we have:	△ ▁
Push a star, and we have:	★ △ ▁
Push a heart, and we have:	♡ ★ △ ▁
Pop the heart, and we have:	★ △ ▁
Push a club, and we have:	♣ ★ △ ▁
Pop the club, and we have:	★ △ ▁
Pop the star, and we have:	△ ▁
Pop the triangle. We're empty again:	▁

Figure 5.10: A stack in action. The horizontal bar marks the bottom of the stack, and the elements are pushed and popped from the top.

that instead of putting elements on one end and taking them off the other, you *add and remove to the same end.* This "end" is called the **top** of the stack. When we add an element to this end, we say we **push** it on the stack, and when we remove the top element, we say we **pop** it off.

You can think of a stack as...well, a stack, whether of books or cafeteria trays or anything else. You can't get anything out of the middle of a stack, but you can take items off and put more items on. Figure 5.10 has an example. The first item pushed is always the last one to be popped, and the most recent one pushed is always ready to be popped back off, and so a stack is also sometimes called a "**LIFO**" (last-in-first-out.)

The depth-first traversal algorithm itself looks like déjà vu all over again. All you do is replace "queue" with "stack":

5.1. GRAPHS

> **Depth-first traversal (DFT)**
> 1. Choose a starting node.
> 2. Mark it and push it on an empty stack.
> 3. While the stack is not empty, do these steps:
>   a) Pop the top node off the stack.
>   b) Visit it.
>   c) Mark and push all of its *unmarked* adjacent nodes (in any order).

The algorithm in action is shown in Figure 5.11. The stack really made a difference! Instead of alternately exploring Chuck's and Izzy's paths, it bullheadedly darts down Chuck's path as far as it can go, all the way to hitting Izzy's back door. Only then does it back out and visit Izzy. This is because the stack always pops off what it just pushed on, whereas whatever got pushed first has to wait until everything else is done before it gets its chance. That first couple of pushes was critical: if we had pushed Chuck before Izzy at the very beginning, then we would have explored *Izzy's* entire world before arriving at Chuck's back door, instead of the other way around. As it is, Izzy got put on the bottom, and so she stayed on the bottom, which is inevitable with a stack.

DFT identifies disconnected graphs in the same way as BFT, and it similarly avoids getting stuck in infinite loops when it encounters cycles. The only difference is the order in which it visits the nodes.

Finding the shortest path

We'll look at two other important algorithms that involve graphs, specifically *weighted* graphs. The first one is called **Dijkstra's shortest-path algorithm.** This is a procedure for finding the shortest path between two nodes, if one exists. It was invented in 1956 by the legendary computer science pioneer Edsger Dijkstra, and is widely used today by, among other things, network routing protocols.

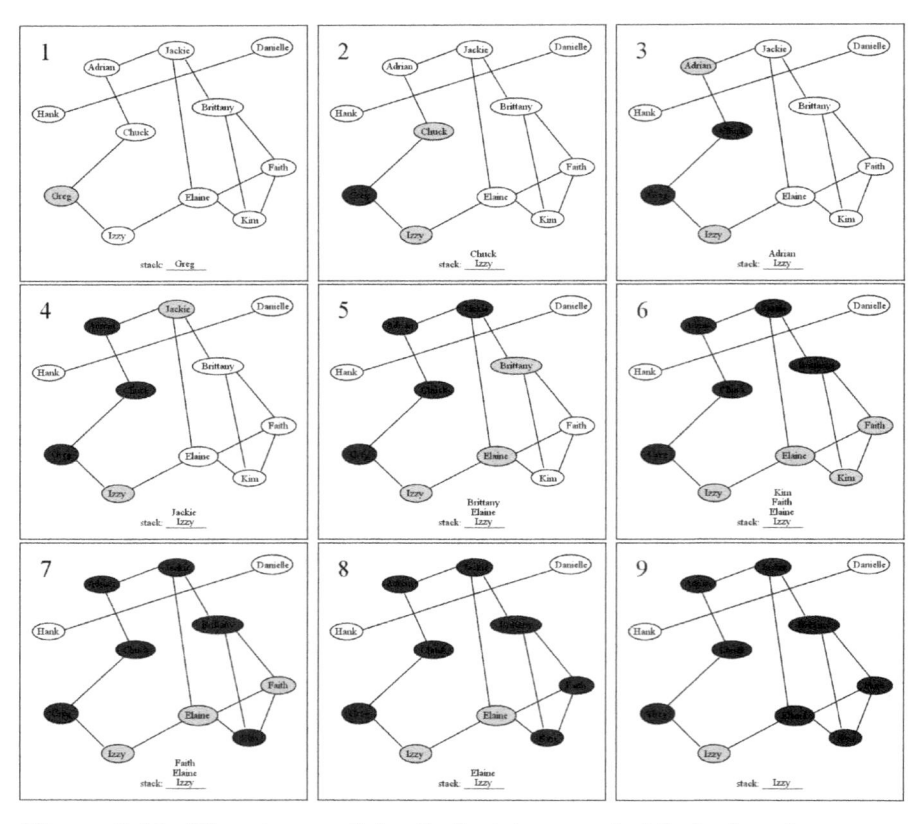

Figure 5.11: The stages of depth-first traversal. Marked nodes are grey, and visited nodes are black. The order of visitation is: G, C, A, J, B, K, F, E, I.

5.1. GRAPHS

Consider Figure 5.12, a simplified map of France circa November 1944. Fresh U.S. troops are arriving by ship at the port town of Bordeaux, and need to reach Strasbourg as quickly as possible to assist the Allies in pushing Nazi squadrons back into Germany. The vertices of this graph are French cities, and the edge weights represent marching distances in kilometers. Although D-Day was successful, the outcome of the War may depend on how quickly these reinforcements can reach the front.

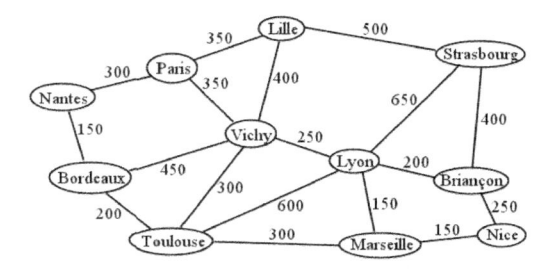

Figure 5.12: A weighted graph, through which we desire to find the shortest path from Bordeaux to Strasbourg.

The question, obviously, is which path the troops should take so as to reach Strasbourg the soonest. With a graph this small, you might be able to eyeball it. (Try it!) But Dijksta's algorithm systematically considers every possible path, and is guaranteed to find the one with the shortest total distance.

The way it works is to assign each node a *tentative* lowest distance, along with a tentative path from the start node to it. Then, if the algorithm encounters a different path to the same node as it progresses, it updates this tentative distance with the new, lower distance, and replaces the "best path to it" with the new one. Dijkstra's algorithm finds the shortest distance from the start node to the end node, but as a bonus, it actually finds the shortest distance from the start node to *every* node as it goes. Thus you are left with the best possible path from your start node to every other node in the graph.

Here's the algorithm in full:

> **Dijkstra's shortest-path algorithm**
>
> 1. Choose a starting node and an ending node.
> 2. Mark the tentative distance for the starting node as 0, and all other nodes as ∞.
> 3. While there are still unvisited nodes, do these steps:
>   a) Identify the *un*visited node with the smallest tentative distance. (If this is ∞, then we're done. All other nodes are unreachable.) Call this node the "current node."
>   b) For each unvisited neighbor of the current node, do these steps:
>   i. Compute the sum of the current node's tentative distance and the distance from the current node to its neighbor.
>   ii. Compare this total to the neighbor's current tentative distance. If it's less than the current tentative distance, update the tentative distance with this new value, and mark an arrow on the path from the current node to the neighbor (erasing any other arrow to the neighbor.)
>   iii. Mark the current node as visited. (Its distance and best path are now fixed.)

Don't worry, this isn't as hard as it sounds. But you do have to have your wits about you and carefully update all the numbers. Let's see it in action for WWII France. In the first frame of Figure 5.13, we've marked each node with a diamond containing the tentative shortest distance to it from Bordeaux. This is 0 for Bordeaux itself (since it's 0 kilometers away from itself, duh), and infinity for all the others, since we haven't explored anything yet, and we want to start off as pessimistic as possible. We'll update these distances to lower values as we find paths to them.

We start with Bordeaux as the "current node," marked in grey. In frame 2, we update the best-possible-path and the distance-of-that-

5.1. GRAPHS

path for each of Bordeaux's neighbors. Nantes, we discover, is no longer "infinity away," but a mere 150 km away, since there is a direct path to it from Bordeaux. Vichy and Toulouse are similarly updated. Note the heavy arrowed lines on the diagram, showing the best path (so far) to each of these cities from Bordeaux.

Step 3a tells us to choose the node with the lowest tentative distance as the next current node. So for frame 3, Nantes fits the bill with a (tentative) distance of 150 km. It has only one unmarked neighbor, Paris, which we update with *450* km. Why 450? Because it took us 150 to get from the start to Nantes, and another 300 from Nantes to Paris. After updating Paris, Nantes is now set in stone — we know we'll never encounter a better route to it than from Bordeaux directly.

Frame 4 is our first time encountering a node that already has a non-infinite tentative distance. In this case, we *don't* further update it, because our new opportunity (Bordeaux–to–Toulouse–to–Vichy) is 500 km, which is longer than going from Bordeaux to Toulouse direct. Lyon and Marseille are updated as normal.

We now have two unmarked nodes that tie for shortest tentative distance: Paris, and Vichy (450 km each). In this case, it doesn't matter which we choose. We'll pick Vichy for no particular reason. Frame 5 then shows some interesting activity. We do not update the path to Paris, since it would be 800 km through Vichy, whereas Paris already had a much better 450 km path. Lille is updated from infinity to 850 km, since we found our first path to it. But Lyon is the really interesting case. It already had a path — Bordeaux–to–Toulouse–to–Lyon — but that path was 800 km, and we have just found a *better* path: Bordeaux–to–Vichy–to–Lyon, which only costs 450 + 250 = 700. This means we remove the arrow from Toulouse to Lyon and draw a new arrow from Vichy to Lyon. Note that the arrow from Bordeaux to Toulouse doesn't disappear, even though it was part of this apparently-not-so-great path to Lyon. That's because the best route to *Toulouse* still *is* along that edge. Just because we wouldn't use it to go to Lyon doesn't mean we don't want it if we were going simply to Toulouse.

In frame 6, we take up the other 450 node (Paris) which we temporarily neglected when we randomly chose to continue with Vichy first. When we do, we discover a better path to Lille than we had before, and so we update its distance (to 800 km) and its path (through Nantes and Paris instead of through Vichy) accordingly.

When we consider Marseille in frame 7, we find another better path: this time to Lyon. Forget that through–Vichy stuff; it turns out to be a bit faster to go through Toulouse and Marseille. In other news, we found a way to Nice.

Hopefully you get the pattern. We continue selecting the unmarked node with the lowest tentative distance, updating its neighbors' distances and paths, then marking it "visited," until we're done with all the nodes. The last frame shows the completed version (with all nodes colored white again so you can read them). The verdict is: our troops should go from Bordeaux through Toulouse, Marseille, Lyon, and Briançon on their way to the fighting in Strasborg, for a total of 1,250 kilometers. Who knew? All other paths are longer. Note also how in the figure, the shortest distance to *every* node is easily identified by looking at the heavy arrowed lines.

Finding the minimal connecting edge set

So we've figured out the shortest path for our troops. But our field generals might also want to do something different: establish supply lines. A supply line is a safe route over which food, fuel, and machinery can be delivered, with smooth travel and protection from ambush. Now we have military divisions stationed in each of the eleven French cities, and so the cities must all be connected to each other via secure paths. Safeguarding each mile of a supply line takes resources, though, so we want to do this in the minimal possible way. How can we get all the cities connected to each other so we can safely deliver supplies between any of them, using the least possible amount of road?

This isn't just a military problem. The same issue came up in ancient Rome when aqueducts had to reach multiple cities. More recently, supplying neighborhoods and homes with power, or networking multiple computers with Ethernet cable, involves the same question. In all these cases, we're not after the shortest route be-

5.1. GRAPHS

tween two points. Instead, we're sort of after the shortest route "between all the points." We don't care how each pair of nodes is connected, provided that they *are* connected. And it's the total length of the required connections that we want to minimize.

To find this, we'll use **Prim's algorithm**, a technique named for the somewhat obscure computer scientist Robert Prim who developed it in 1957, although it had already been discovered much earlier (1930, by the Czech mathematician Vojtech Jarnik). Prim's algorithm turns out to be much easier to carry out than Dijkstra's algorithm, which I find surprising, since it seems to be solving a problem that's just as hard. But here's all you do:

Prim's minimal connecting edge set algorithm

1. Choose a node, any node.
2. While not all the nodes are connected, do these steps:
   a) Identify the node closest to the already-connected nodes, and connect it to those nodes via the shortest edge.

That's it. Prim's algorithm is an example of a **greedy algorithm**, which means that it always chooses the immediately obvious short-term best choice available. Non-greedy algorithms can say, "although doing X would give the highest short-term satisfaction, I can look ahead and see that choosing Y instead will lead to a better overall result in the long run." Greedy algorithms, by contrast, always gobble up what seems best at the time. That's what Prim's algorithm is doing in step 2a. It looks for the non-connected node that's immediately closest to the connected group, and adds it without a second thought. There's no notion of "perhaps I'll get a shorter overall edge set if I forego connecting this temptingly close node right now."

Sometimes, a greedy algorithm turns out to give an optimal result. Often it does not, and more sophisticated approaches can find better solutions. In this case, it happens to work out that the greedy approach does work! Prim's algorithm will always find the set of edges that connects all the nodes and does so with the lowest possible total distance. It's amazing that it can do so, especially since it never backtracks or revises its opinion the way Dijkstra's algorithm does.

Let's follow the algorithm's progress in the WWII example. We can start with any node, so we'll pick Vichy just at random. Frame 1 of Figure 5.14 shows what happens when the algorithm begins with Vichy: we simply examine all its neighbors, and connect the one that's closest to it. Nothing could be simpler. In this case, Lyon is a mere 250 km away, which is closer than anything else is to Vichy, so we connect it and add the Vichy–Lyon edge to our edge set. The figure shows a heavy black line between Vichy and Lyon to show that it will officially be a supply line.

And so it goes. In successive frames, we add Marseille, Nice, and Briançon to the set of connected nodes, since we can do no better than 150 km, 150 km, and 200 km, respectively. Note carefully that in frame 4 we connect Briançon to Lyon – *not* to Nice – because $200 < 250$.[3] Note also that the algorithm can jump around from side to side — we aren't looking for the shortest edge from the most recently added node, but from *any* connected node.

The final result is shown in the last frame. This is the best way to connect all the cities to each other, if "best" means "least total supply line distance," which in this case works out to 2450 total kilometers. But if you look carefully, you'll notice a fascinating thing. *This network of edges does* **not** *contain the shortest path from Bordeaux to Strasbourg!* I find that result dumbfounding. Wouldn't you think that the shortest path between any two nodes would land right on this Prim network? Yet if you compare Figure 5.14 with Figure 5.13 you'll see that the quickest way from Bordeaux to Strasbourg is through Marseille, not Vichy.

So we end up with the remarkable fact that the shortest route between two points has nothing whatsoever to do with the shortest *total* distance between *all* points. Who knew?

---

[3]It's very easy to fall into a trance and always add nodes only to the ends of the growing snake. In fact, I originally did that with this very example!

5.2. TREES

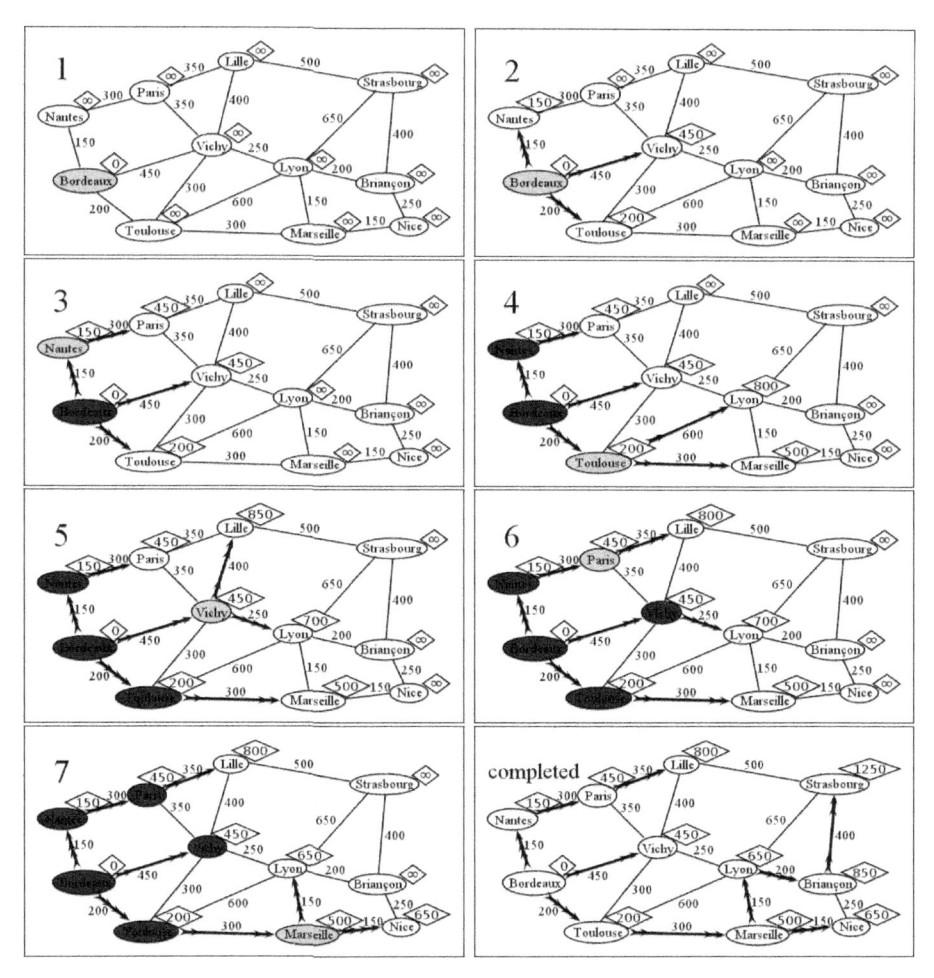

Figure 5.13: The stages of Dijkstra's shortest-path algorithm. The "current node" is shown in grey, with visited nodes (whose best paths and shortest distances have been unalterably determined) in black. The diamond next to each node shows the tentative shortest distance to that node from Bordeaux.

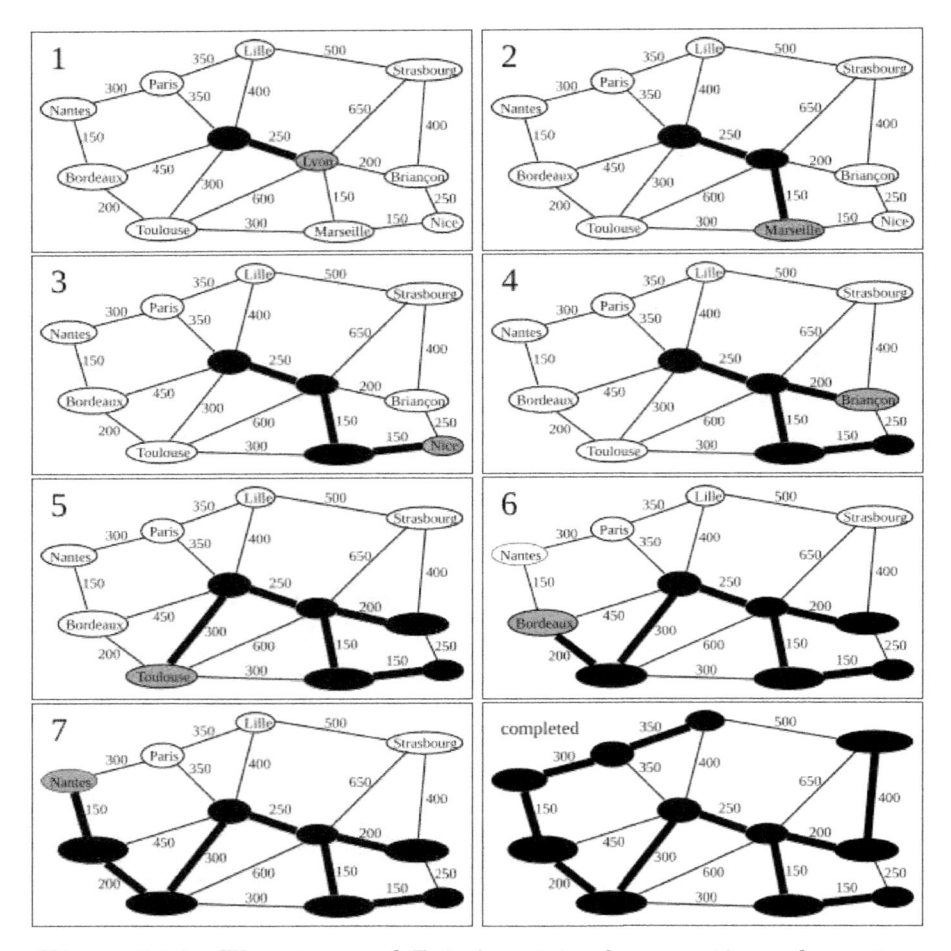

Figure 5.14: The stages of Prim's minimal connecting edge set algorithm. Heavy lines indicate edges that have been (irrevocably) added to the set.

5.2 Trees

A tree is really nothing but a simplification of a graph. There are two kinds of trees in the world: free trees, and rooted trees.[4]

Free trees

A **free tree** is just a connected graph with no cycles. Every node is reachable from the others, and there's only one way to get anywhere. Take a look at Figure 5.15. It looks just like a graph (and it is) but unlike the WWII France graph, it's more skeletal. This is because in some sense, a free tree doesn't contain anything "extra."

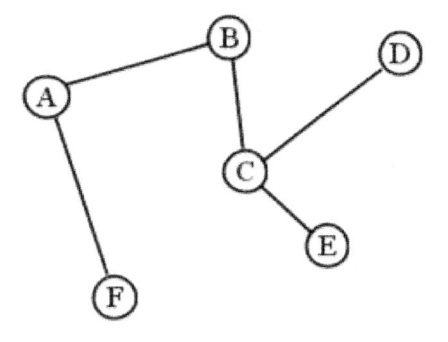

Figure 5.15: A free tree.

If you have a free tree, the following interesting facts are true:

1. There's exactly one path between any two nodes. (Check it!)
2. If you remove any edge, the graph becomes disconnected. (Try it!)
3. If you add any new edge, you end up adding a cycle. (Try it!)
4. If there are n nodes, there are $n-1$ edges. (Think about it!)

---

[4]There appears to be no consensus as to which of these concepts is the most basic. Some authors refer to a free tree simply as a "tree" — as though this were the "normal" kind of tree — and use the term rooted tree for the other kind. Other authors do the opposite. To avoid confusion, I'll try to always use the full term (although I admit I'm one who considers rooted trees to be the more important, default concept).

So basically, if your goal is connecting all the nodes, and you have a free tree, you're all set. Adding anything is redundant, and taking away anything breaks it.

If this reminds you of Prim's algorithm, it should. Prim's algorithm produced exactly this: a *free tree* connecting all the nodes — and specifically the free tree with shortest possible total length. Go back and look at the final frame of Figure 5.14 and convince yourself that the darkened edges form a free tree.

For this reason, the algorithm is often called **Prim's minimal spanning tree algorithm**. A "spanning tree" just means "a free tree that spans (connects) all the graph's nodes."

Keep in mind that there are many free trees one can make with the same set of vertices. For instance, if you remove the edge from A to F, and add one from anything else to F, you have a different free tree.

Rooted trees

Now a **rooted tree** is the same thing as a free tree, except that we elevate one node to become the **root**. It turns out this makes all the difference. Suppose we chose A as the root of Figure 5.15. Then we would have the rooted tree in the left half of Figure 5.16. The A vertex has been positioned at the top, and everything else is flowing under it. I think of it as reaching into the free tree, carefully grasping a node, and then lifting up your hand so the rest of the free tree dangles from there. Had we chosen (say) C as the root instead, we would have a different rooted tree, depicted in the right half of the figure. Both of these rooted trees have all the same edges as the free tree did: B is connected to both A and C, F is connected only to A, *etc.* The only difference is which node is designated the root.

Up to now we've said that the spatial positioning on graphs is irrelevant. But this changes a bit with rooted trees. Vertical positioning is our only way of showing which nodes are "above" others, and the word "above" does indeed have meaning here: it means closer to the root. The altitude of a node shows how many steps it is away

5.2. TREES

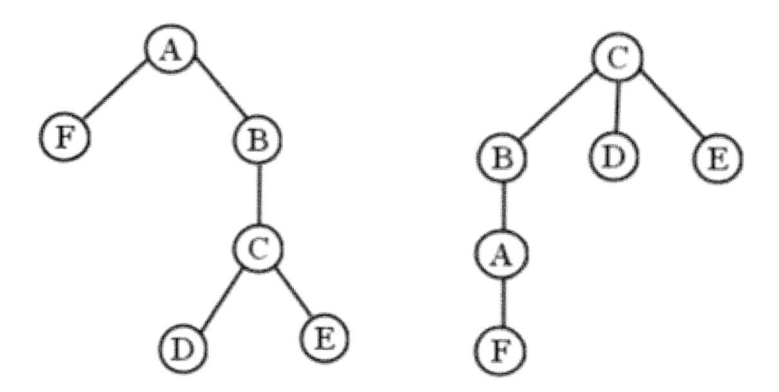

Figure 5.16: Two different rooted trees with the same vertices and edges.

from the root. In the right rooted tree, nodes B, D, and E are all one step away from the root (C), while node F is three steps away.

The key aspect to rooted trees — which is both their greatest advantage and greatest limitation — is that *every node has one and only one path to the root*. This behavior is inherited from free trees: as we noted, every node has only one path to every other.

Trees have a myriad of applications. Think of the files and folders on your hard drive: at the top is the root of the filesystem (perhaps "/" on Linux/Mac or "C:\\" on Windows) and underneath that are named folders. Each folder can contain files as well as other named folders, and so on down the hierarchy. The result is that each file has one, and only one, distinct path to it from the top of the filesystem. The file can be stored, and later retrieved, in exactly one way.

An "org chart" is like this: the CEO is at the top, then underneath her are the VP's, the Directors, the Managers, and finally the rank-and-file employees. So is a military organization: the Commander in Chief directs generals, who command colonels, who command majors, who command captains, who command lieutenants, who command sergeants, who command privates.

The human body is even a rooted tree of sorts: it contains skeletal, cardiovascular, digestive, and other systems, each of which is comprised of organs, then tissues, then cells, molecules, and atoms. In fact, anything that has this sort of part-whole containment hierarchy is just asking to be represented as a tree.

In computer programming, the applications are too numerous to name. Compilers scan code and build a "parse tree" of its underlying meaning. HTML is a way of structuring plain text into a tree-like hierarchy of displayable elements. AI chess programs build trees representing their possible future moves and their opponent's probable responses, in order to "see many moves ahead" and evaluate their best options. Object-oriented designs involve "inheritance hierarchies" of classes, each one specialized from a specific other. *Etc.* Other than a simple sequence (like an array), trees are probably the most common data structure in all of computer science.

Rooted tree terminology

Rooted trees carry with them a number of terms. I'll use the tree on the left side of Figure 5.16 as an illustration of each:

root. The node at the top of the tree, which is A in our example. Note that unlike trees in the real world, computer science trees have their root at the top and grow down. Every tree has a root except the **empty tree**, which is the "tree" that has no nodes at all in it. (It's kind of weird thinking of "nothing" as a tree, but it's kind of like the empty set $\varnothing$, which is still a set.)

parent. Every node except the root has one parent: the node immediately above it. D's parent is C, C's parent is B, F's parent is A, and A has no parent.

child. Some nodes have children, which are nodes connected directly below it. A's children are F and B, C's are D and E, B's only child is C, and E has no children.

5.2. TREES

sibling. A node with the same parent. E's sibling is D, B's is F, and none of the other nodes have siblings.

ancestor. Your parent, grandparent, great-grandparent, *etc.*, all the way back to the root. B's only ancestor is A, while E's ancestors are C, B, and A. Note that F is *not* C's ancestor, even though it's above it on the diagram: there's no connection from C to F, except back through the root (which doesn't count).

descendant. Your children, grandchildren, great-grandchildren, *etc.*, all the way to the leaves. B's descendants are C, D and E, while A's are F, B, C, D, and E.

leaf. A node with no children. F, D, and E are leaves. Note that in a (very) small tree, the root could itself be a leaf.

internal node. Any node that's not a leaf. A, B, and C are the internal nodes in our example.

depth (of a node). A node's depth is the distance (in number of nodes) from it to the root. The root itself has depth zero. In our example, B is of depth 1, E is of depth 3, and A is of depth 0.

height (of a tree). A rooted tree's height is the maximum depth of any of its nodes; *i.e.*, the maximum distance from the root to any node. Our example has a height of 3, since the "deepest" nodes are D and E, each with a depth of 3. A tree with just one node is considered to have a height of 0. Bizarrely, but to be consistent, we'll say that the empty tree has height -1! Strange, but what else could it be? To say it has height 0 seems inconsistent with a one-node tree also having height 0. At any rate, this won't come up much.

level. All the nodes with the same depth are considered on the same "level." B and F are on level 1, and D and E are on level 3. Nodes on the same level are *not* necessarily siblings. If F had a child named G in the example diagram, then G and C would be on the same level (2), but would *not* be siblings because they have different parents. (We might call them "cousins" to continue the family analogy.)

subtree. Finally, much of what gives trees their expressive power is their **recursive** nature. This means that a tree is made up of *other (smaller) trees.* Consider our example. It is a tree with a root of A. But the two children of A are each trees in their own right! F itself is a tree with only one node. B and its descendants make another tree with four nodes. We consider these two trees to be subtrees of the original tree. The notion of "root" shifts somewhat as we consider subtrees — A is the root of the original tree, but B is the root of the second subtree. When we consider B's children, we see that there is yet another subtree, which is rooted at C. And so on. It's easy to see that any subtree fulfills all the properties of trees, and so everything we've said above applies also to it.

Binary trees (BT's)

The nodes in a rooted tree can have any number of children. There's a special type of rooted tree, though, called a **binary tree** which we restrict by simply saying that *each node can have at most two children.* Furthermore, we'll label each of these two children as the "left child" and "right child." (Note that a particular node might well have *only* a left child, or *only* a right child, but it's still important to know which direction that child is.)

The left half of Figure 5.16 is a binary tree, but the right half is not (C has three children). A larger binary tree (of height 4) is shown in Figure 5.17.

Traversing binary trees

There were two ways of traversing a graph: breadth-first, and depth-first. Curiously, there are three ways of traversing a tree: **pre-order**, **post-order**, and **in-order**. All three begin at the root, and all three consider each of the root's children as subtrees. The difference is in the order of visitation.

5.2. TREES

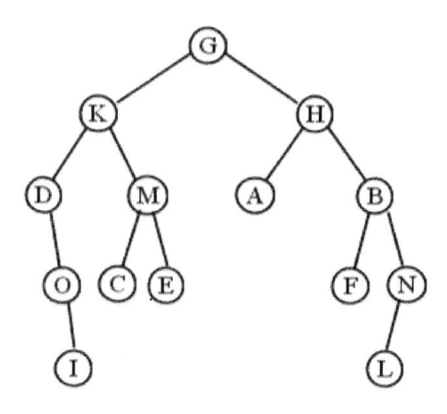

Figure 5.17: A binary tree.

To traverse a tree **pre-order**, we:
1. Visit the root.
2. Treat the left child and all its descendants as a subtree, and traverse it in its entirety.
3. Do the same with the right child.

It's tricky because you have to remember that each time you "treat a child as a subtree" you do *the whole traversal process* on that subtree. This involves remembering where you were once you finish.

Follow this example carefully. For the tree in Figure 5.17, we begin by visiting G. Then, we traverse the whole "K subtree." This involves visiting K itself, and then traversing *its* whole left subtree (anchored at D). After we visit the D node, we discover that it actually *has* no left subtree, so we go ahead and traverse its right subtree. This visits O followed by I (since O has no left subtree either) which finally returns back up the ladder.

It's at this point where it's easy to get lost. We finish visiting I, and then we have to ask "okay, where the heck were we? How did we get here?" The answer is that we had just been at the K node, where we had traversed its left (D) subtree. So now what is it time to do? Traverse the *right* subtree, of course, which is M. This involves visiting M, C, and E (in that order) before returning to the very top, G.

Now we're in the same sort of situation where we could have gotten lost before: we've spent a lot of time in the tangled mess of G's left subtree, and we just have to remember that it's now time to do G's right subtree. Follow this same procedure, and the entire order of visitation ends up being: G, K, D, O, I, M, C, E, H, A, B, F, N, L. (See Figure 5.18 for a visual.)

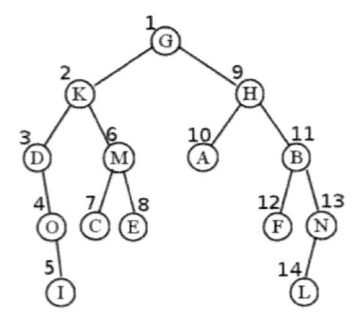

Figure 5.18: The order of node visitation in **pre-order** traversal.

To traverse a tree **post-order**, we:

1. Treat the left child and all its descendants as a subtree, and traverse it in its entirety.
2. Do the same with the right child.
3. Visit the root.

It's the same as pre-order, except that we visit the root after the children instead of before. Still, despite its similarity, this has always been the trickiest one for me. Everything seems postponed, and you have to remember what order to do it in later.

For our sample tree, the first node visited turns out to be I. This is because we have to postpone visiting G until we finish its left (and right) subtree; then we postpone K until we finish its left

5.2. TREES

(and right) subtree; postpone D until we're done with O's subtree, and postpone O until we do I. Then finally, the thing begins to unwind...all the way back up to K. But we can't actually visit K itself yet, because we have to do its right subtree. This results in C, E, and M, in that order. *Then* we can do K, but we still can't do G because we have its whole right subtree's world to contend with. The entire order ends up being: I, O, D, C, E, M, K, A, F, L, N, B, H, and finally G. (See Figure 5.19 for a visual.)

Note that this is not remotely the reverse of the pre-order visitation, as you might expect. G is last instead of first, but the rest is all jumbled up.

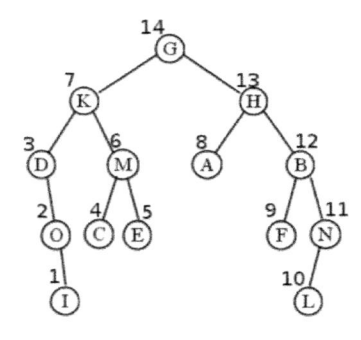

Figure 5.19: The order of node visitation in **post-order** traversal.

Finally, to traverse a tree **in-order**, we:

1. Treat the left child and all its descendants as a subtree, and traverse it in its entirety.
2. Visit the root.
3. Traverse the right subtree in its entirety.

So instead of visiting the root first (pre-order) or last (post-order) we treat it in between our left and right children. This might seem to be a strange thing to do, but there's a method to the madness which will become clear in the next section.

For the sample tree, the first visited node is D. This is because it's the first node encountered that doesn't have a left subtree, which means step 1 doesn't need to do anything. This is followed by O and I, for the same reason. We then visit K before its right subtree, which in turn visits C, M, and E, in that order. The final order is: D, O, I, K, C, M, E, G, A, H, F, B, L, N. (See Figure 5.20.)

If your nodes are spaced out evenly, you can read the in-order traversal off the diagram by moving your eyes left to right. Be careful about this, though, because ultimately the spatial position doesn't matter, but rather the relationships between nodes. For instance, if I had drawn node I further to the right, in order to make the lines between D–O–I less steep, that I node might have been pushed physically to the right of K. But that wouldn't change the order and have K visited earlier.

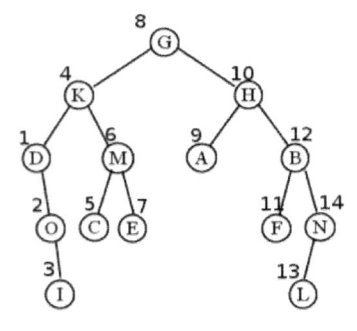

Figure 5.20: The order of node visitation in **in-order** traversal.

Finally, it's worth mentioning that all of these traversal methods make elegant use of **recursion**. Recursion is a way of taking a large problem and breaking it up into similar, but smaller, subproblems. Then, each of those subproblems can be attacked in the same way as you attacked the larger problem: by breaking *them* up into subproblems. All you need is a rule for eventually stopping the "breaking up" process by actually doing something.

Every time one of these traversal processes treats a left or right child as a subtree, they are "recursing" by re-initiating the whole traversal process on a smaller tree. Pre-order traversal, for instance,

5.2. TREES

after visiting the root, says, "okay, let's pretend we started this whole traversal thing with the smaller tree rooted at my left child. Once that's finished, wake me up so I can similarly start it with my right child." Recursion is a very common and useful way to solve certain complex problems, and trees are rife with opportunities.

Sizes of binary trees

Binary trees can be any ragged old shape, like our Figure 5.17 example. Sometimes, though, we want to talk about binary trees with a more regular shape, that satisfy certain conditions. In particular, we'll talk about three special kinds:

full binary tree. A full binary tree is one in which every node (except the leaves) has two children. Put another way, every node has either two children or none: no stringiness allowed. Figure 5.17 is not full, but it would be if we added the three blank nodes in Figure 5.21.

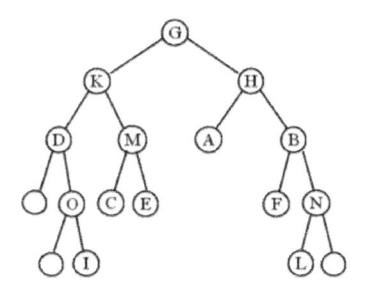

Figure 5.21: A full binary tree.

By the way, it isn't always possible to have a full binary tree with a particular number of nodes. For instance, a binary tree with two nodes, can't be full, since it inevitably will have a root with only one child.

complete binary tree. A complete binary tree is one in which every level has all possible nodes present, except perhaps for the deepest level, which is filled all the way from the left.

Figure 5.21 is not complete, but it would be if we fixed it up as in Figure 5.22.

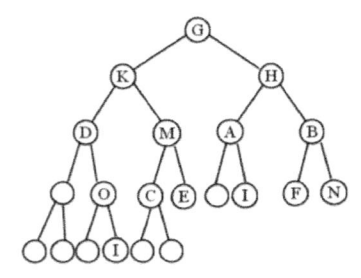

Figure 5.22: A complete binary tree.

Unlike full binary trees, it *is* always possible to have a complete binary tree no matter how many nodes it contains. You just keep filling in from left to right, level after level.

perfect binary tree. Our last special type has a rather audacious title, but a "perfect" tree is simply one that is exactly balanced: every level is completely filled. Figure 5.22 is not perfect, but it would be if we either added nodes to fill out level 4, or deleted the unfinished part of level 3 (as in Figure 5.23.)

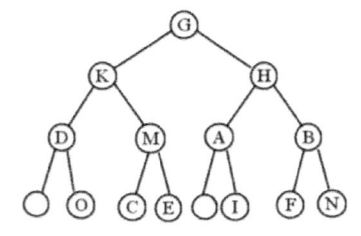

Figure 5.23: A "perfect" binary tree.

Perfect binary trees obviously have the strictest size restrictions. It's only possible, in fact, to have perfect binary trees with $2^{h+1} - 1$ nodes, if h is the height of the tree. So there are perfect binary trees with 1, 3, 7, 15, 31, ... nodes, but none in between. In each such tree, 2^h of the nodes (almost exactly half) are leaves.

5.2. TREES

Now as we'll see, binary trees can possess some pretty amazing powers if the nodes within them are organized in certain ways. Specifically, a binary search tree and a heap are two special kinds of binary trees that conform to specific constraints. In both cases, what makes them so powerful is the rate at which a tree grows as nodes are added to it.

Suppose we have a perfect binary tree. To make it concrete, let's say it has height 3, which would give it 1+2+4+8=15 nodes, 8 of which are leaves. Now what happens if you increase the height of this tree to 4? If it's still a "perfect" tree, you will have added 16 more nodes (all leaves). Thus you have *doubled* the number of leaves by simply adding one more level. This cascades the more levels you add. A tree of height 5 doubles the number of leaves again (to 32), and height 6 doubles it again (to 64).

If this doesn't seem amazing to you, it's probably because you don't fully appreciate how quickly this kind of **exponential growth** can accumulate. Suppose you had a perfect binary tree of height 30 — certainly not an awe-inspiring figure. One could imagine it fitting on a piece of paper...height-wise, that is. But run the numbers and you'll discover that such a tree would have over half a billion leaves, more than one for every person in the United States. Increase the tree's height to a mere 34 — just 4 additional levels — and suddenly you have over 8 billion leaves, easily greater than the population of planet Earth.

The power of exponential growth is only *fully* reached when the binary tree is perfect, since a tree with some "missing" internal nodes does not carry the maximum capacity that it's capable of. It's got some holes in it. Still, as long as the tree is fairly bushy (*i.e.*, it's not horribly lopsided in just a few areas) the enormous growth predicted for perfect trees is still approximately the case.

The reason this is called "exponential" growth is that the quantity we're varying — the height — appears as an *exponent* in the number of leaves, which is 2^h. Every time we add just *one* level, we *double* the number of leaves.

So the number of leaves (call it l) is 2^h, if h is the height of the tree. Flipping this around, we say that $h = \lg(l)$. The function "lg" is a logarithm, specifically a logarithm with base-2. This is what computer scientists often use, rather than a base of 10 (which is written "log") or a base of e (which is written "ln"). Since 2^h grows very, very quickly, it follows that $\lg(l)$ grows very, very slowly. After our tree reaches a few million nodes, we can add more and more nodes without growing the height of the tree significantly at all.

The takeaway message here is simply that an incredibly large number of nodes can be accommodated in a tree with a very modest height. This makes it possible to, among other things, search a huge amount of information astonishingly quickly...provided the tree's contents are arranged properly.

Binary search trees (BST's)

Okay, then let's talk about how to arrange those contents. A **binary search tree** (BST) is any binary tree that satisfies one additional property: *every node is "greater than" all of the nodes in its left subtree, and "less than (or equal to)" all of the nodes in its right subtree.* We'll call this **the BST property**. The phrases "greater than" and "less than" are in quotes here because their meaning is somewhat flexible, depending on what we're storing in the tree. If we're storing numbers, we'll use numerical order. If we're storing names, we'll use alphabetical order. Whatever it is we're storing, we simply need a way to compare two nodes to determine which one "goes before" the other.

An example of a BST containing people is given in Figure 5.24. Imagine that each of these nodes contains a good deal of information about a particular person — an employee record, medical history, account information, what have you. The nodes themselves are indexed by the person's name, and the nodes are organized according to the BST rule. Mitch comes after Ben/Jessica/Jim and before Randi/Owen/Molly/Xander in alphabetical order, and this ordering relationship between parents and children repeats itself all the way down the tree. (Check it!)

Be careful to observe that the ordering rule applies between a node

5.2. TREES

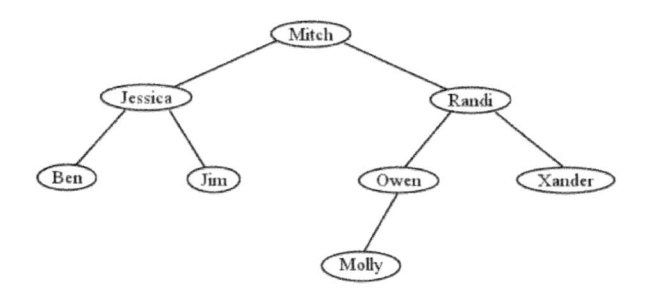

Figure 5.24: A binary search tree.

and the *entire* contents of its subtrees, not merely to its immediate children. This is a rookie mistake that you want to avoid. Your first inclination, when glancing at Figure 5.25, below, is to judge it a BST. It is *not* a binary search tree, however! Jessica is to the left of Mitch, as she should be, and Nancy is to the right of Jessica, as she should be. It seems to check out. But the problem is that Nancy is a descendant of Mitch's *left* subtree, whereas she must properly be placed somewhere in his *right* subtree. And yes, this matters. So be sure to check your BST's all the way up and down.

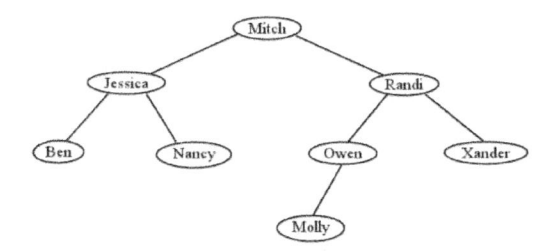

Figure 5.25: **NOT** a binary search tree, though it looks like one at first glance. (Notice Nancy and Mitch)

The power of BST's

All right, so what's all the buzz about BST's, anyway? The key insight is to realize that if you're looking for a node, all you have to do is start at the root and go *the height of the tree down* making one comparison at each level. Let's say we're searching Figure 5.24 for Molly. By looking at Mitch (the root), we know right away that Molly must be in the right subtree, not the left, because she comes *after* Mitch in alphabetical order. So we look at Randi. This time, we find that Molly comes *before* Randi, so she must be somewhere in Randi's left branch. Owen sends us left again, at which point we find Molly.

With a tree this size, it doesn't seem that amazing. But suppose its height were 10. This would mean about 2000 nodes in the tree — customers, users, friends, whatever. With a BST, you'd only have to examine *ten* of those 2000 nodes to find whatever you're looking for, whereas if the nodes were just in an ordinary list, you'd have to compare against 1000 or so of them before you stumbled on the one you were looking for. And as the size of the tree grows, this discrepancy grows (much) larger. If you wanted to find a single person's records in New York City, would you rather search 7 million names, or 24 names?? Because that's the difference you're looking at.

It seems almost too good to be true. How is such a speedup possible? The trick is to realize that with every node you look at, you effectively eliminate *half of the remaining tree* from consideration. For instance, if we're looking for Molly, we can disregard Mitch's entire left half without even looking at it, then the same for Randi's entire right half. If you discard half of something, then half of the remaining half, then half again, it doesn't take you long before you've eliminated almost every false lead.

There's a formal way to describe this speedup, called "Big-O notation." The subtleties are a bit complex, but the basic idea is this. When we say that an algorithm is "O(n)" (pronounced "oh–of–n"), it means that the time it takes to execute the algorithm is *proportional to the number of nodes*. This doesn't imply any specific number of milliseconds or anything — that is highly dependent on the type of computer hardware, you have, the programming language, and a myriad of other things. But what we *can* say about an O(n) algorithm is that if you double the number of nodes, you're going to approximately double the running time. If you quadruple

5.2. TREES

the number of nodes, you're going to quadruple the running time. This is what you'd expect.

Searching for "Molly" in a simple unsorted list of names is an O(n) prospect. If there's a thousand nodes in the list, on average you'll find Molly after scanning through 500 of them. (You might get lucky and find Molly at the beginning, but then of course you might get really unlucky and not find her until the end. This averages out to about half the size of the list in the normal case.) If there's a *million* nodes, however, it'll take you 500,000 traversals on average before finding Molly. Ten times as many nodes means ten times as long to find Molly, and a thousand times as many means a thousand times as long. Bummer.

Looking up Molly in a BST, however, is an O(lg n) process. Recall that "lg" means the logarithm (base-2). This means that doubling the number of nodes gives you a *miniscule* increase in the running time. Suppose there were a thousand nodes in your tree, as above. You wouldn't have to look through 500 to find Molly: you'd only have to look through *ten* (because lg(1000) ≈ 10). Now increase it to a million nodes. You wouldn't have to look through 500,000 to find Molly: you'd only have to look through *twenty*. Suppose you had 6 billion nodes in your tree (approximately the population of the earth). You wouldn't have to look through 3 billion nodes: you'd only have to look through *thirty-three*. Absolutely mind-boggling.

Adding nodes to a BST

Finding things in a BST is lightning fast. Turns out, so is adding things to it. Suppose we acquire a new customer named Jennifer, and we need to add her to our BST so we can retrieve her account information in the future. All we do is follow the same process we would if we were *looking* for Jennifer, but as soon as we find the spot where she would be, we add her there. In this case, Jennifer comes before Mitch (go left), and before Jessica (go left again), and after Ben (go right). Ben has no right child, so we put Jessica in the tree right at that point. (See Figure 5.26.)

This adding process is also an O(lg n) algorithm, since we only need

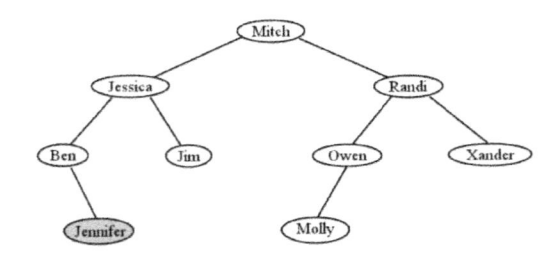

Figure 5.26: The BST after adding Jennifer.

look at a small number of nodes equal to the height of the tree.

Note that a new entry always becomes a *leaf* when added. In fact, this allows us to look at the tree and reconstruct some of what came before. For instance, we know that Mitch must have been the first node originally inserted, and that Randi was inserted before Owen, Xander, or Molly. As an exercise, add your own name to this tree (and a few of your friends' names) to make sure you get the hang of it. When you're done the tree must of course obey the BST property.

Removing nodes from a BST

Removing nodes is a bit trickier than adding them. How do we delete an entry without messing up the structure of the tree? It's easy to see how to delete Molly: since she's just a leaf, just remove her and be done with it. But how to delete Jessica? Or for that matter, Mitch?

Your first inclination might be to eliminate the node and promote one of its children to go up in its place. For instance, if we delete Jessica, you might think we could just elevate Ben up to where Jessica was, and then move Jennifer up under Ben as well. This doesn't work, though. The result would look like Figure 5.27, with Jennifer in the wrong place. The next time we look for Jennifer in the tree, we'll search to the *right* of Ben (as we should), completely missing her. Jennifer has effectively been lost.

One correct way (there are others) to do a node removal is to replace

5.2. TREES

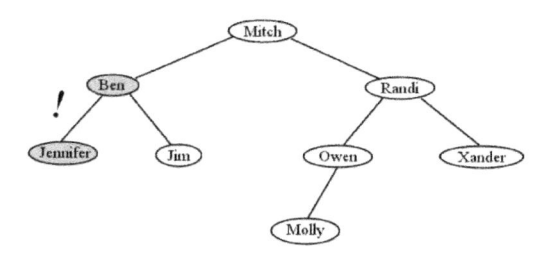

Figure 5.27: A **wrong** (non)-BST after removing Jessica incorrectly.

the node with *the left-most descendant of its right subtree*. (Or, equivalently, the right-most descendant of its left subtree). Let's be careful to define this: to get the left-most descendant of a node's right subtree, we (1) go to the *right* child of the node, and then (2) go as-left-as-we-possibly-can from there, until we come to a node that has no left child. That node (the one without a left child) is officially the left-most descendent of the original node's right subtree.

Example: flip back to Figure 5.17 (p. 117). What is the left-most descendent of G's right subtree? Answer: A. We start by going right from G down to H, and then we go as-left-as-possible...which turns out to be only one node's worth of "left," because we hit A, and A has no left child (or right child, for that matter.) Work these additional examples out for yourself: what is the left-most descendent of K's right subtree? Of D's? Of H's?[5]

Okay, let's return to Figure 5.26 (p. 128) and remove Jessica the *correct* way. We simply find the left-most descendent of her right subtree – namely, Jim – and promote him in place of her. Figure 5.28 shows the result. Note that we replaced her with Jim *not* because it's okay to blindly promote her right child, but because *Jim had no left descendants*, and hence he was the left-most node in her right subtree. (If he *had* left descendents, promoting him would have been just as wrong as promoting Ben. Instead, we would have

---

[5]Answers: The left-most descendent of K's right subtree is **C**, of D's right subtree is **O**, and of H's, **F**.

gone left from Jim until we couldn't go left anymore, and promoted *that* node.)

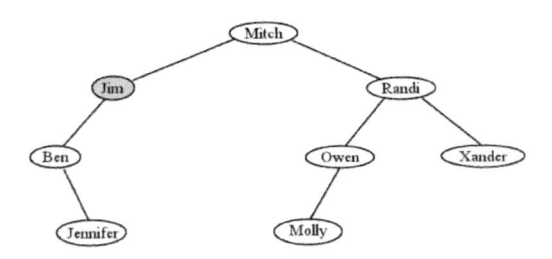

Figure 5.28: The BST after removing Jessica correctly.

As another example, let's go whole-hog and remove the root node, Mitch. The result is as shown in Figure 5.29. It's rags-to-riches for Molly: she got promoted from a leaf all the way to the top. Why Molly? Because she was the left-most descendant of Mitch's right subtree.

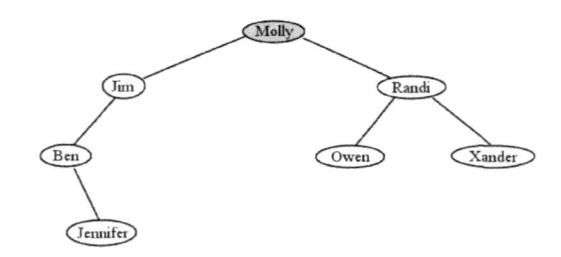

Figure 5.29: The BST after removing Mitch.

To see why this works, just consider that *Molly was immediately after Mitch in alphabetical order.* The fact that he was a king and she a peasant was misleading. The two of them were actually very close: consecutive, in fact, with in-order traversal. So replacing Mitch with Molly avoids shuffling anybody out of alphabetical order, and preserves the all-important BST property.

5.2. TREES

Balancedness

Finally, recall that this amazingly fast lookup is critically dependent on the tree being "bushy." Otherwise, the approximation that $h = \lg(l)$ breaks down. As a laughably extreme example, consider Figure 5.30, which contains the same nodes we've been using. This is a legitimate binary search tree! (Check it!) Yet looking up a node in this monstrosity is obviously not going to be any faster than looking it up in a plain-old list. We're back to O(n) performance.

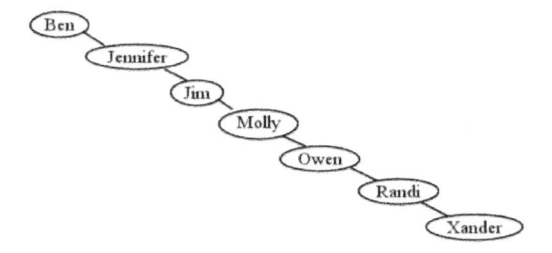

Figure 5.30: An incredibly bad, but still technically legit, BST.

In practice, there are three ways of dealing with this. One approach is to simply not worry about it. After all, as long as we're inserting and removing nodes randomly, with no discernable pattern, the chances of obtaining a tree as lopsided as Figure 5.30 are astronomically small. It's as likely as throwing a deck of cards up in the air and having it land all in a neat stack. The law of entropy tells us that we're going to get a mix of short branches and long branches, and that in a large tree, the unbalancedness will be minimal.

A second approach is to periodically rebalance the tree. If our website goes offline for maintenance every once in a while anyway, we could rebuild our tree from the ground up by inserting the nodes into a fresh tree in a beneficial order. What order should we insert them in? Well, remember that whichever node is inserted first will be the root. This suggests that we'd want to insert the *middle* node first into our tree, so that Molly becomes the new root. This leaves half the nodes for her left subtree and half for her right. If you follow this process logically (and recursively) you'll realize that we'd next want to insert the middle nodes *of each half.* This would equate to Jennifer and Randi (in either order). I think of it like the markings on a ruler: first you insert half an inch, then $\frac{1}{4}$ and $\frac{3}{4}$ inches, then $\frac{1}{8}$, $\frac{3}{8}$, $\frac{5}{8}$, and $\frac{7}{8}$ inches, *etc.* This restores to us a perfectly balanced tree at regular intervals, making any large imbalances even more improbable (and short-lived).

Thirdly, there are specialized data structures you may learn about in future courses, such as AVL trees and red-black trees, which are binary search trees that add extra rules to prevent imbalancing. Basically, the idea is that when a node is inserted (or removed), certain metrics are checked to make sure that the change didn't cause too great an imbalance. If it did, the tree is adjusted so as to minimize the imbalance. This comes at a slight cost every time the tree is changed, but prevents any possibility of a lopsided tree that would cause slow lookups in the long run.

5.3 Final word

Whew, that was a lot of information about structures. Before we continue our walk in the next chapter with a completely different topic, I'll leave you with this summary thought. Let BST be the set of Binary Search Trees, and BT be the set of Binary Trees. Let RT be the set of rooted trees, and T be the set of trees (free or rooted). Finally, let CG be the set of connected graphs, and G the set of all graphs. Then we have:

$$BST \subset BT \subset RT \subset T \subset CG \subset G.$$

It's a beautiful thing.

5.4 Exercises

1. How many vertices are there in the graph below?	6.
2. How many edges are there?	7.
3. What's the degree of vertex B?	3.
4. Is this graph directed?	No. (No arrowheads on the lines.)
5. Is this graph connected?	No – there is no path from A, B, E, or F to either C or D.
6. Is this graph weighted?	No. (No numbers annotating the edges.)
7. Is it a tree?	No. (A tree must be connected, and must also have no cycles, which this graph clearly does: *e.g.*, B–to–A–to–E–to–B.)
8. Is it a DAG?	Not remotely: it is neither directed nor acyclic.
9. If this graph represented an endorelation, how many ordered pairs would it have?	14. (If you said 7, remember that since there are no arrowheads on the lines, this is an undirected graph, which corresponds to a symmetric relation, and hence both (A, E) and (E, A) will be present.)

10. How many vertices and edges are there in the graph below?	7 and 10, respectively.
11. What's the degree of vertex L?	It has an in-degree of 2, and an out-degree of 1.
12. Is this graph directed?	Yes.
13. Is this graph connected?	Depends on what we mean. There are two different notions of "connectedness" for directed graphs. One is **strongly connected**, which means every vertex is reachable from any other by following the arrows in their specified directions. By that definition, this graph is not connected: there's no way to get to H from J, for example. It is **weakly connected**, however, which means that if you *ignore* the arrowheads and consider it like an unidirected graph, it would be connected.
14. Is it a tree?	No. For one thing, a tree can't have any "extra" edges beyond what's necessary to make it connected, and there's redundancy galore here.
15. Is it a DAG?	Allllmost. If you look very carefully, you'll see that there is indeed a cycle: I–to–G–to–L. So if this graph were to represent a recipe or project workflow, it would be impossible to complete.
16. If we reversed the direction of the I–to–G edge, would it be a DAG?	Yes. The steps could now be completed in this order: H, G, L, I, M, K, and finally J.
17. If this graph represented an endorelation, how many ordered pairs would it have?	10.

5.4. EXERCISES

18.	Suppose we traversed the graph below in depth-first fashion, starting with node P. In what order would we visit the nodes? 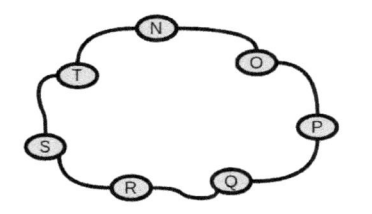	There are two possible answers: P, Q, R, S, T, N, O, or else P, O, N, T, S, R, Q. (The choice just depends on whether we go "left" or "right" initially.) Note in particular that either O or Q is at the very end of the list.
19.	Now we traverse the same graph breadth-first fashion, starting with node P. Now in what order would we visit the nodes?	Again, two possible answers: P, O, Q, N, R, T, S, or else P, Q, O, R, N, S, T. Note in particular that both O and Q are visited very early.
20.	If we traversed the tree below in pre-order fashion, in what order would we visit the nodes? 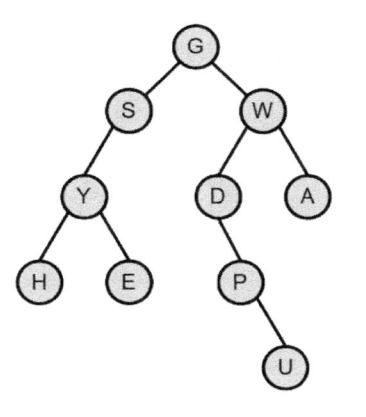	G, S, Y, H, E, W, D, P, U, A.
21.	What if we traversed it in in-order fashion?	H, Y, E, S, G, D, P, U, W, A.
22.	What if we traversed it in post-order fashion?	H, E, Y, S, U, P, D, A, W, G.

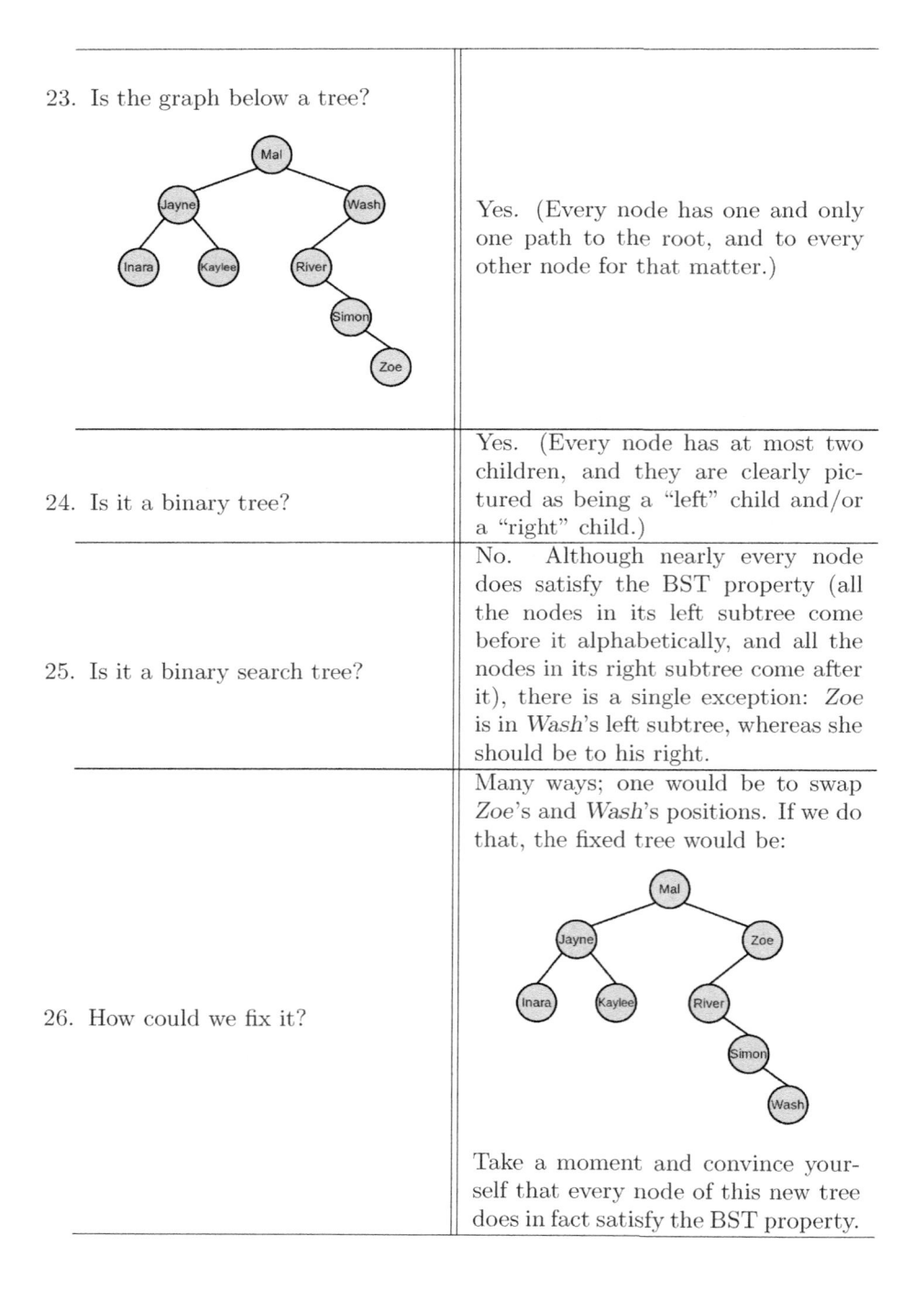

23. Is the graph below a tree? [tree with Mal as root; Mal's children: Jayne, Wash; Jayne's children: Inara, Kaylee; Wash's child: River; River's child: Simon; Simon's child: Zoe]	Yes. (Every node has one and only one path to the root, and to every other node for that matter.)
24. Is it a binary tree?	Yes. (Every node has at most two children, and they are clearly pictured as being a "left" child and/or a "right" child.)
25. Is it a binary search tree?	No. Although nearly every node does satisfy the BST property (all the nodes in its left subtree come before it alphabetically, and all the nodes in its right subtree come after it), there is a single exception: *Zoe* is in *Wash*'s left subtree, whereas she should be to his right.
26. How could we fix it?	Many ways; one would be to swap *Zoe*'s and *Wash*'s positions. If we do that, the fixed tree would be: [tree with Mal as root; Mal's children: Jayne, Zoe; Jayne's children: Inara, Kaylee; Zoe's child: River; River's child: Simon; Simon's child: Wash] Take a moment and convince yourself that every node of this new tree does in fact satisfy the BST property.

5.4. EXERCISES

27. Is the tree balanced?	It's not too bad, but it does have one too many levels in it (it has a height of 4, whereas all its nodes would fit in a tree of height 3).
28. How could we make it more balanced?	Many ways; one would be to rotate the *River–Simon–Wash* threesome so that *Simon* becomes *Zoe*'s left child. *Simon* would then be the parent of *River* (on his left) and *Wash* (on his right).
29. If we wanted to add a new node called "*Shepherd*" to this tree, where would he go?	To *Simon*'s left.
30. If we wanted to remove the "*Mal*" node from this tree, how would we do that?	We can put the left-most node of *Mal*'s right subtree (that would be *River*) in *Mal*'s place, and then make *Simon* (and everything under him) become *Wash*'s left child. The result would look like this: Take a moment and convince yourself that this *Mal*-less tree does in fact satisfy the BST property.

Chapter 6

Counting

If the title of this chapter seems less than inspiring, it's only because the kind of counting we learned as children was mostly of a straightforward kind. In this chapter, we're going to learn to answer some more difficult questions like "how many different semester schedules could a college student possibly have?" and "how many different passwords can a customer choose for this e-commerce website?" and "how likely is this network buffer to overflow, given that its packets are addressed to three different destinations?"

The more impressive-sounding name for this topic is **combinatorics**. In combinatorics, we focus on two tasks: counting things (to find out how many there are), and enumerating things (to systematically list them as individuals). Some things turn out to be hard to count but easy to enumerate, and vice versa.

6.1 The Fundamental Theorem

We start with a basic rule that goes by the audacious name of **The Fundamental Theorem of Counting**.[1] It goes like this:

> If a whole can be divided into k parts, and there's n_i choices for the ith part, then there's $n_1 \times n_2 \times n_3 \times \cdots \times n_k$ ways of doing the whole thing.

Example: Jane is ordering a new Lamborghini. She has twelve different paint colors to choose from (including Luscious Red and Sassy Yellow), three different interiors (Premium Leather, Bonded Leather, or Vinyl), and three different stereo systems. She must also choose between automatic and manual transmission, and she can get power locks & windows (or not). How many different configurations does Jane have to choose from? Put another way, how many different kinds of cars could come off the line for her?

The key is that every one of her choices is independent of all the others. Choosing an Envious Green exterior doesn't constrain her choice of transmission, stereo, or anything else. So no matter which of the 12 paint colors she chooses, she can independently choose any of the three interiors, and no matter what these first two choices were, she can freely choose any of the stereos, *etc*. It's a mix-and-match. Therefore the answer is:

$$12 \times 3 \times 3 \times 2 \times 2 = 432 \text{ choices.}$$

Here's an alternate notation you'll run into for this, by the way:

---

[1] How many other "Fundamental Theorems" of math do you know? Here are a few: the Fundamental Theorem of Arithmetic says that any natural number can be broken down into its prime factors in only one way. The Fundamental Theorem of Algebra says that the highest power of a polynomial is how many roots (zeroes) it has. The Fundamental Theorem of *Linear* Algebra says that the row space and the column space of a matrix have the same dimension. The Fundamental Theorem of Calculus says that integration and differentiation are the inverse of each other.

6.1. THE FUNDAMENTAL THEOREM

$$\prod_{i=1}^{k} n_i$$

which is just a shorter way of writing

$$n_1 \times n_2 \times n_3 \times \cdots \times n_k.$$

As mentioned in section 4.5, the Σ notation is essentially a loop with a counter, and it says to add up the expression to the right of it for each value of the counter. The Π notation is exactly the same, only instead of adding the expressions together for each value of the counter, we're multiplying them. (The reason mathematicians chose the symbols Σ (sigma) and Π (pi) for this, by the way, is that "sigma" and "pi" start with the same letter as "sum" and "product," respectively.)

We can actually get a lot of leverage just with the fundamental theorem. How many different PINs are possible for an ATM card? There are four digits, each of which can be any value from 0 to 9 (ten total values), so the answer is:

$$10 \times 10 \times 10 \times 10 = 10,000 \text{ different PINs.}$$

So a thief at an ATM machine frantically entering PINs at random (hoping to break your account before you call and stop your debit card) would have to try about 5,000 of them on average before cracking the code.

What about middle school bullies who are trying to break into your locker? Well, most combination locks are opened by a three-number sequence, each number of which is anything from 0 to 39. So there are:

$$40 \times 40 \times 40 = 64,000 \text{ different combinations.}$$

That's probably slightly overstated, since I'll bet consecutive repeat numbers are not allowed (Master probably doesn't manufacture a lock with a combination of 17–17–23, for example.) But it does seem at least as secure as a PIN number.

Every car in the state of Virginia must be issued its own license plate number. That's a lot of cars. How many different license plate combinations are available?

This one requires a bit more thought, since not all licenses numbers have the same number of characters. In addition to "SED4756" and "PXY1927" you can also have "DAWG" or "LUVME" or even "U2". How can we incorporate these?

The trick is to divide up our set into mutually exclusive subsets, and then add up the cardinalities of the subsets. If only 7 characters fit on a license plate, then clearly every license plate number has either 1, 2, 3, 4, 5, 6, or 7 characters. And no license plate has *two* of these (*i.e.*, there is no plate that is both 5 characters long *and* 6 characters long). Therefore they're mutually exclusive subsets, and safe to add. This last point is often not fully appreciated, leading to errors. Be careful not to cavalierly add the cardinalities of non-mutually-exclusive sets! You'll end up double-counting items.

So we know that the number of possible license plates is equal to:

$$\text{the \# of 7-character plates} + \\ \text{the \# of 6-character plates} + \\ \text{the \# of 5-character plates} + \\ \cdots + \\ \text{the \# of 1-character plates.}$$

Very well. We can now figure out each one separately. How do we know how many 7-character plates there are? Well, if every character must be either a letter or a digit, then we have 26 + 10 = 36 choices for each character. This implies 36^7 different possible 7-character license plates. The total number of plates is therefore:

$$36^7 + 36^6 + 36^5 + 36^4 + 36^3 + 36^2 + 36 = 80{,}603{,}140{,}212 \text{ plates}$$

which is about ten times the population of the earth, so I think we're safe for now.

6.1. THE FUNDAMENTAL THEOREM 143

Here's an interesting thought experiment to test your intuition about numbers. Look at the above calculation, and ask yourself: "what if the state of Virginia decided, for purposes of consistency, that all license plates *had* to have the full 7 characters? Would that significantly reduce the total number of possible plates?" My first inclination would be to say "yes," because we're adding seven things in that equation, and if we mandated 7-character plates for everyone we'd eliminate 6 out of the 7. Surely we'd be in danger of running out of license plates to give to all the cars! But in fact the new total number of plates would turn out to be:

$$36^7 = 78{,}364{,}164{,}096 \text{ plates.}$$

Wow. We've hardly lost *anything* by scrapping all the less-than-7-character plates. Turns out that in comparison with the 7-character plates, all the other lengths were a drop in the bucket. This is a powerful illustration of exponential growth. When you modify the exponent, going from something like 36^6 to 36^7, you get astronomically larger very, very quickly. This is a good thing to know when all you want is an approximation of some quantity. How many passwords are possible in a system that mandates 6-10 characters per password? Well, you can pretty much ignore all the 6-9 character passwords and just count the 10-character passwords, because there are so many more of those.

One last tweak to the license plate example before we move on. Suppose (again, for the sake of consistency) that Virginia outlawed personalized plates and gave everyone a randomly generated 7-character plate. Furthermore, the last four characters of the plate had to be *digits* instead of letters, so that something like "RFP-6YQ7" would be impossible. Now how many possible plates would there be?

In this case, not each of the k parts of n have an equal number of choices. n_1 through n_3 are still 36, but now n_4 through n_7 are just 10. So this gives us:

$$36 \times 36 \times 36 \times 10 \times 10 \times 10 \times 10 = 466{,}560{,}000 \text{ plates}$$

or only about .006 times as many as before. Better stick with alphanumeric characters for all seven positions.

A simple trick

Sometimes we have something difficult to count, but we can turn it around in terms of something much easier. Often this involves counting the *complement* of something, then subtracting from the total.

For instance, suppose a certain website mandated that user passwords be between 6-10 characters in length — every character being an uppercase letter, lowercase letter, digit, or special character (*, #, @, % or &) — but it also required each password to have *at least one digit or special character*. How many passwords are possible?

Without the "at least one digit or special character" part, it's pretty easy: there are $26 + 26 + 10 + 5 = 67$ different choices for each character, so we have

$$67^{10} + 67^9 + 67^8 + 67^7 + 67^6 = 1{,}850{,}456{,}557{,}795{,}600{,}384 \text{ strings.}$$

But how do we handle the "at least one" part?

One way would be to list all the possible ways of having a password with at least one non-alpha character. The non-alpha could appear in the first position, or the second, or the third, ..., or the tenth, but of course this only works for 10-digit passwords, and in any event it's not like the *other* characters couldn't *also* be non-alpha. It gets messy really fast.

There's a simple trick, though, once you realize that it's easy to count the passwords that *don't* satisfy the extra constraint. Ask yourself this question: out of all the possible strings of 6-10 characters, how many of them *don't* have at least one non-alpha character? (and are therefore illegal, according to the website rules?)

It turns out that's the same as asking "how many strings are there with 6-10 alphabetic (only) characters?" which is of course:

$$52^{10} + 52^9 + 52^8 + 52^7 + 52^6 = 147{,}389{,}519{,}403{,}536{,}384 \text{ (illegal) passwords.}$$

Now, all we have to do is subtract to get

total # of strings − # of illegal passwords = # of legit passwords
1,850,456,557,795,600,384 − 147,389,519,403,536,384 = 1,708,735,865,301,022,720

legitimate passwords. Looks like we don't lose much by requiring the non-alpha character.

The lesson learned is that if counting the elements in some set involves accounting for a lot of different sticky scenarios, it's worth a try to count the elements *not* in the set instead, and see if that's easier.

6.2 Permutations

When we're counting things, we often run into permutations. A **permutation** of n distinct objects is an arrangement of them in a sequence. For instance, suppose all three Davies kids need to brush their teeth, but only one of them can use the sink at a time. What order will they brush in? One possibility is Lizzy, then T.J., then Johnny. Another possibility is T.J., then Lizzy, then Johnny. Another is Johnny, then Lizzy, then T.J. These are all different permutations of the Davies kids. Turns out there are six of them (find all 6 for yourself!).

Counting the number of permutations is just a special application of the Fundamental Theorem of Counting. For the teeth brushing example, we have $n = 3$ different "parts" to the problem, each of which has n_i choices to allocate to it. There are three different Davies kids who could brush their teeth first, so $n_1 = 3$. Once that child is chosen, there are then *two* remaining children who could brush second, so $n_2 = 2$. Then, once we've selected a first-brusher and a second-brusher, there's only one remaining choice for the third-brusher, so $n_3 = 1$. This means the total number of possible brushing orders is:

$$3 \times 2 \times 1 = 6.$$

This pattern comes up so much that mathematicians have established a special notation for it:

$$n \times (n-1) \times (n-2) \times \cdots \times 1 = n! \text{ (``}n\text{-factorial'')}$$

We say there are "3-factorial" different brushing orders for the Davies kids. For our purposes the notion of factorial will only apply for integers, so there's no such thing as 23.46! or π!. (In advanced computer science applications, however, mathematicians sometimes do define factorial for non-integers.) We also define 0! to be 1, which might surprise you.

This comes up a heck of a lot. If I give you a jumbled set of letters to unscramble, like "KRIBS" (think of the Jumble® word game in the newspaper), how many different unscramblings are there? The answer is 5!, or 120, one of which is BRISK. Let's say I shuffle a deck of cards before playing War.[2] How many different games of War are there? The answer is 52!, since any of the cards in the deck might be shuffled on top, then any *but* that top card could be second, then any *but* those two could be third, *etc.* Ten packets arrive near-simultaneously at a network router. How many ways can they be queued up for transmission? 10! ways, just like a larger Davies family.

The factorial function grows really, really fast, by the way, even faster than exponential functions. A five letter word like "BRISK" has 120 permutations, but "AMBIDEXTROUSLY" has 87,178,291,200, ten times the population of the earth. The number of ways to shuffle a deck is

80,658,175,170,944,942,408,940,349,866,698,506,766,127,860,028,660,283,290,685,487,972,352

so I don't think my boys will end up playing the same War game twice any time soon, nor my wife and I the same bridge hand.

---

[2]"War" is a mindless card game which involves no strategy or decision-making on the part of the players. Once you shuffle the initial deck, the entire outcome of the game is fixed.

6.2. PERMUTATIONS

Enumerating permutations

We've discovered that there are 120 permutations of BRISK, but how would we go about listing them all? You can play around with the Davies kids and stumble upon all 6 permutations, but for larger numbers it's harder. We need a systematic way.

Two of the easiest ways to enumerate permutations involve recursion. Here's one:

Algorithm #1 for enumerating permutations

1. Begin with a set of n objects.

   a) If $n = 1$, there is only one permutation; namely, the object itself.

   b) Otherwise, remove one of the objects, and find the permutations of the remaining $n - 1$ objects. Then, insert the removed object at every possible position, creating another permutation each time.

As always with recursion, solving a bigger problem depends on solving smaller problems. Let's start with RISK. We've already discovered from the toothbrushing example that the permutations of ISK are ISK, IKS, SIK, SKI, KIS, and KSI. So to find the permutations of RISK, we insert an R into *each* possible location for *each* of these ISK-permutations. This gives us:

```
RISK
IRSK
ISRK
ISKR
RIKS
IRKS
IKRS
IKSR
RSIK
 ...
```

and so on. Once we have the RISK permutations, we can generate the BRISK permutations in the same way:

$$\boxed{\text{B}}\text{RISK}$$
$$\text{R}\boxed{\text{B}}\text{ISK}$$
$$\text{RI}\boxed{\text{B}}\text{SK}$$
$$\text{RIS}\boxed{\text{B}}\text{K}$$
$$\text{RISK}\boxed{\text{B}}$$
$$\boxed{\text{B}}\text{IRSK}$$
$$\text{I}\boxed{\text{B}}\text{RSK}$$
$$\text{IR}\boxed{\text{B}}\text{SK}$$
$$\text{IRS}\boxed{\text{B}}\text{K}$$
$$\text{IRSK}\boxed{\text{B}}$$
$$\boxed{\text{B}}\text{RSIK}$$
$$\ldots$$

Another algorithm to achieve the same goal (though in a different order) is as follows:

Algorithm #2 for enumerating permutations

1. Begin with a set of n objects.

    a) If $n = 1$, there is only one permutation; namely, the object itself.

    b) Otherwise, remove each of the objects in turn, and prepend that object to the permutations of all the others, creating another permutation each time.

I find this one a little easier to get my head around, but in the end it's personal preference. The permutations of BRISK are: "B followed by all the permutations of RISK, plus R followed by all the permutations of BISK, plus I followed by all the permutations of BRSK, *etc.*" So the first few permutations of a 4-letter word are:

$$\text{R}\,\boxed{\text{I S K}}$$
$$\text{R}\,\boxed{\text{I K S}}$$
$$\text{R}\,\boxed{\text{S I K}}$$

R S K I
R K I S
R K S I
I R S K
I R K S
I S R K
I S K R
I K R S
I K S R
S R I K
...

Then, for the 5-letter word:

B R I S K
B R I K S
B R S I K
B R S K I
B R K I S
B R K S I
B I R S K
B I R K S
...

Partial permutations

Sometimes we want to count the permutations of a set, but only want to choose *some* of the items each time, not all of them. For example, consider a golf tournament in which the top ten finishers (out of 45) all receive prize money, with the first place winner receiving the most, the second place finisher a lesser amount, and so on down to tenth place, who receives a nominal prize. How many different finishes are possible to the tournament?

In this case, we want to know how many different orderings of golfers there are, but it turns out that past tenth place, we don't care what order they finished in. All that matters is the first ten places. If the top ten are 1.Tiger, 2.Phil, 3.Lee, 4.Rory, ..., and

10. Bubba, then it doesn't matter whether Jason finished 11th or 45th.

It's easy to see that there are 45 possible winners, then for each winner there are 44 possible second-placers, *etc.*, so that this total turns out to be:

$45 \times 44 \times 43 \times 42 \times 41 \times 40 \times 39 \times 38 \times 37 \times 36 = 11{,}576{,}551{,}623{,}436{,}800$ finishes.

Each of the finishes is called a **partial permutation**. It's a permutation of k items chosen from n total, and is denoted $p_{n,k}$. The number of such permutations works out to

$$n \times (n-1) \times (n-2) \times \cdots \times (n-k+1).$$

The "$n-k+1$" bit can be confusing, so take your time and think it through. For the golf tournament case, our highest term was 45 and our lowest term was 36. This is because n was 45 and k was 10, and so we only wanted to carry out the multiplication to 36 (not 35), and 36 is 45-10+1.

This can be expressed more compactly in a few different ways. First, we can use factorials to represent it:

$$n \times (n-1) \times (n-2) \times \cdots \times (n-k+1)$$
$$= \frac{n \times (n-1) \times (n-2) \times \cdots \times 1}{(n-k) \times (n-k-1) \times (n-k-2) \times \cdots \times 1}$$
$$= \frac{n!}{(n-k)!}$$

Also, we could use our compact product notation:

$$n \times (n-1) \times (n-2) \times \cdots \times (n-k+1) = \prod_{i=0}^{k-1}(n-i).$$

Finally, as with (non-partial) permutations, this comes up so much that the professionals have invented a special notation for it. It looks like a power, but has an underline under the exponent:

$$n \times (n-1) \times (n-2) \times \cdots \times (n-k+1) = n^{\underline{k}}.$$

6.2. PERMUTATIONS

This is pronounced "n-to-the-k-falling," and was invented by one of the most brilliant computer scientists in history, Donald Knuth.

To keep straight what $n^{\underline{k}}$ means, think of it as the same as plain exponentiation, except that the product diminishes instead of staying the same. For example, "17-to-the-6th" is

$$17^6 = 17 \cdot 17 \cdot 17 \cdot 17 \cdot 17 \cdot 17$$

but "17-to-the-6th-falling" is

$$17^{\underline{6}} = 17 \cdot 16 \cdot 15 \cdot 14 \cdot 13 \cdot 12.$$

In both cases, you're multiplying the same number of terms, it's just that in the second case, these terms are "falling."

Anyway, notation aside, partial permutations abound in practice. A late night movie channel might show four classic films back to back every evening. If there are 500 films in the studio's library, how many nightly TV schedules are possible? Answer: $500^{\underline{4}}$, since there are 500 choices of what to show at 7pm, then 499 choices for 9pm, 498 for 11pm, and 497 for the 1am late show.

The fastest 41 auto racers will qualify for Sunday's race, and will be placed from Pole Position on down depending on their qualifying time. If 60 cars participate in the qualifying heat, then there are $60^{\underline{41}}$ different possible starting configurations for Sunday.

Middle schoolers entering sixth grade will be assigned a semester schedule that consists of five "blocks" (periods), each of which will have one of thirteen classes (science, math, orchestra, study hall, *etc.*) How many schedules are possible? You guessed it, $13^{\underline{5}}$. Notice that this is the correct answer only because no repeats are allowed: we don't want to schedule any student for American History more than once. If a student *could* take the same class more than once in a day, then there would be 13^5 (not "falling") different possible schedules.

6.3 Combinations

All the stuff with permutations has emphasized *order*. Somebody gets first place in the golf tournament, and somebody else gets second, and you bet your bottom dollar that it matters which is which. What if it turns out we don't care about the order, though? Maybe we don't care who got what place, but just *which* golfers were in the top ten. Maybe we don't care which film is showing in which time slot, but only *which* films are in tonight's movie lineup.

This counting scenario involves something called *combinations* rather than permutations. A **combination** of k objects out of a possible n is a choice of any set of k of them, without regard to order. For instance, suppose all three Davies kids want to play on the Wii, but only two can play at a time. Who will get to play first after school? One possibility is Lizzy and T.J., another is Lizzy and Johnny, and the last one is T.J. and Johnny. These are the three (and only three) combinations of 2 objects out of 3.

To see how to count these in general, let's return to the golf tournament example. Suppose that in addition to winning money, the top three finishers of our local tournament will also advance to the regional tournament. This is a great honor, and brings with it far greater additional winning potential than the local money did. Question: how many different possible trios might we send to regional competition?

At first glance, this seems just like the "how many prize money allocations" problem from before, except that we're taking 3 instead of 10. But there is a twist. In the former problem, it mattered who was first vs. second vs. third. Now *the order is irrelevant.* If you finish in the top three, you advance, period. You don't "advance more forcefully" for finishing first locally instead of third.

It's not as obvious how to count this, but of course there is a trick. The trick is to count the partial permutations, *but then realize how much we overcounted, and then compensate for it accordingly.*

If we count the partial permutations of 3 out of 45 golfers, we have $45^{\underline{3}}$ such permutations. One of those partial permutations is:

6.3. COMBINATIONS

1.Phil 2.Bubba 3.Tiger

Another one is:

1.Phil 2.Tiger 3.Bubba

and yet another is:

1.Tiger 2.Phil 3.Bubba

Now the important thing to recognize is that in our present problem — counting the possible number of regional-bound golf trios — all three of these *different* partial permutations represent the *same* combination. In all three cases, it's Bubba, Phil, and Tiger who will represent our local golf association in the regional competition. So by counting all three of them as separate partial permutations, we've overcounted the combinations.

Obviously we want to count Bubba/Phil/Tiger only once. Okay then. How many times did we overcount it when we counted partial permutations? The answer is that we counted this trio *once for every way it can be permuted*. The three permutations, above, were examples of this, and so are these three:

1.Tiger 2.Bubba 3.Phil
1.Bubba 2.Tiger 3.Phil
1.Bubba 2.Phil 3.Tiger

This makes a total of six times that we (redundantly) counted the same combination when we counted the partial permutations. Why 6? Because that's the value of 3!, of course. There are 3! different ways to arrange Bubba, Phil, and Tiger, since that's just a straight permutation of three elements. And so we find that every threesome we want to account for, we have counted 6 times.

The way to get the correct answer, then, is obviously to correct for this overcounting by dividing by 6:

$$\frac{45^{\underline{3}}}{3!} = \frac{45 \times 44 \times 43}{6} = 14{,}190 \text{ different threesomes.}$$

And in general, that's all we have to do. To find the number of combinations of k things taken from a total of n things we have:

$$\frac{n^{\underline{k}}}{k!} = \frac{n!}{(n-k)!k!} \text{ combinations.}$$

This pattern, too, comes up so often that mathematicians have invented (yet) another special notation for it. It looks a bit strange at first, almost like a fraction without a horizontal bar:

$$\binom{n}{k} = \frac{n!}{(n-k)!k!}.$$

This is pronounced "n-choose-k".

Again, examples abound. How many different 5-card poker hands are there? Answer: $\binom{52}{5}$, since it doesn't matter what order you're dealt the cards, only which five cards you get. If there are 1024 sectors on our disk, but only 256 cache blocks in memory to hold them, how many different combinations of sectors can be in memory at one time? $\binom{1024}{256}$. If we want to choose 4 or 5 of our top 10 customers to participate in a focus group, how many different combinations of participants could we have? $\binom{10}{4} + \binom{10}{5}$, since we want the number of ways to pick 4 of them plus the number of ways to pick 5 of them. And for our late night movie channel, of course, there are $\binom{500}{4}$ possible movie lineups to attract audiences, if we don't care which film is aired at which time.

Binomial coefficients

The "n-choose-k" notation $\binom{n}{k}$ has another name: values of this sort are called **binomial coefficients**. This is because one way to generate them, believe it or not, is to repeatedly multiply a binomial times itself (or, equivalently, take a binomial to a power.)

A binomial, recall, is a polynomial with just two terms:

$$x + y.$$

6.3. COMBINATIONS

The coefficients for this binomial are of course 1 and 1, since "x" really means "$1 \cdot x$." Now if we multiply this by itself, we get:

$$(x+y) \cdot (x+y) = x^2 + 2xy + y^2,$$

the coefficients of the terms being 1, 2, and 1. We do it again:

$$(x^2 + 2xy + y^2) \cdot (x+y) = x^3 + 3x^2y + 3xy^2 + y^3$$

to get 1, 3, 3, and 1, and do it again:

$$(x^3 + 3x^2y + 3xy^2 + y^3) \cdot (x+y) = x^4 + 4x^3y + 6x^2y^2 + 4xy^3 + y^4$$

to get 1, 4, 6, 4, and 1. At this point you might be having flashbacks to Pascal's triangle, which perhaps you learned about in grade school, in which each entry in a row is the sum of the two entries immediately above it (to the left and right), as in Figure 6.1. (If you never learned that, don't worry about it.)

```
          1
         1 1
        1 2 1
       1 3 3 1
      1 4 6 4 1
     1 5 10 10 5 1
```

Figure 6.1: The first six rows of Pascal's triangle.

Now you might be wondering where I'm going with this. What do fun algebra tricks have to do with counting combinations of items? The answer is that the values of $\binom{n}{k}$ are *precisely the coefficients of these multiplied polynomials.* Let n be 4, which corresponds to the last polynomial we multiplied out. We can then compute all the combinations of items taken from a group of four:

$$\binom{4}{0} = 1, \binom{4}{1} = 4, \binom{4}{2} = 6, \binom{4}{3} = 4, \text{ and } \binom{4}{4} = 1.$$

In other words, there is exactly *one* way of taking no items out of 4 (you simply don't take any). There are *four* ways of taking one item out of 4 — you could take the first, or the second, or the third, or the fourth. There are *six* ways of taking two items out of four; namely:

1. the first and second
2. the first and third
3. the first and fourth
4. the second and third
5. the second and fourth
6. the third and fourth

And so on.

Now in some ways we're on a bit of a tangent, since the fact that the "n-choose-k" values happen to work out to be the same as the binomial coefficients is mostly just an interesting coincidence. But what I really want you to take notice of here — and what Pascal's triangle makes plain — is the *symmetry* of the coefficients. This surprises a lot of students. What if I asked you which of the following numbers was greater: $\binom{1000}{18}$ or $\binom{1000}{982}$? Most students guess that the second of these numbers is far greater. In actual fact, though, they both work out to $\frac{1000!}{18!982!}$ and are thus exactly the same. And in the above example, we see that $\binom{4}{0}$ is equal to $\binom{4}{4}$, and that $\binom{4}{1}$ is equal to $\binom{4}{3}$.

Why is this? Well, you can look back at the formula for $\binom{n}{k}$ and see how it works out algebraically. But it's good to have an intuitive feel for it as well. Here's how I think of it. Go back to the Davies kids and the Wii. We said there were three different ways to choose 2 kids to play on the Wii first after school. In other words, $\binom{3}{2} = 3$. Very well. But if you think about it, there must then also be three different ways to *leave out* exactly *one* kid. If we change what we're counting from "combinations of players" to "combinations of non-players" — both of which must be equal, since no matter what happens, we'll be partitioning the Davies kids into players and non-players — then we see that $\binom{3}{1}$ must also be 3.

And this is true across the board. If there are $\binom{500}{4}$ different lineups of four movies, then there are the same number of lineups of 496 movies, since $\binom{500}{4} = \binom{500}{496}$. Conceptually, in the first case we choose a group of four and show them, and in the second case we choose a group of four and show *everything but them.*

Also notice that the way to get the greatest number of combinations of n items is for k to be half of n. If we have 100 books in our library, there are a lot more ways to check out 50 of them then there are to check out only 5, or to check out 95. Strange but true.

Lastly, make sure you understand the extreme endpoints of this phenomenon. $\binom{n}{0}$ and $\binom{n}{n}$ are both always 1, no matter what n is. That's because if you're picking *no* items, you have no choices at all: there's only one way to come up empty. And if you're picking *all* the items, you also have no choices: you're forced to pick everything.

6.4 Summary

Most of the time, counting problems all boil down to a variation of one of the following three basic situations:

- n^k — this is when we have k different things, each of which is free to take on one of n completely independent choices.

- $n^{\underline{k}}$ — this is when we're taking a sequence of k different things from a set of n, but no repeats are allowed. (A special case of this is $n!$, when $k = n$.)

- $\binom{n}{k}$ — this is when we're taking k different things from a set of n, but the order doesn't matter.

Sometimes it's tricky to deduce exactly which of these three situations apply. You have to think carefully about the problem, and ask yourself whether repeated values would be allowed, and whether it matters what order the values appear in. This is often subtle.

As an example, suppose my friend and I work out at the same gym. This gym has 18 different weight machines to choose from, each of which exercises a different muscle group. Each morning, we each do a quick 30-minute workout session divided into six 5-minute blocks, and we work with one of the machines during each block, taking turns spotting each other. One day my friend asks me, "hey Stephen, have you ever wondered: how many different workout routines are possible for us?"

I was, of course, wondering exactly that. But the correct answer turns out to hinge very delicately on exactly what "a workout routine" is. If we could select any weight machine for any 5-minute block, then the answer is 18^6, since we have 18 choices for our first block, 18 choices for our second, and so on. (This comes to 34,012,224 different routines, if you're interested).

However, on further inspection, we might change our mind about this. Does it make sense to choose the same machine more than once in a 30-minute workout? Would we really complete a workout that consisted of "1.Biceps 2.Abs, 3.Pecs, 4.Biceps, 5.Biceps, 6.Biceps?" If not (and most trainers would probably recommend against such monomaniacal approaches to excercise) then the real answer is only $18^{\underline{6}}$, since we have 18 choices for our first block, and then only 17 for the second, 16 for the third, *etc.* (This reduces the total to 13,366,080.)

But perhaps the phrase "a workout routine" means something different even than that. If I tell my physical therapist what "my workout routine" consisted of this morning, does he really care whether I did triceps first, last, or in the middle? He probably only cares about *which* machines (and therefore which muscle groups) I worked out that morning, not what order I did them in. If this is true, then our definition of a workout routine is somewhat different than the above. It's no longer a consecutive sequence of machine choices, but rather a *set* of six machine choices. There would only be $\binom{18}{6}$ of those, or a mere 18,564. So as you can see, the answer radically depends on the precise interpretation of the concepts, which means that to successfully do combinatorics, you have to slow down and think very carefully.

6.5 Exercises

1. Inside a dusty chest marked "Halloween costumes" in the family attic, there are four different outfits (a wizard's cape, army fatigues, and two others), five different headgears (a batman helmet, a headband, a tiara, *etc.*), and nine different accessories (a wand, a lightsaber, a pipe, and many others). If a child were to choose a costume by selecting one outfit, one headgear, and one accessory, how many costume choices would he/she have?	$4 \times 5 \times 9 = 180$.
2. What if the child were permitted to skip one or more of the items (for instance, choosing a costume with an outfit and accessory, but no headgear)?	$5 \times 6 \times 10 = 300$, since now "no choice at all" is effectively another choice for each of the categories.[3] Kind of amazing how much that increases the total!

---

[3] Note, by the way, that this approach does *not* work for situations like the license plate example on p.142. Namely, you can't say "if a license plate can have fewer than 7 characters, we can just add 'no character at this position' as one of the options for that position," and calculate $37^7 = 94{,}931{,}877{,}133$ possible plates. That number is too high. Why? (Hint: for some of those choices, you can get the same license plate in more than one way. Hint 2: if we choose 'A' for the first license plate character, 'no character' for the second, followed by 'NTMAN' we get the license plate 'ANTMAN'. But what other choices could we have made, that would also have resulted in 'ANTMAN'?)

3. Go back to when the child did have to choose something from each category, but now say they can have *any* number of accessories (so they could have the wizard's cape, a batman helmet, plus a lightsaber, pipe, and scepter). Now how many costumes are there?	This is $4 \times 5 \times 2^9$, or a whopping 10,240 for those of you keeping score. The 9 changed to a 2^9 because now for *each* accessory, a costume might include it, or exclude it. That's two independent choices for each accessory.
4. Okay, that's overkill. A kid only has two hands, after all, so handling nine accessories would be a dextrous challenge. Let's say instead that a child can choose *up to three* accessories (but must have at least one). Now how many costume choices are there?	Now it's $4 \times 5 \times (\binom{9}{1} + \binom{9}{2} + \binom{9}{3})$, which is equal to $4 \times 5 \times (9 + 36 + 84)$, or 2,580 possible costumes.
5. When it's finally time to go trick-or-treating, we join up with our next-door neighbors and split up the families into somewhat haphazard groups. There are eleven total children, and six adults. Now let's say each group must have between 3 and 5 members, and must have at least one adult (to stay safe) and at least one kid (otherwise what's the point?) How many different groups are possible?	Ignoring the at-least-one-child-and-adult constraint for the moment, the total number of groups would seem to be $\binom{17}{3} + \binom{17}{4} + \binom{17}{5} = 680 + 2380 + 6188 = 9,248$ possible groups. But of course this is an overcount, since it includes groups with no children and groups with no adults. We'll use the trick from p. 144 to subtract those out. How many size-3-to-5 groups with no adults (all kids) are there? $\binom{11}{3} + \binom{11}{4} + \binom{11}{5} = 957$. And how many size-3-to-5 groups with no kids (all adults)? $\binom{6}{3} + \binom{6}{4} + \binom{6}{5} = 41$. Therefore, by the p. 144 trick, the total number of legal groups is $9248 - 957 - 41 = 8,250$. Final answer.

6.5. EXERCISES

6. To encourage rivalry and gluttony, we're going to give a special certificate to the child who collects the most candy at the end of the night. And while we're at it, we'll give 2nd-place and 3rd-place certificates as well. How many different ways could our 1st-2nd-3rd contest turn out?	This is a partial permutation: there are eleven possible winners, and ten possible runners-up for each possible winner, and nine possible 3rd-placers for each of those top-twos. The answer is therefore $11^{\underline{3}}$, or 990. Wow! I wouldn't have guessed that high.
7. Finally, what if we want *every* kid to get a certificate with their name and place-of-finish on it. How many possibilities? (Assume no ties.)	This is now a full-blown permutation: 11!. It comes to 39,916,800 different orders-of-finish, believe it or not. I told you: this counting stuff can explode fast.

Chapter 7

Numbers

Wow, last chapter was about "counting," and this one is about "numbers." It sure seems like we're regressing back to first grade or earlier. And indeed, this chapter will contain a repeat of some elementary school concepts! But this is so we can re-examine the foundations and generalize them somewhat. The mechanical processes you've always used with numbers — adding, subtracting, comparing, checking whether something divides evenly, working with place value — are all correct, but they're all hard-coded for *decimal* numbers. The word "decimal," in this chapter, won't mean "a number with a decimal point, like 5.62" but rather a number *expressed in base 10*. And what does "expressed in base 10" mean? It means that the digits, from right to left, represent a "one's place," a "ten's place," a "hundred's place," and so on. This is what we all learned in grade school, and perhaps you thought that's just how numbers "were." But it turns out that 1, 10, 100, 1000, ..., is just one choice of place values, and that we could equally as well choose many other things, like 1, 2, 4, 8, ..., or 1, 16, 256, 4096, ..., or even 1, 23, 529, 12167, ..., as long as those values are of a certain type (successive powers of the base).

It's the concept of bases, and specifically bases other than 10, that will cause us to rethink some things. It'll feel unnatural at first, but soon you'll discover that there are aspects of how you work with numbers that are unnecessarily specific, and that it's freeing to treat them in a more general way.

7.1 What is a "number?"

Before we do anything with bases, let's talk about the concept of **number**, generally. The question "what is a number?" sounds like the dumbest question I could possibly ask you. Yet I predict that unless you've studied this material before, you have a whole bunch of tangled thoughts in your head regarding what "numbers" are, and those tangled thoughts are of two kinds. Some of them are about numbers *per se*. Others are about *base-10 numbers*. If you're like most people, you think of these two sets of concepts as equally "primary," to the point where a number seems to *be* a base-10 number. It's hard to conceive of it in any other way. It's this prejudice that I want to expose and root out at the beginning.

Most people, if I asked them to name a number, would come up with something like "seventeen." This much is correct. But if I asked them what their mental image was of the number "seventeen," they would immediately form the following unalterable picture:

$$17$$

To them, the number "seventeen" is intrinsically a two-character-long entity: the digit 1 followed by the digit 7. That *is* the number. If I were to tell them that there are other, equally valid ways of representing the number seventeen — using more, less, or the same number of digits — they'd be very confused. Yet this is in fact the case. And the only reason that the particular two-digit image "17" is so baked into our brains is that we were hard-wired from an early age to think in decimal numbers. We cranked through our times tables and did all our carrying and borrowing in base 10, and in the process we built up an incredible amount of inertia that is hard to overcome. A big part of your job this chapter will be to "unlearn" this dependence on decimal numbers, so that you can work with numbers in other bases, particularly those used in the design of computers.

7.1. WHAT IS A "NUMBER?"

When you think of a number, I want you to try to erase the sequence of digits from your mind. Think of a number as what is is: a **quantity**. Here's what the number seventeen *really* looks like:

○ ○
○ ○ ○
○ ○ ○
○   ○   ○
○ ○ ○
○ ○
○

It's just an *amount*. There are more circles in that picture than in some pictures, and less than in others. But in no way is it "two digits," nor do the particular digits "1" and "7" come into play any more or less than any other digits.

Let's keep thinking about this. Consider this number, which I'll label "A":

(A)   ○
    ○ ○ ○
    ○ ○
     ○ ○

Now let's add another circle to it, creating a different number I'll call "B":

(B)   ○
      ○ ○ ○
     ○ ○
      ○ ○ ○

And finally, we'll do it one more time to get "C":

(C)   ○ ○
     ○ ○ ○
      ○ ○ ○
       ○ ○

(Look carefully at those images and convince yourself that I added one circle each time.)

When going from A to B, I added one circle. When going from B to C, I also added one circle. Now I ask you: was going from B to C any more "significant" than going from A to B? Did anything qualitatively different happen?

The answer is obviously no. Adding a circle is adding a circle; there's nothing more to it than that. But if you had been writing these numbers out as base-10 representations, like you're used to doing, you might have thought differently. You'd have gone from:

(A) 8

to

(B) 9

to

(C) 10

When going from B to C, your "odometer" wrapped around. You had to go from a one-digit number to a two-digit number, simply because you ran out of room in one digit. This can lead to the *illusion* that something fundamentally different happens when you go from B to C. *This is completely an illusion.* Nothing different happens to the *number* just because the way we write it down changes.

Human beings have a curious habit of thinking that odometer changes are significant. When the temperature breaks 100, it suddenly feels "more hotter" than it did when it merely rose from 98 to 99. When the Dow Jones Industrial Average first reached 10,000, and when Pete Rose eclipsed 4,000 career hits, and when the year 2000 dawned, we tended to think that something truly important had taken place. But as we'll see, the point at which these milestones occur is utterly and even laughably aribitrary: it simply has to do with what number we've chosen as our *base*. And we quite honestly could have chosen any number at all.

7.2 Bases

As I mentioned, a **base** is simply a number that's an anchor for our place value system. It represents *how many distinct symbols we will use to represent numbers*. This implicitly sets the value of the largest quantity we can hold in one digit, before we'd need to "roll over" to two digits.

In base 10 (decimal), we use ten symbols: 0, 1, 2, 3, 4, 5, 6, 7, 8, and 9. Consequently, the number nine is the highest value we can hold in a single digit. Once we add another element to a set of nine, we have no choice but to add another digit to express it. This makes a "ten's place" because it will represent the number of sets-of-10 (which we couldn't hold in the 1's place) that the value contains.

Now why is the next place over called the "hundred's place" instead of, say, the "twenty's place"? Simply because twenty — as well as every other number less than a hundred — comfortably fits in two digits. We can have up to 9 in the one's place, and also *up to 9 in the ten's place*, giving us a total of ninety-nine before we ever have to cave in to using three digits. The number one hundred is exactly the point at which we *must* roll over to three digits; therefore, the sequence of digits 1-0-0 represents one hundred.

If the chosen base isn't obvious from context (as it often won't be in this chapter) then when we write out a sequence of digits we'll append the base as a subscript to the end of the number. So the number "four hundred and thirty-seven" will be written as 437_{10}.

The way we interpret a decimal number, then, is by counting the right-most digits as a number of *individuals*, the digit to its left as the number of *groups of ten* individuals, the digit to *its* left as the number of groups of hundred individuals, and so on. 5472_{10} is just a way of writing $5 \times 1000 + 4 \times 100 + 7 \times 10 + 2 \times 1$.

If we use exponential notation (remember that anything to the 0th power is 1), this is equivalent to:

$$5472_{10} = 5 \times 10^3 + 4 \times 10^2 + 7 \times 10^1 + 2 \times 10^0.$$

By the way, we will often use the term **least significant digit** to refer to the right-most digit (2, in the above example), and **most significant digit** to refer to the left-most (5). "Significant" simply refers to how much that digit is "worth" in the overall magnitude of the number. Obviously 239 is less than 932, so we say that the hundreds place is more significant than the other digits.

All of this probably seems pretty obvious to you. All right then. Let's use a base other than ten and see how you do. Let's write out a number *in base 7*. We have seven symbols at our disposal: 0, 1, 2, 3, 4, 5, and 6. Wait, you ask — why not 7? Because there is no digit for seven in a base 7 system, just like there is no digit for ten in a base 10 system. Ten is the point where we need *two* digits in a decimal system, and analogously, seven is the point where we'll need two digits in our base 7 system. How will we write the value seven? Just like this: **10**. Now stare at those two digits and practice saying "seven" as you look at them. All your life you've been trained to say the number "ten" when you see the digits 1 and 0 printed like that. But those two digits only represent the number ten *if you're using a base 10 system.* If you're using a base 34 system, "10" is how you write "thirty-four."

Very well, we have our seven symbols. Now how do we interpret a number like 6153_7? It's this:

$$6153_7 = 6 \times 7^3 + 1 \times 7^2 + 5 \times 7^1 + 3 \times 7^0.$$

That doesn't look so strange: it's very parallel to the decimal string we expanded, above. It looks weirder when we actually multiply out the place values:

$$6153_7 = 6 \times 343 + 1 \times 49 + 5 \times 7 + 3 \times 1.$$

So in base 7, we have a "one's place," a "seven's place," a "forty-nine's place," and a "three hundred forty-three's place." This seems unbelievably bizarre — how could a number system possibly hold together with such place values? — but I'll bet it wouldn't look funny at all if we had been born with 7 fingers. Keep in mind that in the equation above, we wrote out the place values as decimal numbers! Had we written them as base-7 numbers (as we certainly would have if base 7 was our natural numbering system), we would have written:

$$6153_7 = 6 \times 1000_7 + 1 \times 100_7 + 5 \times 10_7 + 3 \times 1_7.$$

This is exactly equivalent numerically. Because after all, 1000_7 *is* 343_{10}. A quantity that looks like an oddball in one base system looks like the roundest possible number in another.

7.3 Hexadecimal (base 16)

Now objectively speaking, it turns out that ten is a pretty weird base too. I know it doesn't seem like it, but that's only because we're so used to it. Really, if you're repeatedly adding little circles to a drawing, ten is a funny place to decide to draw the line and go to more digits. It's only divisible by 2 and 5 (of all things), it's not a perfect square, and all this makes it kind of an awkward choice.

In computer science, it turns out to be very (very) convenient to use a base that is *a power of two*. This means a base that is "two-to-the-something." In earlier computing days, octal (base 8) was a common choice. But for various reasons, that turns out to be less convenient than using base 16, or **hexadecimal**.[1] Any time you're working with hardware, operating systems, device drivers, bit masks, or anything else low level, you'll encounter numbers written in base 16 a heck of a lot. So let's study this particular base in some detail.

Base 16 will need sixteen digits, of course. Unfortunately, we ten-fingered people have only invented ten symbols that are obviously numerical: the digits 0 through 9. So what do we do for the other six? It turns out that the originators of this system took perhaps the most obvious approach: repurposing the letters of the alphabet. So we add the "digits" A through F (sometimes written as capitals, sometimes in lower-case) to our set of symbols. These, then, are the quantities that each individual digit represents:

---

[1] Sometimes numbers written in base 16 are called "**hex numbers**."

0	zero
1	one
2	two
3	three
4	four
5	five
6	six
7	seven
8	eight
9	nine
A	ten
B	eleven
C	twelve
D	thirteen
E	fourteen
F	fifteen

The inventors of hexadecimal notation didn't have to use the alphabet, of course; they could have chosen a star for ten, a square for eleven, a happy face for twelve, *etc.*, but that wouldn't have been very easy to type. So we're stuck with the letters, for better or for worse. Practice staring at that letter A and saying the word "ten." Because that's what it means. In hexadecimal, the sequence of digits 10 does *not* mean "ten." It means "sixteen."

Those are the symbols. What are the place values? Well, they are (from the right) the 16^0's place, the 16^1's place, the 16^2's place, and so on. Written decimally, those work out to be the 1's place, the 16's place, the 256's place, the 4096's place, and so on. Again, those numbers seem strange only because when they are *written decimally* they don't come out very "round."

The value of a number like 72E3 is computed as:

$$72E3_{16} = 7 \times 4096_{10} + 2 \times 256_{10} + 14 \times 16_{10} + 3 \times 1_{10} = 29{,}411_{10}.$$

Notice we treated the "E" just like another digit, which it is. We also called 72E3 "a number," which it is. Get used to the idea that numbers — totally legitimate numbers — can have letters for some of their digits.

7.3. HEXADECIMAL (BASE 16)

In hexadecimal, what's the highest value that can fit in one digit? Answer: F (which is fifteen.) What's the highest that can fit in two digits? FF (which is two hundred fifty-five.) What about three digits? FFF (which is sixty-five thousand five hundred thirty-five.) And so on. If you count in hexadecimal, you do the same thing as in decimal, only you "roll over the odometer" when you get to F, not when you get to 9.

Converting to and from decimal

So we know how to take a hexadecimal number (like $72E3_{16}$) and find its decimal equivalent: we just interpret each place's value as 1, 16, 256, 4096, and so on. What about going the other way? If we had a decimal number, how would we write its value hexadecimally?

First, let's learn two operations (if you don't already know them) that come in handy when working with integers. The first is called the **modulo operator** (written "**mod**"), and simply gives the *remainder* when dividing two numbers. This is a concept you probably learned in elementary school but might not have used since then. As we get older (and use calculators), we tend to think of a division operation like 13 ÷ 3 as being 4.333.... But that's when we want a real-valued (instead of integer-valued) answer. If we only want integers, then we say that 13 ÷ 3 is "4 with a remainder of 1." (The "4" is called the **quotient**.) This means that if you have 13 objects, you can take four groups of 3's out of them, and then have 1 object left over. The way we write this operation mathematically is "13 mod 3." In this case, it turns out that 13 mod 3 = 1.

Let's think through what the mod operator yields for different values. We know that 13 mod 3 = 1. What about 14 mod 3? That is equal to 2, since we can (again) take out four groups of 3's, but then we'd have *two* left over. What about 15 mod 3? That yields 0, since 3 goes in to 15 evenly, leaving no remainder at all. 16 mod 3 again gives us 1, just like 13 did. If you think it through, you'll realize that 19 mod 3 will also be 1, as will 22 mod 3 and 25 mod 3. These numbers that give the same remainder are said to be "**congruent** mod 3." The numbers 2, 5, 8, 11, 14, *etc.* are also all congruent (to each other) mod 3, since they all give remainder 2.

Another observation is that the value of n mod k always gives a value between 0 and $k-1$. We may not know at a glance what 407,332,117 mod 3 is, but we know it can't be 12, or 4, or even 3, because if we had that many elements left after taking out groups of 3's, we could still take out *another* group of 3. The remainder only gives us what's left after taking out groups, so by definition there cannot be an entire group (or more) left in the remainder.

The other operation we need is simply a "round down" operation, traditionally called "**floor**" and written with brackets: "$\lfloor \ \rfloor$". The floor of an integer is itself. The floor of a non-integer is the integer just below it. So $\lfloor 7 \rfloor = 7$ and $\lfloor 4.81 \rfloor = 4$. It's that simple.

The reason we use the floor operator is just to get the whole number of times one number goes into another. $\lfloor 13 \div 3 \rfloor = 4$, for example. By using mod and floor, we get the quotient and remainder of a division, both integers. If our numbers are 25 and 7, we have $\lfloor 25 \div 7 \rfloor = 3$ and 25 mod 7 = 4. Notice that this is equivalent to saying that $25 = 3 \times 7 + 4$. We're asking "how many groups of 7 are in 25?" and the answer is that 25 is equal to *3* groups of 7, plus 4 extra.

The general procedure for converting from one base to another is to repeatedly use mod and floor to strip out the digits from right to left. Here's how you do it:

Express a numeric value in a base

1. Take the number mod the base. Write that digit down.

2. Divide the number by the base and take the floor:

   a) If you get zero, you're done.

   b) If you get non-zero, then make this non-zero number your new value, move your pencil to the left of the digit(s) you've already written down, and return to step 1.

7.3. HEXADECIMAL (BASE 16)

As an example, let's go backwards to the hex number 72E3 as in our example above, which we already computed was equal to 29,411 in decimal. Starting with 29,411, then, we follow our algorithm:

1. (Step 1) We first compute 29,411 mod 16. This turns out to be 3. Many scientific calculators can perform this operation, as can programming languages like Java and data analysis languages like R. Or, you could do long division (459,494 ÷ 16) by hand and see what the remainder is. Or, you could divide on an ordinary calculator and see whether the part after the decimal point is 0, or $\frac{1}{16}^{th}$, or $\frac{2}{16}^{ths}$, *etc.* Or, you could sit there and subtract 16 after 16 after 16 from 29,411 until there are no more 16's to take out, and see what the answer is. At any rate, the answer is 3. So we write down 3:

$$3$$

2. (Step 2) We now divide 29,411 by 16 and take the floor. This produces $\lfloor 29{,}411 \div 16 \rfloor = 1838$. Since this is not zero, we perform step 2b: make 1838 our new value, move our pencil to the left of the 3, and go back to step 1.

3. (Step 1) Now compute 1838 mod 16. This gives us the value 14, which is of course a base 10 number. The equivalent hex digit is E. So we now write down E to the left of the 3:

$$E3$$

4. (Step 2) Dividing 1838 by 16 and taking the floor gives us 114. Since this is again not zero, we perform step 2b: make 114 our new value, move our pencil to the left of the E, and go back to step 1.

5. (Step 1) Next we compute 114 mod 16. This turns out to be 2, so we write down a 2:

$$2E3$$

6. (Step 2) Computing $\lfloor 114 \div 16 \rfloor$ produces 7, which is again not zero, so 7 becomes our new value and we go back once again to step 2b.

7. (Step 1) 7 mod 16 is simply 7, so we write it down:

$$72E3$$

8. (Step 2) Finally, $\lfloor 7 \div 16 \rfloor$ is zero, so we go to step 2a and we're done. The page has 72E3 written on it in big bold letters, which is the correct answer.

Adding hex numbers

Suppose we have two hexadecimal numbers, and we want to add them together to get a hexadecimal result. How do we do it? One way is to first convert them both to decimal, then add them like you learned in first grade, then convert the answer back to hex. But we can stay "natively hex" as long as we add each pair of digits correctly.

Let's try it. Suppose we want to compute this sum:

$$\begin{array}{r} 48D4_{16} \\ +5925_{16} \\ \hline ?_{16} \end{array}$$

We proceed in the first-grade way from right to left. Adding the one's-place values, we get $4 + 5 = 9$:

$$\begin{array}{r} 48D4_{16} \\ +5925_{16} \\ \hline 9_{16} \end{array}$$

Easy enough. Now we add the next digit to the left (the sixteen's-place, mind you, not the ten's place) and we find D + 2. Now what in the world is "D+2"? It's actually easy: all you have to do is the same thing you did when you were a child and you had to add something like 4 + 5. You hadn't memorized the answer yet, and so you started with four fingers held up, and counted off "1...2...3...4...5," sticking up another finger each time. Then, you looked at your hands, and behold! nine fingers.

We'll do the same thing here: start with the number "D," and count two additional places: "E...F." The answer is F. That is the number that's two greater than D. Lucky for us, it still fits in one digit. So now we have:

$$\begin{array}{r} 48D4_{16} \\ +5925_{16} \\ \hline F9_{16} \end{array}$$

So far so good. The next pair of digits is 8 + 9. Here's where you want to be careful. You're liable to look at "8+9" and immediately say "17!" But 8 + 9 is *not* 17 in hexadecimal. To figure out what it is, we start with the number 8, and count: "9...A...B...C...D...E...F...10...11...". The answer is "11," which of course is how you write "seventeen" in hex. So just like in grade school, we write down 1 and carry the 1:

$$\begin{array}{r} 1 \\ 48D4_{16} \\ +5925_{16} \\ \hline 1F9_{16} \end{array}$$

Finally, our last digit is 4 + 5, plus the carried 1. We start with four and count off five: "5...6...7...8...9." Then we add the carry, and count "...A." The answer is A, with no carry, and so we have our final answer:

$$\begin{array}{r} 1 \\ 4\,8D4_{16} \\ +\,592\,5_{16} \\ \hline \mathbf{A1F9_{16}} \end{array}$$

7.4 Binary (base 2)

The other base we commonly use in computer science is base 2, or **binary**. This is because the basic unit of information in a computer is called a **bit**, which has only two values, conventionally called either "true" and "false" or "1" and "0". Numbers (as well as everything else) are ultimately represented as colossal sequences of 1's and 0's, which are of course binary numbers.

The rules for interpreting place value are the same:

$$\begin{aligned} 110101_2 &= 1 \times 2^5 + 1 \times 2^4 + 0 \times 2^3 + 1 \times 2^2 + 0 \times 2^1 + 1 \times 2^0 \\ &= 1 \times 32 + 1 \times 16 + 0 \times 8 + 1 \times 4 + 0 \times 2 + 1 \times 1 \\ &= 53_{10}. \end{aligned}$$

So in binary we have a one's-place, a two's-place, a four's-place, an eight's-place, and so on. We call the right-most place the **least significant bit (LSB)** and the left-most the **most significant bit (MSB)**.

Counting up from zero is really just the same as any other base, although it feels a little strange in binary because you "roll over" so often:

0_2	zero
1_2	one
10_2	two
11_2	three
100_2	four
101_2	five
110_2	six
111_2	seven
1000_2	eight
1001_2	nine
$\vdots$	$\vdots$

Converting to and from decimal

Converting from binary to decimal was demonstrated above (with $110101_2 = 53_{10}$.) To go the other way, we follow the algorithm from page 172. Let's try it for the decimal number 49:

1. (Step 1) We first compute 49 mod 2. Doing "mod 2" is easy: you just see whether the number is even or odd. In this case, it's odd, so the remainder is a 1:

7.4. BINARY (BASE 2)

1

2. (Step 2) Now divide 49 by 2 and take the floor, which gives $\lfloor 49 \div 2 \rfloor = 24$. It's not zero, so we perform step 2b: make 24 our new value, move our pencil to the left of the 1, and go back to step 1.

3. (Step 1) Compute 24 mod 2. Since 24 is even, this is zero, which we write down to the left of the 1:

01

4. (Step 2) Divide 24 by 2 and take the floor, which gives $\lfloor 24 \div 2 \rfloor = 12$. Make 12 our new value, move our pencil to the left of the 0, and go back to step 1.

5. (Step 1) Compute 12 mod 2. Since 12 is even, this is zero, which we write down:

001

6. (Step 2) Divide 12 by 2 and take the floor, which gives $\lfloor 12 \div 2 \rfloor = 6$. Make 6 our new value, move our pencil to the left of the 0, and go back to step 1.

7. (Step 1) Compute 6 mod 2. Since 6 is even, this is zero, which we write down:

0001

8. (Step 2) Divide 6 by 2 and take the floor, which gives $\lfloor 6 \div 2 \rfloor = 3$. Make 3 our new value, move our pencil to the left of the 0, and go back to step 1.

9. (Step 1) Compute 3 mod 2. Since 3 is odd, this is one, which we write down:

10001

10. (Step 2) Divide 3 by 2 and take the floor, which gives $\lfloor 3 \div 2 \rfloor = 1$. This still isn't zero, so make 1 our new value, move our pencil to the left of the 0, and go back to step 1.

11. (Step 1) Compute 1 mod 2. Since 1 is odd, this is one, which we write down:

110001

12. (Step 2) Divide 1 by 2 and take the floor, which gives $\lfloor 1 \div 2 \rfloor = 0$. We're done. The final answer is 110001_2. Double-checking our work, we verify that indeed one 32 plus one 16 plus one 1 gives 49, which is what we started with.

Converting to and from hex

That was pretty tedious. But converting back and forth from binary to *hex* is a snap. That's because 16 is exactly 2^4, and so one hex digit is exactly equal to four binary digits. This isn't the case with base 10, where one decimal digit is equal to three binary digits... *plus* a little extra. This "not quite a whole number of digits" thing is what makes converting from decimal to binary (or decimal to hex, for that matter) so awkward.

We most commonly deal with sets of eight bits at a time, which is called a **byte**. (This is the fundamental unit of storage on pretty much every computer on earth.) Suppose I had the following byte:

10000110_2

Because one hex digit is exactly equal to four bits, this byte is exactly equal to:

86_{16}

7.4. BINARY (BASE 2)

This is because the byte can be neatly split into two parts: 1000, which corresponds to the hex digit 8, and 0110, which corresponds to the hex digit 6. These two halves are called **nibbles** — one byte has two nibbles, and each nibble is one hex digit. At a glance, therefore, with no multiplying or adding, we can convert from binary to hex.

Going the other direction is just as easy. If we have:

$$3E_{16}$$

we just convert each hex digit into the corresponding nibble:

$$00111110_2$$

After you do this a while, you get to the point where you can instantly recognize which hex digit goes with which nibble value. Until then, though, here's a handy table:

nibble	hex digit
0000	0
0001	1
0010	2
0011	3
0100	4
0101	5
0110	6
0111	7
1000	8
1001	9
1010	A
1011	B
1100	C
1101	D
1110	E
1111	F

In case you're wondering, yes this is worth memorizing.

Adding binary numbers

Adding two binary numbers is the same as adding in decimal, hexadecimal, or any other base: you just have to know when to "roll over the odometer," which in this case is almost instantly, since the highest value a bit can hold is 1! Let's give it a shot:

$$\begin{array}{r} 111001_2 \\ +011010_2 \\ \hline ?_2 \end{array}$$

A child could follow the rules: when we add two zeroes, we get zero. Adding a one to a zero gives one. Adding two ones gives zero, and a carry to the next significant digit. And adding two ones plus a carry gives a one and a carry. See if you can follow the flow:

$$\begin{array}{r} 1\,1 \\ 111001_2 \\ +011010_2 \\ \hline 1\,010011_2 \end{array}$$

Capacity

How large a value can a byte store? There are 8 bits, and each one can independently have either of two values (0 or 1), so by the Fundamental Theorem of Counting, there are 2^8 different combinations. This works out to 256, but we can't actually store the number 256 in a byte if we're using the bit pattern 00000000_2 (or 00_{16}) to represent zero. The highest value would be 11111111_2 (or FF_{16}), which is 256_{10}.

How do we store a number larger than that? Simply use more than one byte, of course. If we used two bytes of memory, and treated them as concatenated one after the other, that would give us 16 bits, allowing us to store up to the number $0000000000000000_2 = FFFF_{16}$ = $65{,}535_{10}$. We'd call one of these bytes — the one representing the 2^0's place up to the 2^7's place — the least significant *byte*, and the other one — containing places 2^8 through 2^{15} — the most significant byte. Extending to more than two bytes to accommodate even larger numbers is done in the obvious way.

Binary representation schemes

That's mostly all there is to it. But there's one thing we haven't discussed yet, and that's *negative* numbers. We know how to represent any positive number (or zero) with an ordinary place value scheme. But how do we store a number like −5?

There are three different schemes for treating negative numbers, each with its strengths and weaknesses.

Unsigned

The simplest scheme is called **unsigned**, and it simply means that we don't *allow* negative numbers. For one byte, we have 256 different bit patterns at our disposal, and we might just choose to allocate them all to represent positive numbers, so as to get the widest range. This makes sense for, say, a C++ program variable called `heightInInches` which we know can never meaningfully be negative (no one has a negative height).

The advantage of this scheme is simply that we can represent the greatest possible range of positive numbers, which is sometimes the goal. Each of the alternative schemes carves off a chunk of these available bit patterns and devotes them to representing negative numbers, leaving fewer left over for positive numbers. There's no free lunch: you have to decide how you want to "spend" your available bit patterns depending on what values you need to represent.

Sign-magnitude

The **sign-magnitude** scheme is probably the first thing you'd think of to solve the negative number representation problem. We need to store the sign of the number somehow, and a sign is inherently a two-valued thing (either positive or negative), so why not peel off one of the bits and use it to represent the sign? The remaining bits can then be used in the ordinary way to represent the magnitude of the number.

The way this is most often done is to take the left-most bit and use it as the **sign bit**. This bit now has *no other meaning*. It can't "double" as the 128's place, because then there'd be no way to distinguish between, say, 129 and −129 (each would be represented with 10000001.) No, the sign bit must be considered "spent money," and its expressive power cannot be reclaimed to also represent part of the magnitude. By convention, if the sign bit is 0 this represents a *positive* number, and a sign bit of 1 represents a *negative* number. (That might seem counterintuitive, but hey, that's the way it is.)

So this number in sign-magnitude:

00100110

represents the decimal number 38. That's because the sign bit (bolded, on the far left) is 0, which means the number is positive. The magnitude of the number is contained in the other 7 bits, which gives $32 + 4 + 2 = 38$. This number, on the other hand:

10100110

represents −38. The magnitude is the same, but the sign bit is 1 so this pattern now "means" a negative number.

Clearly we have reduced our range of positive numbers in exchange for the ability to also store negatives. We have 7 bits of range instead of 8, so instead of 255, our highest possible value is merely 127. On the other end, the lowest possible value is −127.

If you have sharp eyes, you may have noticed a discrepancy in the counting. With the sign-magnitude approach, we can hold numbers in the range −127 to 127. But wait: that's only 255 different values, not 256! Why did we lose one value of expressive power? The answer is that the sign-magnitude scheme has *two ways* of representing *zero*. The bit pattern 00000000 is obviously zero, but so is 10000000 (which you might call "negative zero.") Using two different patterns to represent the same value is a little wasteful, but the situation is actually worse than that. Having to account for both patterns means that computer hardware using the sign-magnitude scheme is inevitably more complicated. To compare two

7.4. BINARY (BASE 2) 183

bytes to see if they're equal, you'd think we'd just compare each bit position, and if they were all the same, the bytes would be declared equal, otherwise no. Alas, this is no longer quite that simple. The two zero patterns must be considered numerically equal, so our digital logic now has to contain a special case. "To be equal, all the bits have to be the same... oh, but actually not if the right-most seven are all zeroes in both bytes. In that case, it doesn't matter what the left-most bit contains." Maddening.

Two's-complement

This shortcoming in the sign-magnitude scheme is remedied with the **two's-complement** scheme, which is the one actually used most often in practice. It'll seem weird at first — certainly not as intuitive as the first two — but it leads to a critically important feature that we'll look at shortly.

First, the rules. To interpret a two's-complement number, you:

1. Look at the left-most bit (just like in sign-magnitude). If it's a 0, you have a positive number. If it's a 1, you have a negative number.

2. If it's a positive number, the other 7 bits give you the magnitude (just like in sign-magnitude).

3. If, however, it's a negative number, then to discover the magnitude of that negative number you must *flip all the bits and add one*. This will give you a positive number which is the absolute value of your negative number.

Easy example: take the byte 00100110. The left-most bit is a 0, which means it's a positive number, and as we discovered above, the remaining 7 bits give a magnitude of 38. So this is the number 38.

Harder example: take the byte 10100110. The left-most bit is a 1, which means it's negative. Okay: negative *what*? How do we find the magnitude? Well, we "flip" all the bits (*i.e.*, invert each one from 0 to 1 or vice versa) to get:

$$01011001$$

and then add one to the result:

$$\begin{array}{r} 1 \\ 01011001 \\ +1 \\ \hline 01011010 \end{array}$$

This black magic produces the value 01011010_2, which converts to 90_{10}. **This means that the original number, 10100110, corresponds to the value –90.**

"Flipping all the bits and adding one" is the cookbook procedure for taking the complement (negative) of a number in the two's-complement scheme. It works in reverse, too. Let's start with 90 this time and crank through the process again, making sure we get –90.

Start with the binary representation of 90_{10}:

$$01011010$$

Flip all the bits to get:

$$10100101$$

and finally add one to the result:

$$\begin{array}{r} 1 \\ 10100101 \\ +1 \\ \hline 10100110 \end{array}$$

We get 10100110, which was precisely the number we originally began with, and which we have already determined represents –90.

Now you may ask what we gain from all this. Surely this scheme is considerably more convoluted than the simple idea of reserving one bit as a sign bit, and treating the rest as a magnitude. But it turns out there is indeed a method to the madness. Strange as

7.4. BINARY (BASE 2)

it sounds, a two's-complement representation scheme allows us to *perform addition and subtraction with a single operation.*

In first grade (or so), you learned the procedure for adding multi-digit numbers, which we've followed several times in this chapter. It involves adding the digits right-to-left and possibly "carrying." Then in second grade (or so), you learned the procedure for *subtracting* multi-digit numbers. It involves subtracting the digits right-to-left and possibly "borrowing." If you're like me, you found adding easier than subtracting. It's easy to just carry the one, but to borrow requires looking at the digit to the left, making sure that you *can* borrow from it (*i.e.*, that it's not already 0), borrowing from further left until you actually find an available non-zero value, hoping the number on the bottom is actually less than the one on the top (because otherwise you have to switch the order and then add a negative sign to the result), and keeping all of that straight as you march down the line.

Even if you didn't find subtracting more difficult than adding, though, you can't argue that it's still a completely *different* algorithm, with different rules to follow. In computer hardware, we have to implement different circuitry to perform each operation, which is more difficult, costly, error-prone, and power-draining.

The wonderful thing about two's-complement, however, is that with this scheme we actually *never need to use the subtraction algorithm.* If we want to subtract two numbers — say, $24 - 37$ — we can instead take the complement of the second number and then add them. Instead of $24 - 37$ we compute $24 + (-37)$.

Let's see it in action. Using conversion procedures, we can figure out that 24_{10} is:

$$00011000$$

and that *positive* 37_{10} is:

$$00100101$$

If we wanted to compute $24 + 37$, we'd just add these. But instead we're looking for $24 - 37$, so we'll take the complement of 37 to find

-37. Flip all the bits of 37:

$$11011010$$

and add one:

$$\begin{array}{r} 1\,1011010 \\ +1 \\ \hline 1\,1011011 \end{array}$$

and so now we've determined that in the two's-complement scheme, -37 is represented by 11011011_2.

We're now ready to compute $24 + (-37)$:

$$\begin{array}{rl} 1\,1 & \\ 00011000 & \leftarrow \textit{this is } 24_{10} \\ +11011011 & \leftarrow \textit{this is } -37_{10} \\ \hline 11110011 & \end{array}$$

So we have our two's-complement answer, 11110011. What value does that correspond to? Well, the left-most bit is a 1, so it's a negative number. To find out what it's the negative *of*, flip all the bits and add one:

$$\begin{array}{rl} 0\,0001100 & \leftarrow \textit{flip the bits to get} \\ +1 & \leftarrow \textit{add one} \\ \hline 0\,0001101 & \end{array}$$

This is positive 13, which means the number we inverted to get it — 11110011 — must represent -13. And that is indeed the correct answer, for $24 - 37 = -13$.

One last word on two's-complement: what is the *range* of numbers we can represent? It turns out to be -128 to 127. The highest value is 01111111, which is 127. You might think the lowest value would be represented as 11111111, but if you work it out, you'll find that this is actually the number -1. The lowest number is actually the bit pattern 10000000, which is -128.

Overflow

One last sticky detail we need to cover has to do with **overflow**. When we add two numbers, there is the possibility that the result

7.4. BINARY (BASE 2)

will contain one more digit than the original numbers did. You've probably seen this on a hand calculator when you press "=" and get an "E" (for "error") in the display. If there are only ten digits on your display, adding two ten-digit numbers will (sometimes) result in an eleven-digit number that your calculator can't display, and it's alerting you to that fact so you don't misinterpret the result. Here, we might add two 8-bit quantities and end up with a 9-bit quantity that can't fit in one byte. This situation is called overflow, and we need to detect when it occurs.

The rules for detecting overflow are different depending on the scheme. For *unsigned* numbers, the rule is simple: if a 1 is carried out from the MSB (far left-side), then we have overflow. So if I were to try to add 155_{10} and 108_{10}:

```
   1111
   10011011   ← 155₁₀
  +01101100   ← 108₁₀
  ─────────
  1 00001111
```

then I get a carry out left into the 9th digit. Since we can only hold eight digits in our result, we would get a nonsensical answer (15_{10}), which we can detect as bogus because the carry out indicated overflow.

Sign-magnitude works the same way, except that I have one fewer bit when I'm adding and storing results. (Instead of a byte's worth of bits representing magnitude, the left-end bit has been reserved for a special purpose: indicating the number's sign. Therefore, if I add the remaining 7-bit quantities and get a carry out left into the *eighth* digit, that would indicate overflow.)

Now with two's-complement, things are (predictably) not that easy. But it turns out they're *almost* as easy. There's still a simple rule to detect overflow, it's just a different rule. The rule is: if the carry *in to* the last (left-most) bit is *different* than the carry *out from* the last bit, then we have overflow.

Let's try adding 103_{10} and 95_{10} in two's-complement, two numbers which fit in our -128 to 127 range, but whose sum will not:

$$
\begin{array}{r}
\text{carry-in} \rightarrow \texttt{1111111} \\
\texttt{01100111} \leftarrow 103_{10} \\
+ \quad \texttt{01011111} \leftarrow 95_{10} \\
\hline
\text{carry-out} \rightarrow \texttt{011000110}
\end{array}
$$

The carry-in to the last bit was 1, but the carry-out was 0, so for two's-complement this means we detected overflow. It's a good thing, too, since 11000110 in two's-complement represents -57_{10}, which is certainly not 103 + 95.

Essentially, if the carry-in is not equal to the carry-out, that means we added two positive numbers and came up with a negative number, or that we added two negatives and got a positive. Clearly this is an erroneous result, and the simple comparison tells us that. Just be careful to realize that the rule for detecting overflow depends *totally* on the particular representation scheme we're using. A carry-out of 1 always means overflow... *in the unsigned scheme.* For two's-complement, we can easily get a carry-out of 1 with no error at all, provided the carry-in is *also* 1.

"It's all relative"

Finally, if we come up for air out of all this mass of details, it's worth emphasizing that there is no intrinsically "right" way to interpret a binary number. If I show you a bit pattern — say, 11000100 — and ask you what value it represents, you can't tell me without knowing how to interpret it.

If I say, "oh, that's an unsigned number," then you'd treat each bit as a digit in a simple base 2 numbering scheme. You'd add $2^7 + 2^6 + 2^2$ to get 196, then respond, "ah, then that's the number 196_{10}." And you'd be right.

But if I say, "oh, that's a sign-magnitude number," you'd first look at the leftmost bit, see that it's a 1, and realize you have a negative number. Then you'd take the *remaining* seven bits and treat them as digits in a simple base 2 numbering scheme. You'd add $2^6 + 2^2$ to get 68, and then respond, "ah, then that's the number -68_{10}." And you'd be right.

7.4. BINARY (BASE 2)

But then again, if I say, "oh, that's a two's-complement number," you'd first look at the leftmost bit, see that it's a 1, and realize you're dealing with a negative number. What is it the negative of? You'd flip all the bits and add one to find out. This would give you 00111100, which you'd interpret as a base 2 number and get 60_{10}. You'd then respond, "ah, then that's the number -60_{10}." And you'd be right.

So what does 11000100 represent then?? Is it 196, -68, or -60? The answer is *any of the three*, depending on what representation scheme you're using. None of the data in computers or information systems has intrinsic meaning: it all has to be interpreted according to the syntactic and semantic rules that we invent. In math and computer science, anything can be made to mean anything: after all, we invent the rules.

7.5 Exercises

1. If I told you that the decimal number (*i.e.*, base-10 number) 2022 was equal to 13621_6, would you call me a liar without even having to think too hard?	Yes, you should. A number in base-6 can't have any digits in it other than 0 through 5, and the "number" I tried to give you had a 6 in it.
2. If I told you that the decimal number 2022 was equal to 1413_6, would you call me a liar without even having to think too hard?	Yes, you should. Think about it: in base 6, each digit's place value (except the one's place) is worth *less* than it is in base 10. Instead of a ten's place, hundred's place, and thousand's place, we have a woosy six's place, thirty-six's place, and two-hundred-and-sixteen's place. So there's no way that a number whose base-6 digits are 1, 4, 1, and 3 would be as large as a number whose base-*10* digits are 2, something, something, and something. Put another way, if the base is smaller, the number itself has to "look bigger" to have a chance of evening that out.
3. If I told you that the decimal number 2022 was equal to $8FA8_{16}$, would you call me a liar without even having to think too hard?	Yes, you should, because of the mirror reflection of the above logic. Every digit of a hexadecimal number (again, except the one's place) is worth *more* than it is in base 10. So a four-digit hex number beginning with an 8 is going to be way bigger than a wimpy four-digit decimal number beginning with 2.
4. If I told you that the decimal number 2022 was equal to 12310_6, would you call me a liar without even having to think too hard?	No, you shouldn't, because you do have to think hard for this one. As it happens, I *am* a liar (the true answer is 13210_6), but there's no easy way to know that at a glance.
5. If I told you that the decimal number 2022 was equal to $7E6_{16}$, would you call me a liar without even having to think too hard?	No, you shouldn't, because you do have to think hard for this one. (And in fact, it's correct! Work it out.)

7.5. EXERCISES

6. If I told you that 98,243,917,215 mod 7 was equal to 1, would you call me a liar without even having to think too hard?	No, you shouldn't. It turns out that the answer is 3, not 1, but how would you know that without working hard for it?
7. If I told you that 273,111,999,214 mod 6 was equal to 6, would you call me a liar without even having to think too hard?	Yes, you should. Any number mod 6 will be in the range 0 through 5, never 6 or above. (Think in terms of repeatedly taking out groups of six from the big number. The mod is the number of stones you have left when there are no more whole groups of six to take. If towards the end of this process there are six stones left, that's not a remainder, because you can get another whole group!)
8. Are the numbers 18 and 25 equal?	Of course not. Don't waste my time.
9. Are the numbers 18 and 25 congruent mod 7?	Yes. If we take groups of 7 out of 18 stones, we'll get two such groups (a total of 14 stones) and have 4 left over. And then, if we do that same with 25 stones, we'll get three such groups (a total of 21 stones) and again have 4 left over. So they're not congruent mod 7.
10. Are the numbers 18 and 25 congruent mod 6?	No. If we take groups of *6* out of 18 stones, we'll get three such groups with nothing left over. But if we start with 25 stones, we'll take out 4 such groups (for a total of 24 stones) and have one left over. So they're not congruent mod 6.
11. Are the numbers 617,418 and 617,424 equal?	Of course not. Don't waste my time.

12. Are the numbers 617,418 and 617,424 congruent mod 3?	Yes. The number 617,418 is exactly 6 less than 617,424. Let's say there are k stones left over after removing groups of three from 617,418. (k must be 0, 1, or 2, of course.) Now if we did the same remove-groups-of-three thing but starting with 617,424 instead, we'll have two more groups of three than we did before, but then also have exactly k stones left over.
13. Are the numbers 617,418 and 617,424 congruent mod 2?	Yes. The number 617,418 is exactly 6 less than 617,424. If there are k stones left over after removing pairs of stones from 617,418, we'd get three additional pairs if we had instead started with 617,424, but then also have exactly k stones left over.
14. Are the numbers 617,418 and 617,424 congruent mod 5?	No. Five doesn't go evenly into six.
15. Are the numbers 617,418 and 617,424 congruent mod 6?	Yes. The number 617,418 is exactly 6 less than 617,424. If there are k stones left over after removing groups of six from 617,418, we'd get one additional group if we had instead started with 617,424, and then have exactly k stones left over.
16. What's $1_{16} + 2_{16}$?	3_{16}.
17. What's $1_{16} + 9_{16}$?	A_{16}.
18. What's $1_{16} + E_{16}$?	F_{16}.
19. What's $1_{16} + F_{16}$?	10_{16}. This is the first time we've had to "carry."
20. What's $11_{16} + 22_{16}$?	33_{16}.
21. What's $11_{16} + 99_{16}$?	AA_{16}.
22. What's $11_{16} + EE_{16}$?	FF_{16}.
23. What's $11_{16} + EF_{16}$?	100_{16}. (As in exercise 19, we must carry.)

7.5. EXERCISES

24. What's the binary number 1011001110101010_2 in hexadecimal? Or is that too hard a question to eyeball?	Naw, it's easy. By inspection, it's $B3AA_{16}$, since each of the four 4-bit nibbles goes one-for-one with a hex digit. (You can look up nibble values on p. 179 if you want, but again it's definitely worth memorizing.)
25. What's the binary number 1011001110101010_2 in decimal? Or is that too hard a question to eyeball?	Ugh. Ain't nobody got time for that.
26. What's the hex number $F4CE_{16}$ in decimal? Or is that too hard a question to eyeball?	Too hard.
27. What's the hex number $F4CE_{16}$ in binary? Or is that too hard a question to eyeball?	Simple: 1111001011001110_2. Read it right off the chart (p. 179).
28. If I told you that the bit pattern 1010 was meant to represent an unsigned number, what value would it represent?	Ten. $(8 + 2 = 10)$.
29. If I told you that the bit pattern 1010 was meant to represent a sign-magnitude number, what value would it represent?	Negative two. The left-most bit is 1, so it's negative; and the remaining bits are 010, which when interpreted in binary are the number 2.
30. If I told you that the bit pattern 1010 was meant to represent a two's-complement number, what value would it represent?	Negative six. The left-most bit is 1, so it's negative. This means in order to figure out the value, we have to flip all the bits and add one. Flipping them yields 0101, and adding one to that gives 0110 (we had to do one carry). Since the binary number 0110 is positive six, that must mean that what we started with – 1010 – must be negative six.

Chapter 8

Logic

To a great extent, logic governs the way your mind works, even among so-called "irrational people." If we want to capture logical processes and represent them in a computer program, we need a way to express these thoughts in a form suitable for automated reasoning. This is primarily why computer scientists study logic.

Interestingly, the material in this chapter covers the very bottom and the very top of the technology stack. At the bottom, we have actual physical hardware that consists of circuits turning bits on and off. The rules that govern when we want to turn which bits on and off are based on "logic gates," or tiny physical devices that implement the logical principles of this chapter on a micro scale. At the other end of the spectrum, we have highly abstract programs aiming towards "artificial intelligence." These systems are centered around a "knowledge base" of accumulated facts, and regularly examine those known facts to make decisions and draw additional conclusions. What does a knowledge base consist of? You guessed it: logical statements that are described in this chapter.

8.1 Propositional logic

The simpler — but less powerful — of the two logic systems we'll study is called **propositional logic**. It has this name because the core building block is the **proposition**. A proposition is simply a statement that has a "truth value," which means that it is either true or false. The statement "all plants are living beings" could be a proposition, as could "Barack Obama was the first African-American President" and "Kim Kardashian will play the title role in *Thor: Love and Thunder*." By contrast, questions like "are you okay?" cannot be propositions, nor can commands like "hurry up and answer already!" or phrases like "Lynn's newborn schnauzer," because they are not statements that can be true or false. (Linguistically speaking, propositions have to be in the indicative mood.)

We normally use capital letters (what else?) to denote propositions, like:

Let A be the proposition that UMW is in Virginia.

Let B be the proposition that the King of England is female.

Let C be the proposition that dogs are carnivores.

Don't forget that a proposition doesn't have to be true in order to be a valid proposition (B is still a proposition, for example). It just matters that it is labeled and that it has the potential to be true or false.

Propositions are considered **atomic**. This means that they are *indivisible*: to the logic system itself, or to a computer program, they are simply an opaque chunk of truth (or falsity) called "A" or whatever. When we humans read the description of A, we realize that it has to do with the location of a particular institution of higher education, and with the state of the union that it might reside (or not reside) in. All this is invisible to an artificially intelligent agent, however, which treats "A" as nothing more than a stand-in label for a statement that has no further discernible structure.

So things are pretty boring so far. We can define and label propositions, but none of them have any connections to the others. We change that by introducing **logical operators** (also called **logical connectives**) with which we can build up compound constructions out of multiple propositions. The six connectives we'll learn are:

8.1. PROPOSITIONAL LOGIC

∧ — "and"
∨ — "or"
⊕ — "xor" (exclusive "or")

¬ — "not"
⇒ — "implies" (or "if... then ...")
⇔ — "equiv" (equivalent)

Just as the ordinary algebraic operators (+, -, *etc.*) can be used to join numbers and produce another number, and just as the set operators can be used to join sets and produce another set, the logical operators can be used to join propositions and produce another proposition. The expression "34 + 59" produces the number 93. The expression "{X,Y}∪{Y,Z}" produces the set {X,Y,Z}. And the expression "A ∧ B" produces the value *false*, since although UMW is located in Virginia, the King is not female.

Let's run through the six operators, some of which are intuitive and some of which are not:

∧ **("and")** The proposition X∧Y is true when both X and Y are true propositions. "A∧C" represents the proposition "UMW is in Virginia *and* dogs are carnivores," which has a truth value of *true* since both components are true. This operation is sometimes called a **conjunction**. Notice that the "∧" sign somewhat resembles the "∩" sign for set intersection. This is not an accident. An element is in the intersection of two sets if it is a member of the first *and* the second set. Hence mathematicians have chosen symbols which reinforce this connection.

∨ **("or")** The proposition X∨Y is true when either X or Y (or both) are true propositions. "B∨C" represents the proposition "The King of England is female *or* dogs are carnivores," which has a truth value of *true* since the second component is true. This operation is sometimes called a **disjunction**. The ∨ looks somewhat like the "∪" sign for set union, since an element is in the union of two sets if it is an element of the first set *or* the second set (or both). This operator is sometimes called an "inclusive or" since it is true if both propositions are true.

⊕ (**"xor"**) The ⊕ operator is just like ∨ except that it's *exclusive*: the proposition X⊕Y is true when *either* X *or* Y (but not both) are true propositions. "B∨C" and "B⊕C" are both true, but "A⊕C" is false, since UMW is in Virginia *and* dogs are carnivores.

¬ (**"not"**) This operator is different from the others in that it's *unary*, which means that it only operates on one proposition instead of two. All it does is flip the value from true to false (or vice versa.) The proposition "A" is true, but the proposition "¬A" is false. "¬B," on the other hand, is true. This operation is sometimes called a **negation**.

⇒ (**"implies"**) Okay, now for the toughest one. We're going to spend significant time thinking through this one carefully, because it's both important (in some ways, the most important of the operators) and also potentially baffling. I've studied this stuff for years, and I still sometimes get stuck when trying to figure out ⇒.

If we say "X⇒Y," we're claiming that *"if* X is true, *then* Y is true." Note carefully that *we are not claiming that X itself is true*. We're simply asserting that *if* it's true, then Y must necessarily also be true. We call the first part of a ⇒ proposition the **premise**, and the second part the **conclusion**. Here, X is the premise and Y the conclusion.

So far, it seems easy. It gets a little slippery when you realize that the *only* claim "X⇒Y" is making is: *"if* X is true, then Y *must be* true". If X is *not* true, then "X⇒Y" is making no claim at all.

Confusingly enough, this means that except for the one scenario where X is true but Y is false, the statement "X⇒Y itself" is *always true*. So, besides the obviously sensible case when X and Y are both true, X⇒Y is true even when: (1) X is false and Y is true, and (2) X is false and Y is false. Or, to put it succinctly: X⇒Y is true *whenever either X is false or Y is true or both*.

8.1. PROPOSITIONAL LOGIC

For example, A⇒C is a true proposition, believe it or not. In English, it says "UMW being in Virginia implies that dogs are carnivores." The proposition B⇒A is also true: "The King of England being female implies that UMW is in Virginia." What possible sense can we make out of these nonsensical claims?

The key to understanding it, for me at least, is twofold. First, remember that to a computer (or a logic system), there is no *meaning* to the propositions: they're simply atomic building blocks, each of which is true or false. So the fact that to a human, the content of the propositions might have nothing to do with each other — English Kings and dogs — is irrelevant to a computer: it just thinks indifferently in terms of "X" and "Y," and has no idea what real-world entities any of this refers to. Second, think in terms of ruling out counterexamples. When I assert X⇒Y, what I'm saying is "it's impossible for X to be true and Y false, because X's truthfulness would imply Y's truthfulness." Just as when I assert X∨Y I'm promising that either X or Y is true (or both), when I assert X⇒Y I'm promising that either X is false or Y is true (or both).

In this way, it starts to make sense when someone says, "Iowa being in the Southern hemisphere implies that Batman's cape is red." That assertion is like a promise: "*if* it turns out that Iowa is in the Southern hemisphere, then I guarantee Batman's cape is red." But since Iowa *isn't* in the Southern hemisphere, all bets are off. The conclusion was conditional on the premise.

The reason this operator is so important is that in artificial intelligence, the name of the game is concluding new facts from known existing facts, so that knowledge is increased. Every time a 'bot learns that X⇒Y is true, and then also learns that the premise (X) is true, it can conclude that the conclusion (Y) is true, even if it was never explicitly told that Y was true. This rule of logic is called *modus ponens*, and is the workhorse of automated knowledge bases.

⇔ (**"equiv"**) Finally, the proposition X⇔Y is true whenever X and Y have the same value: they're either both true, or both false. This can be seen as "implies in both directions," since X⇔Y means "if X is true, then Y is true; and if Y is true, then X is true." This operator is also the inverse of ⊕, since X⊕Y is true only if X and Y are different, and X⇔Y is true only if they're the same.

These operators, which each produce another proposition (called a **compound proposition**) from the proposition(s) they operate on, can be combined to form complex expressions. For instance:

- ¬B is the proposition that the King of England is not female. (This is true.)

- A ∧ ¬B is the proposition that UMW is in Virginia and also the King of England is not female. (This is also true.)

- C ⊕ (A ∧ ¬ B) is the proposition that *either* dogs are carnivores *or* UMW is in Virginia and the King of England is not female. (This is false, because both halves of the xor are true.)

- (C ⊕ (A ∧¬ B)) ⇒ ¬A is the proposition that if *either* dogs are carnivores *or* UMW resides in Virginia and the King of England is not female, then UMW must not reside in Virginia. (This is true, since dogs are carnivores *and* UMW resides in Virginia and the King of England is not female, so the left-hand side of the ⇒ is false, which means that the entire expression is true regardless of the truth value of the right-hand side (which is also false, since UMW doesn't *not* reside in Virginia.)

- Etc.

Truth tables

Several times in this book, we've drawn the distinction between *intension* — the inner, conceptual meaning — and *extension* — the exhaustive list of examples. A set can have both an intension like "the prime numbers less than ten" and an extension like $\{2,3,5,7\}$. A relation can have an intension like "*isDaughterOf*" and an extension like "{(Lisa,Homer), (Lisa,Marge), (Maggie,Homer), (Maggie,Marge)}." So, too, with the logical connectives. When we say that the "∧" operator means "both propositions must be true," we're specifying the conceptual meaning of the "and" operator. Another way to describe it, however, would be to just list its value for all the possible inputs.

Such an exhaustive list is called a **truth table**. We specify every possible combination of inputs, and list the output for each one of them. Here's the truth table for "∧":

X	Y	X∧Y
0	0	0
0	1	0
1	0	0
1	1	1

We use "1" to represent true and "0" for false, just to make the table more compact. The "∧" operator works on two propositions, either of which can have a truth value or 0 or 1. There are therefore, by the Fundamental Theorem of Counting, four different combinations of inputs, and so our truth table has four rows. The right-most column shows the output for each of these sets of inputs. It indicates that X∧Y is 1 only when both inputs are 1, and 0 otherwise. Even if we didn't grasp the simple concept that "∧" is supposed to represent the concept of "and," we could just look up the value of X∧Y if we knew the truth values of X and Y.

Sometimes we show more than one output in a truth table. For instance, this truth table shows the values for the other five operators:

X	Y	X∨Y	X⊕Y	¬X	X⇒Y	X⇔Y
0	0	0	0	1	1	1
0	1	1	1	1	1	0
1	0	1	1	0	0	0
1	1	1	0	0	1	1

Take a moment and look carefully through the entries in that table, and make sure you agree that this correctly represents the outputs for the five operators. (Note that "¬", being a unary operator, only has X as an input, which means that the value of Y is effectively ignored for that column.)

Now sometimes we have a more complex expression (like the (C ⊕ (A ∧¬B)) ⇒ ¬A example from above) and we want to know the truth value of the entire expression. Under what circumstances — *i.e.*, for what truth values of A, B, and C — is that expression true? We can use truth tables to calculate this piece by piece.

Let's work through that example in its entirety. First, we set up the inputs for our truth table:

A	B	C
0	0	0
0	0	1
0	1	0
0	1	1
1	0	0
1	0	1
1	1	0
1	1	1

In this case, there are three inputs to the expression (A, B, and C) and so we have 2^3, or eight, rows in the truth table.

Now we work our way through the expression inside out, writing down the values of intermediate parts of the expression. We need to know the value of ¬B to figure some other things out, so let's start with that one:

8.1. PROPOSITIONAL LOGIC

A	B	C	¬B
0	0	0	1
0	0	1	1
0	1	0	0
0	1	1	0
1	0	0	1
1	0	1	1
1	1	0	0
1	1	1	0

Now we can compute $A \wedge \neg B$, a component of the expression:

A	B	C	¬B	A∧¬B
0	0	0	1	0
0	0	1	1	0
0	1	0	0	0
0	1	1	0	0
1	0	0	1	1
1	0	1	1	1
1	1	0	0	0
1	1	1	0	0

This produces a 1 only for rows where A is true *and* B is false. Knowing this allows us to compute the value of $(C \oplus (A \wedge \neg B))$:

A	B	C	¬B	A∧¬B	(C⊕(A∧¬B))
0	0	0	1	0	0
0	0	1	1	0	1
0	1	0	0	0	0
0	1	1	0	0	1
1	0	0	1	1	1
1	0	1	1	1	0
1	1	0	0	0	0
1	1	1	0	0	1

which is true only when the value of C is different than the value of $(A \wedge \neg B)$. We're almost there now. All we need is $\neg A$:

A	B	C	¬B	A∧¬B	(C⊕(A∧¬B))	¬A
0	0	0	1	0	0	1
0	0	1	1	0	1	1
0	1	0	0	0	0	1
0	1	1	0	0	1	1
1	0	0	1	1	1	0
1	0	1	1	1	0	0
1	1	0	0	0	0	0
1	1	1	0	0	1	0

and we can finally obtain our answer:

A	B	C	¬B	A∧¬B	(C⊕(A∧¬B))	¬A	(C⊕(A∧¬B))⇒¬A
0	0	0	1	0	0	1	**1**
0	0	1	1	0	1	1	**1**
0	1	0	0	0	0	1	**1**
0	1	1	0	0	1	1	**1**
1	0	0	1	1	1	0	**0**
1	0	1	1	1	0	0	**1**
1	1	0	0	0	0	0	**1**
1	1	1	0	0	1	0	**0**

That last step is the hardest one. We look at the third output column (C⊕(A∧¬B)) and the fourth (¬A) and mark down a 1 for each row in which the third is 0 or the fourth is 1. (Review the truth table for the "⇒" operator if you have doubts about this.) The final result is that our complex expression is true for all possible values of A, B, and C, except when they have the values 1, 0, and 0, or else 1, 1, and 1, respectively. In our original example, we know that UMW *is* in Virginia, the King is *not* female, and dogs *are* carnivores, so our input values are 1, 0, and 1 for A, B, and C. Therefore, for those inputs, this expression is true.

Tautologies

Let's work through this process for a different example. Suppose I want to know under what circumstances the expression ¬Z ∧ (X ⇔ Y) ∧ (X ⊕ Z) ⇒ (X ∧ ¬ Z) evaluates to true. When we follow the above procedure, it yields the following truth table:

8.1. PROPOSITIONAL LOGIC

X	Y	Z	$\neg Z$	$X \Leftrightarrow Y$	$\neg Z \wedge (X \Leftrightarrow Y)$	$X \oplus Z$	A^1	$(X \wedge \neg Z)$	B^1
0	0	0	1	1	1	0	0	0	1
0	0	1	0	1	0	1	0	0	1
0	1	0	1	0	0	0	0	0	1
0	1	1	0	0	0	1	0	0	1
1	0	0	1	0	0	1	0	1	1
1	0	1	0	0	0	0	0	0	1
1	1	0	1	1	1	1	1	1	1
1	1	1	0	1	0	0	0	0	1

(If you're looking for some practice, cranking through this example on your own and then comparing your answers to the above truth table isn't a bad idea at all.)

You'll notice that the "answer" column has *all* 1's. This means that the expression is always true, no matter what the values of the individual propositions are. Such an expression is called a **tautology**: it's always true. The word "tautology" has a negative connotation in regular English usage: it refers to a statement so obvious as to not tell you anything, like "all triangles have three sides," or "the fatal overdose was deadly." But in logic, tautologies are quite useful, since they represent reliable identities.

The tautology above was a contrived example, and not useful in practice. Here are some important others, though:

X	$\neg X$	$X \vee \neg X$
0	1	**1**
1	0	**1**

Sometimes called **the law of the excluded middle**, this identity states that either a proposition or its negative will always be true. (There is no third option.)

---

[1]Here, "A" stands for $\neg Z \wedge (X \Leftrightarrow Y) \wedge (X \oplus Z)$ and "B" is "$\neg Z \wedge (X \Leftrightarrow Y) \wedge (X \oplus Y) \Rightarrow (X \wedge \neg Z)$," which were too long to fit in the table heading.

X	Y	X∨Y	¬(X∨Y)	¬X	¬Y	¬X∧¬Y	¬(X∨Y)⇔(¬X∧¬Y)
0	0	0	1	1	1	1	1
0	1	1	0	1	0	0	1
1	0	1	0	0	1	0	1
1	1	1	0	0	0	0	1

This is one of **De Morgan's Laws**, which we've seen previously with regards to sets (p. 21). Here is the other:

X	Y	X∧Y	¬(X∧Y)	¬X	¬Y	¬X∨¬Y	¬(X∧Y)⇔(¬X∨¬Y)
0	0	0	1	1	1	1	1
0	1	0	1	1	0	1	1
1	0	0	1	0	1	1	1
1	1	1	0	0	0	0	1

The first can be expressed as "the negation of the disjunction is equal to the conjunction of the negations," and the second as "the negation of the conjunction is equal to the disjunction of the negations." If that helps at all.

One last identity is this one:

X	Y	Z	Y∨Z	X∧(Y∨Z)	X∧Y	X∧Z	(X∧Y)∨(X∧Z)	A^2
0	0	0	0	0	0	0	0	1
0	0	1	1	0	0	0	0	1
0	1	0	1	0	0	0	0	1
0	1	1	1	0	0	0	0	1
1	0	0	0	0	0	0	0	1
1	0	1	1	1	0	1	1	1
1	1	0	1	1	1	0	1	1
1	1	1	1	1	1	1	1	1

This is none other than the distributive law, which we also saw for set union and intersection (p. 20) and which you should also remember from introductory algebra: $x \cdot (y + z) = x \cdot y + x \cdot z$.

It's interesting, actually, when you compare the distributive law from algebra to the distributive law for logic:

$$x \cdot (y + z) = x \cdot y + x \cdot z$$
$$X \wedge (Y \vee Z) \Leftrightarrow (X \wedge Y) \vee (X \wedge Z)$$

---

[2]Here, "A" is X∧(Y∨Z)⇔(X∧Y)∨(X∧Z).

The "∧" operator is analogous to "·" (times), while "∨" corresponds to "+" (plus). In fact, if you look at the truth tables for these two operators again, you'll see an uncanny resemblance:

X	Y	X∧Y	X∨Y
0	0	0	0
0	1	0	1
1	0	0	1
1	1	1	*(1)*

Except for the *(1)* that I put in parentheses, this truth table is exactly what you'd get if you mathematically *multiplied* (∧) and *added* (∨) the inputs! At some level, logically "and-ing" *is* multiplying, while "or-ing" is adding. Fascinating.

8.2 Predicate logic

Propositional logic can represent a lot of things, but it turns out to be too limiting to be practically useful. And that has to do with the atomic nature of propositions. Every proposition is its own opaque chunk of truthhood or falsity, with no way to break it down into constituent parts. Suppose I wanted to claim that every state in the union had a governor. To state this in propositional logic, I'd have to create a brand new proposition for each state:

Let G1 be the proposition that Alabama has a governor.

Let G2 be the proposition that Alaska has a governor.

Let G3 be the proposition that Arizona has a governor.

...

and then, finally, I could assert:

$$G1 \land G2 \land G3 \land \cdots \land G50.$$

That's a lot of work just to create a whole bunch of individual propositions that are essentially the same. What we need is some kind of proposition *template*, with which we can "mint" new propositions of a similar form by plugging in new values.

This is exactly what a **predicate** is, which forms the basis for **predicate logic**, or "*first-order* predicate logic," to be more exact.[3] A predicate is a formula that yields a proposition for each value of its inputs. For instance, I can define a predicate called "HasGovernor" as follows:

Let HasGovernor(x) be the proposition that x is a state that has a governor.

Then I can assert:

HasGovernor(Virginia)

to state that Virginia has a governor. This mechanism alleviates the need to define fifty nearly-identical propositions. Instead, we define one predicate.

If you're a programmer, you can think of a predicate as a function that returns a proposition (which, in turn, can be thought of as a function that returns a boolean value). Whether you're a programmer or not, you can think of a predicate as a function (in the chapter 3 sense) mapping objects to propositions:

HasGovernor : $\Omega \to P$,

where P is the set of all propositions. Note that the domain of this function is Ω, the entire domain of discourse. This means that you can give any input at all to the predicate. For instance, we can assert:

¬HasGovernor(mayonnaise)

---

[3]Or, if you want to sound really nerdy, you can call it **first-order predicate calculus**, which is a synonym.

8.2. PREDICATE LOGIC

which is perfectly true.[4]

You may recall the word "predicate" from your middle school grammar class. Every sentence, remember, has a subject and a predicate. In "Billy jumps," "Billy" is the subject, and "jumps" the predicate. In "The lonely boy ate spaghetti with gusto," we have "the lonely boy" as the subject and "ate spaghetti with gusto" as the predicate. Basically, a predicate is anything that can describe or affirm something about a subject. Imagine asserting "JUMPS(Billy)" and "ATESPAGHETTIWITHGUSTO(lonely boy)."

A predicate can have more than one input. Suppose we define the predicate ISFANOF as follows:

Let ISFANOF(x, y) be the proposition that x digs the music of rock band y.

Then I can assert:

$$\text{ISFANOF(Stephen, Led Zeppelin)}$$
$$\text{ISFANOF(Rachel, The Beatles)}$$
$$\text{ISFANOF(Stephen, The Beatles)}$$
$$\neg\text{ISFANOF(Stephen, The Rolling Stones)}$$

We could even define TRAVELEDTOBYMODEINYEAR with a bunch of inputs:

Let TRAVELEDTOBYMODEINYEAR(p, d, m, y) be the proposition that person p traveled to destination d by mode m in year y.

The following statements are then true:

TRAVELEDTOBYMODEINYEAR(Stephen, Richmond, car, 2017)

---

[4]By the way, when I say you can give any input at all to a predicate, I mean any individual element from the domain of discourse. I don't mean that a *set* of elements can be an input. This limitation is why it's called "first-order" predicate logic. If you allow sets to be inputs to predicates, it's called "second-order predicate logic," and can get quite messy.

TraveledToByModeInYear(Rachel, Germany, plane, 2014)

¬TraveledToByModeInYear(Johnny, Mars, spaceship, 1776)

Defining multiple inputs gives us more precision in defining relationships. Imagine creating the predicate "AteWithAttitude" and then asserting:

AteWithAttitude(lonely boy, spaghetti, gusto)

¬AteWithAttitude(Johnny, broccoli, gusto)

AteWithAttitude(Johnny, broccoli, trepidation)

Predicates and relations

The astute reader may have noticed that the IsFanOf predicate, above, seems awfully similar to an *isFanOf* relation defined between sets P (the set of people) and R (the set of rock bands), where isFanOf $\subseteq P \times R$. In both cases, we have pairs of people/bands for which it's true, and pairs for which it's false.

Indeed these concepts are identical. In fact, a relation can be defined as *the set of ordered pairs (or tuples) for which a predicate is true.* Saying "IsFanOf(Rachel, The Beatles)" and "¬IsFanOf(Stephen, The Rolling Stones)" is really just another way of saying "Rachel isFanOf The Beatles" and "Stephen ~~isFanOf~~ The Rolling Stones."

Quantifiers

One powerful feature of predicate logic is the ability to make grandiose statements about many things at once. Suppose we did want to claim that every state had a governor. How can we do it?

We'll add to our repertoire the notion of **quantifiers**. There are two kinds of quantifiers in predicate logic, the first of which is called the **universal quantifier**. It's written "$\forall$" and pronounced "for all." Here's an example:

$$\forall x \; \text{HasGovernor}(x).$$

8.2. PREDICATE LOGIC

This asserts that for *every* x, HASGOVERNOR is true. Actually, this isn't quite right, for although Michigan and California have governors, mayonnaise does not. To be precise, we should say:

$$\forall x \in S \ \text{HASGOVERNOR}(x),$$

where S is the set of all fifty states in the U.S.

We can use a quantifier for any complex expression, not just a simple predicate. For instance, if H is the set of all humans, then:

$$\forall h \in H \ \text{ADULT}(h) \oplus \text{CHILD}(h)$$

states that every human is either an adult or a child, but not both. (Imagine drawing an arbitrary line at a person's 18th birthday.) Another (more common) way to write this is to dispense with sets and define another predicate HUMAN. Then we can say:

$$\forall h \ \text{HUMAN}(h) \Rightarrow \text{ADULT}(h) \oplus \text{CHILD}(h).$$

Think this through carefully. We're now asserting that this expression is true for *all* objects, whether they be Duchess Kate Middleton, little Prince Louis, or a bowl of oatmeal. To see that it's true for all three, let h first be equal to Kate Middleton. We substitute Kate for h and get:

$$\text{HUMAN(Kate)} \Rightarrow \text{ADULT(Kate)} \oplus \text{CHILD(Kate)}$$
$$\text{true} \Rightarrow \text{true} \oplus \text{false}$$
$$\text{true} \Rightarrow \text{true}$$
$$\text{true} \ \checkmark$$

Remember that "implies" ($\Rightarrow$) is true as long as the premise (left-hand side) is false and/or the conclusion (right-hand side) is true. In this case, they're both true, so we have a true end result. Something similar happens for Prince Louis:

$$\text{HUMAN(Louis)} \Rightarrow \text{ADULT(Louis)} \oplus \text{CHILD(Louis)}$$
$$\text{true} \Rightarrow \text{false} \oplus \text{true}$$
$$\text{true} \Rightarrow \text{true}$$
$$\text{true} \ \checkmark$$

So these two cases both result in true. But perhaps surprisingly, we also get true for oatmeal:

$$\text{HUMAN(oatmeal)} \Rightarrow \text{ADULT(oatmeal)} \oplus \text{CHILD(oatmeal)}$$
$$\text{false} \Rightarrow \text{false} \oplus \text{false}$$
$$\text{false} \Rightarrow \text{false}$$
$$\text{true} \checkmark$$

Whoa, how did *true* pop out of that? Simply because the premise was false, and so all bets were off. We effectively said *"if* a bowl of oatmeal is human, *then* it will either be an adult or a child. But it's not, so never mind." Put another way, the bowl of oatmeal did *not* turn out to be a counterexample, and so we're confident claiming that this expression is true "for *all* h": ∀h.

The other kind of quantifier is called the **existential quantifier**. As its name suggests, it asserts the *existence* of something. We write it "∃" and pronounce it "there exists." For example,

$$\exists x \ \text{HASGOVERNOR}(x)$$

asserts that there is *at least one* state that has a governor. This doesn't tell us how *many* states this is true for, and in fact despite their name, quantifiers really aren't very good at "quantifying" things for us, at least numerically. As of 2008, the statement

$$\exists x \ \text{PRESIDENT}(x) \wedge \text{AFRICAN-AMERICAN}(x)$$

is true, and always will be, no matter how many more African-American U.S. presidents we have. Note that in compound expressions like this, a variable (like x) always stands for a *single* entity wherever it appears. For hundreds of years there have existed African-Americans, and there have existed Presidents, so the expression above would be ridiculously obvious if it meant only "there have been Presidents, and there have been African-Americans." But the same variable x being used as inputs to *both* predicates is what seals the deal and makes it represent the much stronger statement "there is at least one individual who is personally *both* African-American *and* President of the United States at the same time."

8.2. PREDICATE LOGIC

It's common practice to negate quantifiers, both universal and existential. As of 2022, the following statement is still true:

$$\neg \exists p \ \text{PRESIDENT}(p) \wedge \text{FEMALE}(p).$$

This conveys that there does *not* exist a female president. As another example, if one day Missouri overhauls its government structure and replaces it with a mobocracy, perhaps we'll state:

$$\neg \forall x \ \text{HASGOVERNOR}(x).$$

Interchanging quantifiers

Some illuminating themes can be seen when we examine the relationship that the two types of quantifiers have to each other. Consider this one first:[5]

$$\forall x \ P(x) \Leftrightarrow \neg \exists x \ \neg P(x), \tag{8.1}$$

where P is any predicate (or for that matter, any expression involving many predicates). That's sensible. It states: "if P is true of all things, then there does *not* exist anything that it *isn't* true for." Three other equivalences come to light:[6]

$$\neg \forall x \ P(x) \Leftrightarrow \exists x \ \neg P(x) \tag{8.2}$$

$$\forall x \ \neg P(x) \Leftrightarrow \neg \exists x \ P(x) \tag{8.3}$$

$$\neg \forall x \ \neg P(x) \Leftrightarrow \exists x \ P(x) \tag{8.4}$$

In words, identity 8.2 says "if it's not true for everything, then it must be false for something." Identity 8.3 says "if it's false for everything, then there's nothing it's true for." And identity 8.4 says "if it's not false for everything, then it must be true for something." All of these are eminently logical, I think you'll agree. They also imply that there are nearly always multiple correct ways to state something. In our apocalyptic vision of Missouri, for example, we stated "$\neg \forall x \ \text{HASGOVERNOR}(x)$," but we could just as well have stated "$\exists x \ \neg \text{HASGOVERNOR}(x)$," which amounts to the same thing.

---

[5](8.1) Everybody was driving. $\Leftrightarrow$ Nobody exists who was not driving.
[6](8.2) Not everybody was driving. $\Leftrightarrow$ At least one person was not driving.
(8.3) Everybody was not driving. $\Leftrightarrow$ Nobody was driving.
(8.4) Not everybody was not driving. $\Leftrightarrow$ At least one person was driving.

Order matters

When you're facing an intimidating morass of ∀'s and ∃'s and ∨'s and ⇒'s and God knows what else, it's easy to get lost in the sauce. But you have to be very careful to dissect the expression to find out what it means. Consider this one:

$$\forall x \in \mathbb{R} \exists y \in \mathbb{R} \ x + 1 = y. \tag{8.5}$$

This statement is *true*. It says that for every single real number (call it x), it's true that you can find some other number (call it y) that's one greater than it. If you generate some examples it's easy to see this is true. Suppose we have the real number $x = 5$. Is there some other number y that's equal to $x + 1$? Of course, the number 6. What if $x = -32.4$? Is there a number y that satisfies this equation? Of course, $y = -31.4$. Obviously no matter what number x we choose, we can find the desired number y just by adding one. Hence this statement is true *for all* x, just like it says.

What happens, though, if we innocently switch the order of the quantifiers? Let's try asserting this:

$$\exists y \in \mathbb{R} \forall x \in \mathbb{R} \ x + 1 = y. \tag{8.6}$$

Is this also true? Look carefully. It says "there exists some magic number y that has the following amazing property: no matter what value of x you choose, this y is one greater than x!" Obviously this is not true. There *is* no such number y. If I choose $y = 13$, that works great as long as I choose $x = 12$, but for any other choice of x, it's dead in the water.

The lesson learned here is that the order of quantifiers matters. You have to take each quantifier/variable pair in turn, and think to yourself, "okay, this statement is asserting that *once I choose* the first variable, the rest of the expression is true for that choice."

The value of precision

This fluency with the basic syntax and meaning of predicate logic was our only goal in this chapter. There are all kinds of logical rules that can be applied to predicate logic statements in order to

8.2. PREDICATE LOGIC

deduce further statements, and you'll learn about them when you study artificial intelligence later on. Most of them are formalized versions of common sense. "If you know A is true, and you know A⇒B is true, then you can conclude B is true." Or "if you know X∧Y is false, and then you discover that Y is true, you can then conclude that X is false." *Etc.* The power to produce new truth from existing truth is the hallmark of AI systems, and why this stuff really matters.

If you can imagine a program doing this sort of automated reasoning, it will become clear why the precision of something like predicate logic — instead of the sloppiness of English — becomes important. English is a beautiful and poetic language, but its ambiguity is notorious. For example, back in chapter 3 we used the phrase "some employee belongs to every department" when describing relations. Now consider that English sentence. What does "some employee belongs to every department" actually mean? Does it mean that there is some special employee who happens to hold membership in every department in the company? Or does it mean that no department is empty: all departments have at least *one* person in them, for crying out loud? The English could mean either. In predicate logic, we're either asserting:

$$\exists x \; \text{EMPLOYEE}(x) \land \forall y \; \text{BELONGSTO}(x, y)$$

or

$$\forall y \; \exists x \; \text{EMPLOYEE}(x) \land \text{BELONGSTO}(x, y)$$

These are two very different things. A human being would realize that it's the second one the speaker means, drawing from a whole range of experience and common sense and context clues. But a 'bot has available none of these, and so it demands that the language clearly and unambiguously state exactly what's meant.

English is rife with these ambiguities, especially involving pronouns. **"After John hit George he ran away."** What happened? Did John run away after striking George, fearing that George would retaliate? Or did George run away after getting hit, fearing additional abuse? It's unclear what "he" refers to, so we can't say from the sentence alone.

Here's a funny one I'll end with. Consider the sentence "**He made her duck**." What is intended here? Did some guy reach out with his hand and forcefully push a woman's head down out of the way of a screaming projectile? Or did he prepare a succulent dish of roasted fowl to celebrate her birthday? Oh, if the computer could only know. If we'd used predicate logic instead of English, it could!

8.3 Exercises

Let B be the proposition that Joe Biden was elected president in 2020, C be the proposition that Covid-19 was completely and permanently eradicated from the earth in 2021, and R be the proposition that *Roe v. Wade* was overturned in 2022.	True.
1. What's $B \vee C$?	
2. What's $B \wedge C$?	False.
3. What's $B \wedge R$?	True.
4. What's $B \wedge \neg R$?	False.
5. What's $\neg C \vee \neg R$?	True.
6. What's $\neg(C \vee \neg R)$?	True.
7. What's $\neg(\neg C \vee R)$?	False.
8. What's $\neg C \vee B$?	True.
9. What's $\neg C \oplus B$?	False.
10. What's $\neg C \oplus \neg B$?	True.
11. What's $\neg\neg\neg\neg B$?	True.
12. What's $\neg\neg\neg\neg\neg B$?	False.
13. What's $\neg\neg\neg\neg\neg C$?	True.
14. What's $B \vee C \vee R$?	True.
15. What's $B \wedge C \wedge R$?	False.
16. What's $B \wedge \neg C \wedge R$?	True.
17. What's $B \Rightarrow R$?	True. (Even though there is plainly no causality there.)
18. What's $R \Rightarrow B$?	True. (Ditto.)
19. What's $B \Rightarrow C$?	False. (The premise is true, so the conclusion must also be true for this sentence to be true.)
20. What's $C \Rightarrow B$?	**True**. (The premise is false, so all bets are off and the sentence is true.)

21. What's $C \Rightarrow \neg R$?	**True.** (The premise is false, so all bets are off and the sentence is true.)
22. What's $C \Leftrightarrow B$?	False. (The truth values of the left and right sides are not the same.)
23. What's $C \Leftrightarrow \neg B$?	True. (The truth values of the left and right sides *are* the same.)
24. I make this assertion: "$X \wedge \neg Y \wedge \neg(Z \Rightarrow Q)$." And since I'm the professor, you can assume I'm correct about this. From this information alone, can you determine a unique set of values for the four variables? Or is there more than one possibility for them?	There is actually only one solution. Here's one way to tell. We know that X must be true, since it's being "and-ed" in to another expression. We know that Y must be false, since its *opposite* is similarly being "and-ed" in. Finally, we also know that Z must be true and Q must be false, since the only way an implication ($\Rightarrow$) can be false is if its premise is true and its conclusion is false. And the implication here *must* be false if the professor is telling the truth, because its *opposite* is being "and-ed" in to the three other things. So the one and only answer is: $X = 1, Y = 0, Z = 1, Q = 0$. (You can figure this all out with truth tables too, of course, and for most examples you would. I just wanted to make an exercise that you could figure out in your head without pencil and paper.)
25. What if I get rid of Q and replace it with X, thus making my assertion: "$X \wedge \neg Y \wedge \neg(Z \Rightarrow X)$." Now what is/are the solutions?	Now it's impossible, and if you study the previous item, you'll see why. The only way that item 24 could be true was if the conclusion of the implication (namely, Q) was false. But X had to be true. So whether X is true or false in this new assertion, something will go haywire: either it'll be true and the third and-ed thing will be false, or else it'll be false and the first and-ed thing will be false. There's no way the professor could be telling the truth here.
At the time of this writing, all professors are human, and that's what I'll be assuming in these exercises. 26. True or false: $\forall x \; \text{Professor}(x)$.	False. This says "everyone and everything is a professor," which is clearly not true. (Consider what you ate for lunch as a counterexample.)
27. True or false: $\forall x \; \text{Human}(x)$.	False. This says "everyone and everything is human," which is clearly not true. (Consider the book in front of you as a counterexample.)

8.3. EXERCISES

28. True or false: $\neg \forall x$ HUMAN(x).	True. This says "it's *not* the case that everyone and everything is human." And that certainly is not the case.
29. True or false: $\forall x\ \neg$HUMAN(x).	False. This says "nothing is human," which is clearly not true. (Consider yourself as a counterexample.)
30. True or false: $\exists x\ \neg$HUMAN(x).	True. This says "there's at least one thing in the universe which is not human." (Consider your lunch.)
31. True or false: $\neg \exists x$ HUMAN(x).	False. This says "nothing is human," just like item 29 did.
32. True or false: $\forall x$ HUMAN$(x) \wedge$ PROFESSOR(x).	Not even close. This says "everything in the universe is a human professor." (Even though I would exist in such a world, what a sad, limited place it would be.)
33. True or false: $\forall x$ HUMAN$(x) \Rightarrow$ PROFESSOR(x).	False. This says "every person is a professor." (Consider LeBron James.) Keep in mind: "$\forall$" and "$\wedge$" don't really play well together.
34. True or false: $\exists x$ PROFESSOR$(x) \Rightarrow$ HUMAN(x).	This is technically true, but for a stupid reason, and whoever wrote it almost certainly didn't intend what they wrote. It says, "there's at least one thing in the universe which either (a) isn't a professor, or (b) if it *is* a professor, is also human." Keep in mind: "$\exists$" and "$\Rightarrow$" don't really play well together. To drill this lesson home, realize that you could substitute almost *any* predicates for PROFESSOR() and HUMAN() in that statement and it would still be true. (Try swapping out PROFESSOR() for CONDIMENT() and HUMAN() for ASTROLOGICALSIGN(). Now try x=EuropeanUnion and voila! the statement is true. The EU is not a condiment, nor is it an astrological sign, so both sides of the implication are false, and never forget: false $\Rightarrow$ false = **true**.)

35. True or false: $\forall x \ \text{Professor}(x) \Rightarrow \text{Human}(x)$.	True at last! This is what we were trying to say all along. Every professor is a person.
36. True or false: $\neg \exists x \ \text{Professor}(x) \Rightarrow \neg \text{Human}(x)$.	True! This is an equivalent statement to item 35. There's nothing in the universe that is a professor yet not a human. (At least, at the time of this writing.)

Chapter 9

Proof

We've seen a lot of pretty sights on our cool brisk walk. We've caught a glimpse of the simple elegance of sets and relations, the precision of probabilistic reasoning, the recursive structure of trees, the explosive nature of combinatorics, and much more. None of these things have we plumbed to the depths, but we've appreciated their beauty and taken note of where they stood along our blazed trail. You'll remember this hike when you run into such concepts again and again in future computer science and math courses, and in your career beyond academics.

Now we have one more stop to make before returning to the trailhead, and that deals with the notion of *proof*. As we've studied these various mathematical entities, I've pointed out certain of their properties. A free tree has one more vertex than edge, for example. The cardinality of the union of two sets is at least as big as each of their individual unions. If you flip-all-the-bits-and-add-one in a two's complement scheme, and then perform that flip-and-add operation again, you'll return to the original number. But with a few exceptions, we haven't *proven* any of these things. I've just stated them, and you've taken them on faith.

In order to establish reliable truth, of course, professional mathematicians aren't satisfied with unsubstantiated statements. They need to be convinced that the claims we make do truly hold, and provably so, in all circumstances. What they seek is a **proof** of a claim: an irrefutable sequence of logical steps that leads inescapably from our premises to our conclusion. There are several ways to construct a convincing proof, and this chapter will highlight some of them.

Most authors of discrete math texts, by the way, interweave the concept of proof throughout the entire book. I'm taking a radical departure by deferring this fundamental idea until the very end. Why did I make this choice? A couple of reasons. First, as I said at the very beginning, my target audience for this book is future practitioners, not theoretical researchers. I think most practicing computer scientists need fluency with the tools of discrete math, not the ability to devise new fundamental theorems about them. We mostly need to use, not to prove. The second reason is that I've found that interspersing proofs throughout the presentation often distracts the reader from the concepts at hand, since the focus shifts slightly from the concept being discussed (the function, the directed graph, what have you) to the proof *about* the concept. When the proof itself takes center stage, it forces the actual subject matter to share the limelight. And with technical material like this, we need all the light we can get.

9.1 Proof concepts

A proof is essentially a chain of reasoning, in which each step can be logically deduced from the ones that preceded it. It's a way of putting your thought process on display so it can be scrutinized to make sure it holds water. Any step of your reasoning which was unwarranted will be exposed, and perhaps reveal that the conclusion you thought was true isn't necessarily dependable after all.

Here's an example from everyday life. I'm driving home from work one afternoon, and I believe that my wife and children will be gone when I arrive. I'll be coming home to an empty house.

Now why do I believe this? Well, if I unravel my reasoning, it goes like this. First, today is Wednesday. On Wednesday nights, my wife and children normally go to church for dinner and service. Second, my wife likes to call me ahead of time if this plan changes. My cell

9.1. PROOF CONCEPTS

phone is in my pocket, and has not rung, and so I conclude that the plan has not changed. I look at my watch, and it reads 5:17pm, which is after the time they normally leave, so I know I'm not going to catch them walking out the door. This is, roughly speaking, my thought process that justifies the conclusion that the house will be empty when I pull into the garage.

Notice, however, that this prediction depends precariously on several facts. What if I spaced out the day of the week, and this is actually Thursday? All bets are off. What if my cell phone battery has run out of charge? Then perhaps she *did* try to call me but couldn't reach me. What if I set my watch wrong and it's actually 4:17pm? *Etc.* Just like a chain is only as strong as its weakest link, a whole proof falls apart if even one step isn't reliable.

Knowledge bases in artificial intelligence systems are designed to support these chains of reasoning. They contain statements expressed in formal logic that can be examined to deduce *only* the new facts that logically follow from the old. Suppose, for instance, that we had a knowledge base that currently contained the following facts:

1. $A \Rightarrow C$
2. $\neg(C \wedge D)$
3. $(F \vee \neg E) \Rightarrow D$
4. $A \vee B$

These facts are stated in propositional logic, and we have no idea what any of the propositions really *mean*, but then neither does the computer, so hey. Fact #1 tells us that if proposition A (whatever that may mean) is true, then we know C is true as well. Fact #2 tells us that we know $C \wedge D$ is false, which means at least one of the two must be false. And so on. Large knowledge bases can contain thousands or even millions of such expressions. It's a complete record of everything the system "knows."

Now suppose we learn an additional fact: $\neg B$. In other words, the system interacts with its environment and comes to the conclusion that proposition B must be false. What else, if anything, can now be safely concluded from this?

It turns out that we can now conclude that *F is also false.* How do we know this? Here's how:

1. Fact #4 says that either A or B (or both) is true. But we just discovered that B was false. So if it ain't B, it must be A, and therefore we conclude that **A must be true**. (For the curious, this rule of common sense is called a "disjunctive syllogism.")

2. Now if A is true, we know that C must also be true, because fact #1 says that A implies C. So we conclude that **C is true.** (This one goes by the Latin phrase *"modus ponens."*)

3. Fact #2 says that C∧D must be *false.* But we just found out that C was true, so it must be D that's false in order to make the conjunction false. So we conclude that **D is false.** (This is a disjunctive syllogism in disguise, combined with De Morgan's law.)

4. Finally, fact #3 tells us that if either F were true or E were false, then that would imply that D would be true. But we just found out that D is false. Therefore, neither F nor ¬E can be true. (This step combines *"modus tollens"* with "disjunction elimination.") So we conclude that **F must be false**. Q.E.D.

(The letters *"Q.E.D."* at the end of a proof stand for a Latin phrase meaning, "we just proved what we set out to prove." It's kind of a way to flex your muscles as you announce that you're done.)

Not all proofs are performed in formal logic like this; some use algebra, set theory, or just plain English. But the idea is the same: start with what you know, proceed to derive new knowledge using only legal operations, and end with your conclusion.

The things we're allowed to start with are called **axioms** (or **postulates**). An axiom is a presupposition or definition that is *given*

9.2. TYPES OF PROOF

to be true, and so it is legal grounds from which to start. A proof can't even get off the ground without axioms. For instance, in step 1 of the above proof, we noted that either A or B must be true, and so if B isn't true, then A must be. But we couldn't have taken this step without knowing that disjunctive syllogism is a valid form of reasoning. It's not important to know all the technical names of the rules that I included in parentheses. But it is important to see that we made use of an axiom of reasoning on every step, and that if any of those axioms were incorrect, it could lead to a faulty conclusion.

When you create a valid proof, the result is a new bit of knowledge called a **theorem** which can be used in future proofs. Think of a theorem like a subroutine in programming: a separate bit of code that does a job and can be invoked at will in the course of doing other things. One theorem we learned in chapter 2 was the distributive property of sets; that is, that $X \cap (Y \cup Z) = (X \cap Y) \cup (X \cap Z)$. This can be proven through the use of Venn diagrams, but once you've proven it, it's accepted to be true, and can be used as a "given" in future proofs.

9.2 Types of proof

There are a number of accepted "styles" of doing proofs. Here are some important ones:

Direct proof

The examples we've used up to now have been **direct proof**s. This is where you start from what's known and proceed directly by positive steps towards your conclusion.

Direct proofs remind me of a game called "word ladders," invented by Lewis Carroll, that you might have played as a child:

```
WARM
||||
????
||||
```

COLD

You start with one word (like WARM) and you have to come up with a sequence of words, *each of which differs from the previous by only one letter*, such that you eventually reach the ending word (like COLD). It's sort of like feeling around in the dark:

>WARM
>WAR<u>T</u>
>WA<u>L</u>T
>W<u>I</u>LT
>WIL<u>D</u>
>| | | |
>. . . .

This attempt seemed promising at first, but now it looks like it's going nowhere. ("WOLD?" "CILD?" Hmm....) After starting over and playing around with it for a while, you might stumble upon:

>WARM
>W<u>O</u>RM
>WOR<u>D</u>
><u>C</u>ORD
>CO<u>L</u>D

This turned out to be a pretty direct path: for each step, the letter we changed was exactly what we needed it to be for the target word COLD. Sometimes, though, you have to meander away from the target a little bit to find a solution, like going from BLACK to WHITE:

>BLACK
><u>C</u>LACK
>C<u>R</u>ACK
><u>T</u>RACK
>TR<u>I</u>CK
>TRIC<u>E</u>

9.2. TYPES OF PROOF

<pre>
            TRI<u>T</u>E
            <u>W</u>RITE
            WH<u>I</u>TE
</pre>

Here, we had to temporarily change our first letter three different times — two of which seemingly brought us no nearer to WHITE — in order to successfully forge a path through the tangled forest.

Knowing which direction to set out on is a matter of intuition plus trial and error. Given the axioms of any system (whether algebra, predicate logic, sets, *etc.*) there are an unfathomable number of different ways to proceed. The vast majority of them are bound to lead to dead ends. This is why a valid proof, when it is finished, is often an elegant and beautiful thing. It's a thin braid of jewels glistening in the midst of a whole lot of mud.

Indirect proof

Also known as a **proof by contradiction** or *reductio ad absurdum*, the **indirect proof** starts in a completely opposite way. It says, "okay, I'm trying to prove X. Well, suppose for the sake of argument I assume that the opposite — *not* X — is true. Where would that lead me?" If you follow all the rules and it leads you to a contradiction, this tells you that the original assumption of ¬X must have been false. And this in turn proves that X must be true.

We do this all the time in our thinking. Say you're driving down the highway. How do you *know* that the alternator in your car engine is working? A direct proof would require that you open the hood and examine the part, testing to ensure it works properly. An indirect proof simply says, "well, suppose it *weren't* working properly. Then, my car engine wouldn't operate. But here I am, driving down the road, and the engine obviously *does* operate, so that tells me that the alternator must be working properly."

One of the most famous indirect proofs dates from Euclid's *Elements* in 300 B.C. It proves that the square root of 2 is an irrational number, a great surprise to mathematicians at the time (most of whom doubted the very existence of irrational numbers). Remember that an irrational number is one that *cannot* be expressed as the ratio of two integers, no matter what the integers are.

Proving this directly seems pretty hard, since how do you prove that there *aren't* any two integers whose ratio is $\sqrt{2}$, no matter how hard you looked? I mean, 534,927 and 378,250 are pretty dang close:

$$\left(\frac{534,927}{378,250}\right)^2 = 2.000005.$$

How could we possibly prove that no matter how hard we look, we can never find a pair that will give it to us exactly?

One way is to assume that $\sqrt{2}$ *is* a rational number, and then prove that down that path lies madness. It goes like this. Suppose $\sqrt{2}$ is rational, after all. That means that there must be two integers, call them a and b, whose ratio is exactly equal to $\sqrt{2}$:

$$\frac{a}{b} = \sqrt{2}.$$

This, then, is the starting point for our indirect proof. We're going to proceed under this assumption and see where it leads us.

By the way, it's clear that we could always reduce this fraction to lowest terms in case it's not already. For instance, if $a = 6$ and $b = 4$, then our fraction would be $\frac{6}{4}$, which is the same as $\frac{3}{2}$, so we could just say $a = 3$ and $b = 2$ and start over. Bottom line: if $\sqrt{2}$ is rational, then we can find two integers a and b that have no common factor (if they do have a common factor, we'll just divide it out of both of them and go with the new numbers) whose ratio is $\sqrt{2}$.

Okay then. But now look what happens. Suppose we square both sides of the equation (a perfectly legal thing to do):

$$\frac{a}{b} = \sqrt{2}$$

$$\left(\frac{a}{b}\right)^2 = (\sqrt{2})^2$$

$$\frac{a^2}{b^2} = 2$$

$$a^2 = 2b^2.$$

Now if a^2 equals 2 times something, then a^2 is an even number. But a^2 can't be even unless a itself is even. (Think hard about that one.) This proves, then, that a is even. Very well. It must be equal to twice some other integer. Let's call that c. We know that $a = 2c$, where c is another integer. Substitute that into the last equation and we get:

$$(2c)^2 = 2b^2$$
$$4c^2 = 2b^2$$
$$2c^2 = b^2.$$

So it looks like b^2 must be an even number as well (since it's equal to 2 times something), and therefore b is also even. But wait a minute. We started by saying that a and b *had no common factor*. And now we've determined that they're both even numbers! This means they both have a factor of 2, which contradicts what we started with. The only thing we introduced that was questionable was the notion that there *are* two integers a and b whose ratio was equal to $\sqrt{2}$ to begin with. That must be the part that's faulty then. Therefore, $\sqrt{2}$ is *not* an irrational number. Q.E.D.

9.3 Proof by induction

One of the most powerful methods of proof — and one of the most difficult to wrap your head around — is called **mathematical induction**, or just "induction" for short. I like to call it "proof by recursion," because this is exactly what it is. Remember that we discussed recursion in the context of rooted trees (see p.116). A tree can be thought of as a node with several children — each of which are, in turn, trees. Each of *them* is the root node of a tree comprised of yet smaller trees, and so on and so forth. If you flip back to the left-hand side of Figure 5.16 on p.113, you'll see that A is the root of one tree, and its two children, F and B, are roots of their own smaller trees in turn. If we were to traverse this tree in (say) pre-order, we'd visit the root, then visit the left and right subtrees in turn, treating each of them as their *own* tree. In this way we've broken up a larger problem (traversing the big tree) into smaller problems (traversing the smaller trees F and B). The A node has very little to do: it just visits itself, then defers all the rest of the work onto its children. This idea of pawning off most of the work onto smaller subproblems *that you trust will work* is key to the idea of inductive proofs.

Mathematical induction is hard to wrap your head around because it feels like cheating. It seems like you never actually prove anything: you defer all the work to someone else, and then declare victory. But the chain of reasoning, though delicate, is strong as iron.

Casting the problem in the right form

Let's examine that chain. The first thing you have to be able to do is express the thing you're trying to prove as *a predicate about natural numbers*. In other words, you need to form a predicate that has one input, which is a natural number. You're setting yourself up to prove that the predicate is true *for all natural numbers*. (Or at least, all natural numbers of at least a certain size.)

Suppose I want to prove that in the state of Virginia, all legal drinkers can vote. Then I could say "let $\text{VOTE}(n)$ be the proposition that a citizen of age n can vote."

If I want to prove an algebraic identity, like $\sum_{i=1}^{x} i = \frac{x(x+1)}{2}$, then I have to figure out which variable is the one that needs to vary across the natural numbers. In this case it's the x variable in my equation.

9.3. PROOF BY INDUCTION

So I'll say "let P(n) be the proposition that $\sum_{i=1}^{n} i = \frac{n(n+1)}{2}$." (The choice of the letter "n" isn't important here — it just needs to be a letter that stands for a number. We could have chosen anything, even sticking with x. Later, we'll use "k" as a stand-in, so keep your eyes peeled for that.)

If I want to prove that the number of leaves in a perfect binary tree is one more than the number of internal nodes, I'd have to think about which *quantity* I can parameterize on (*i.e.*, which quantity I can use for my n.) In this case, I'd probably use the *height* of the tree. I'd say "let P(n) be the proposition that the number of leaves in a perfect binary tree of height n is one more than the number of internal nodes."

These are just examples. In any case, you need to cast your proof in a form that allows you to make statements in terms of the natural numbers. Then you're ready to begin the process of proving by induction that your predicate is true for *all* the natural numbers.

Proof by induction: weak form

There are actually two forms of induction, the weak form and the strong form. Let's look at the **weak form** first. It says:

1. *If* a predicate is true for a certain number,

2. *and* its being true for some number would reliably mean that it's also true for the next number (*i.e.*, one number greater),

3. *then* it's true for all numbers.

All you have to do is prove those two things, and you've effectively proven it for every case.

The first step is called the **base case**, and the "certain number" we pick is normally either 0 or 1. The second step, called the **inductive step**, is where all the trouble lies. You have to look really, really carefully at how it's worded, above. We are *not* assuming that the predicate is true for any old number! We are simply considering, *if* it's true for any old number, whether that would necessarily imply it's also true for the next number. In terms of the predicate, we're asking "does $P(k)$ imply $P(k+1)$?" In other words: "we aren't sure if $P(k)$ is true. But if it is — a big "if," of course — would that logically demand that $P(k+1)$ was also true?" If you can prove that it does, then you're in business.

The whole thing is set up like a row of dominos. If one domino falls, then the one after it will also fall. And if that one falls, then so will the next. All that is needed is a base case to tip over the first domino, and by this trail of causality, *all* the dominos will fall.

One terminology note: the entire second step is called the inductive step, but the first half of it (the part where we assume that $P(k)$ is true) is called the **inductive hypothesis**. We never prove the inductive hypothesis; rather, we assume it, and then see if that allows us to deduce that $P(k+1)$ would also be true.

Example 1

Let's work this out for the drinking/voting example. Let VOTE(n) be the proposition that a citizen of age n can vote. Our proof goes like this:

1. **base case.** VOTE(21) is true, because a 21-year old is old enough to vote in the state and national elections.

2. **inductive step.** VOTE(k)$\Rightarrow$VOTE(k+1). Why? Because nobody's gettin' any younger. If you can vote in a particular year, then you're also old enough to vote next year. Unless the laws change, there will never be a case when someone old enough to vote this year turns out to be too young to vote next year.

3. **conclusion.** Wow. $\forall n \geq 21$ VOTE(n). We're done. *Q.E.D.* and all that.

The only specific example we showed was true was VOTE(21). And yet we managed to prove VOTE(n) for *any* number $n \geq 21$.

9.3. PROOF BY INDUCTION

Let's look back at that inductive step, because that's where all the action is. It's crucial to understand what that step does *not* say. It doesn't say "VOTE(k) is true for some number k." If it did, then since k's value is arbitrary at that point, we would basically be assuming the very thing we were supposed to prove, which is circular reasoning and extremely unconvincing. But that's not what we did. Instead, we made the inductive hypothesis and said, "okay then, let's assume for a second a 40-year-old can vote. We don't know for sure, but let's say she can. Now, if that's indeed true, can a 41-year-old also vote? The answer is yes." We might have said, "okay then, let's assume for a second a 7-year-old can vote. We don't know for sure, but let's say she can. Now, if that's indeed true, can an 8-year-old also vote? The answer is yes." Note carefully that we did *not* say that 8-year-olds can vote! We merely said that *if* 7-year-olds can, why then 8-year-olds must be able to as well. Remember that X⇒Y is true if either X is false or Y is true (or both). In the 7/8-year-old example, the premise X turns out to be false, so this doesn't rule out our implication.

The result is a row of falling dominos, up to whatever number we wish. Say we want to verify that a **25-year-old** can vote. Can we be sure? Well:

1. If a 24-year-old can vote, then that would sure prove it (by the inductive step).

2. So now we need to verify that a 24-year-old can vote. Can he? Well, if a 23-year-old can vote, then that would sure prove it (by the inductive step).

3. Now everything hinges on whether a 23-year-old can vote. Can he? Well, if a 22-year-old can vote, then that would sure prove it (by the inductive step).

4. So it comes down to whether a 22-year-old can vote. Can he? Well, if a 21-year-old can vote, then that would sure prove it (by the inductive step).

5. And now we need to verify whether a 21-year-old can vote. Can he? Yes (by the base case).

Example 2

A famous story tells of Carl Friedrich Gauss, perhaps the most brilliant mathematician of all time, getting in trouble one day as a schoolboy. As punishment, he was sentenced to tedious work: adding together all the numbers from 1 to 100. To his teacher's astonishment, he came up with the correct answer in a moment, not because he was quick at adding integers, but because he recognized a trick. The first number on the list (1) and the last (100) add up to 101. So do the second number (2) and the second-to-last (99). So do 3 and 98, and so do 4 and 97, *etc.*, all the way up to 50 and 51. So really what you have here is 50 different sums of 101 each, so the answer is $50 \times 101 = 5050$. In general, if you add the numbers from 1 to x, where x is any integer at all, you'll get $\frac{x}{2}$ sums of $x+1$ each, so the answer will be $\frac{x(x+1)}{2}$.

Now, use mathematical induction to prove that Gauss was right (*i.e.*, that $\sum_{i=1}^{x} i = \frac{x(x+1)}{2}$) for all numbers x.

First we have to cast our problem as a predicate about natural numbers. This is easy: we say "let P(n) be the proposition that $\sum_{i=1}^{n} i = \frac{n(n+1)}{2}$."

Then, we satisfy the requirements of induction:

1. **base case.** We prove that P(1) is true simply by plugging it in. Setting $n = 1$ we have

$$\sum_{i=1}^{1} i \stackrel{?}{=} \frac{1(1+1)}{2}$$

$$1 \stackrel{?}{=} \frac{1(2)}{2}$$

$$1 = 1 \ \checkmark$$

2. **inductive step.** We now must prove that P(k)$\Rightarrow$P($k+1$). Put another way, we *assume* P(k) is true, and then use that assumption to prove that P($k+1$) is also true.

9.3. PROOF BY INDUCTION

Let's be crystal clear where we're going with this. Assuming that P(k) is true means we can count on the fact that

$$1 + 2 + 3 + \cdots + k = \frac{k(k+1)}{2}.$$

What we need to do, then, is prove that P($k+1$) is true, which amounts to proving that

$$1 + 2 + 3 + \cdots + (k+1) = \frac{(k+1)((k+1)+1)}{2}.$$

Very well. First we make the inductive hypothesis, which allows us to assume:

$$1 + 2 + 3 + \cdots + k = \frac{k(k+1)}{2}.$$

The rest is just algebra. We add $k+1$ to both sides of the equation, then multiply things out and factor it all together. Watch carefully:

$$\begin{aligned}
1 + 2 + 3 + \cdots + k + (k+1) &= \frac{k(k+1)}{2} + (k+1) \\
&= \frac{1}{2}k^2 + \frac{1}{2}k + k + 1 \\
&= \frac{1}{2}k^2 + \frac{3}{2}k + 1 \\
&= \frac{k^2 + 3k + 2}{2} \\
&= \frac{(k+1)(k+2)}{2} \\
&= \frac{(k+1)((k+1)+1)}{2}. \quad \checkmark
\end{aligned}$$

3. **conclusion.** Therefore, $\forall n \geq 1$ P(n).

Example 3

Another algebra one. You learned in middle school that $(ab)^n = a^n b^n$. Prove this by mathematical induction.

Solution: Let P(n) be the proposition that $(ab)^n = a^n b^n$.

1. **base case.** We prove that P(1) is true simply by plugging it in. Setting $n = 1$ we have

$$(ab)^1 \stackrel{?}{=} a^1 b^1$$
$$ab = ab \quad \checkmark$$

2. **inductive step.** We now must prove that P(k)⇒P($k+1$). Put another way, we *assume* P(k) is true, and then use that assumption to prove that P($k+1$) is also true.

Let's be crystal clear where we're going with this. Assuming that P(k) is true means we can count on the fact that

$$(ab)^k = a^k b^k.$$

What we need to do, then, is prove that P($k+1$) is true, which amounts to proving that

$$(ab)^{k+1} = a^{k+1} b^{k+1}.$$

Now we know by the very definition of exponents that:

$$(ab)^{k+1} = ab(ab)^k.$$

Adding in our inductive hypothesis then lets us determine:

$$(ab)^{k+1} = ab(ab)^k$$
$$= ab \cdot a^k b^k$$
$$= a \cdot a^k \cdot b \cdot b^k$$
$$= a^{k+1} b^{k+1} \quad \checkmark$$

3. **conclusion.** Therefore, $\forall n \geq 1$ P(n).

9.3. PROOF BY INDUCTION

Example 4

Let's switch gears and talk about structures. Prove that the number of leaves in a perfect binary tree is one more than the number of internal nodes.

Solution: let P(n) be the proposition that a perfect binary tree of height n has one more leaf than internal node. That is, if l_k is the number of *l*eaves in a tree of height k, and i_k is the number of *i*nternal nodes in a tree of height k, let P(n) be the proposition that $l_n = i_n + 1$.

1. **base case.** We prove that P(0) is true simply by inspection. If we have a tree of height 0, then it has only one node (the root). This sole node is a leaf, and is not an internal node. So this tree has 1 leaf, and 0 internal nodes, and so $l_0 = i_0 + 1$. ✓

2. **inductive step.** We now must prove that P(k)⇒P($k+1$). Put another way, we *assume* P(k) is true, and then use that assumption to prove that P($k+1$) is also true.

   Let's be crystal clear where we're going with this. Assuming that P(k) is true means we can count on the fact that

   $$l_k = i_k + 1.$$

   What we need to do, then, is prove that P($k+1$) is true, which amounts to proving that

   $$l_{k+1} = i_{k+1} + 1.$$

   We begin by noting that the number of nodes *on level k* of a perfect binary tree is 2^k. This is because the root is only one node, it has two children (giving 2 nodes on level 1), both those children have two children (giving 4 nodes on level 2), all four of those children have two children (giving 8 nodes on level 3), *etc.* Therefore, $l_k = 2^k$, and $l_{k+1} = 2^{k+1}$.

   Further, we observe that $i_{k+1} = i_k + l_k$: this is just how trees work. In words, suppose we have a perfect binary tree of height k, and we add another level of nodes to it, making it a perfect binary tree of height $k+1$. Then *all* of the first tree's nodes (whether internal or leaves) become internal nodes of bigger tree.

Combining these two facts, we have $i_{k+1} = i_k + 2^k$. By the inductive hypothesis, we assume that $2^k = i_k + 1$, and we now must prove that $2^{k+1} = i_{k+1} + 1$. Here goes:

$$i_{k+1} = i_k + 2^k \qquad \text{(property of trees)}$$
$$i_{k+1} = 2^k - 1 + 2^k \qquad \text{(using inductive hypothesis)}$$
$$i_{k+1} + 1 = 2^k + 2^k$$
$$i_{k+1} + 1 = 2(2^k)$$
$$i_{k+1} + 1 = 2^{k+1}. \quad \checkmark$$

3. **conclusion.** Therefore, $\forall n \geq 0$ P(n).

Proof by induction: strong form

Now sometimes we actually need to make a stronger assumption than just "the single proposition P(k) is true" in order to prove that P($k+1$) is true. In all the examples above, the $k+1$ case flowed directly from the k case, and only the k case. But sometimes, you need to know that *all* the cases less than $k+1$ are true in order to prove the $k+1$ case. In those situations, we use the **strong form** of mathematical induction. It says:

1. *If* a predicate is true for a certain number,

2. *and* its being true for *all numbers up to and including some number* would reliably mean that it's also true for the next number (*i.e.*, one number greater),

3. *then* it's true for all numbers.

It's exactly the same as the weak form, except that the inductive hypothesis is stronger. Instead of having to prove

9.3. PROOF BY INDUCTION

$$P(k) \Rightarrow P(k+1),$$

we get to prove

$$(\forall i \leq k \ P(i)) \Rightarrow P(k+1).$$

At first glance that might not seem any easier. But if you look carefully, you can see that we've *added information* to the left hand side of the implication. No longer do we need to rely on the single fact that P(5) is true in order to prove P(6). Now we get to take advantage of the fact that P(1), P(2), P(3), P(4), and P(5) are *all* known to be true when we try to prove P(6). And that can make a world of difference.

Example 1

The Fundamental Theorem of Arithmetic says that every natural number (greater than 2) is expressible as the product of one or more primes. For instance, 6 can be written as "$2 \cdot 3$", where 2 and 3 are primes. The number 7 is itself prime, and so can be written as "7." The number 9,180 can be written as "$2 \cdot 2 \cdot 3 \cdot 3 \cdot 3 \cdot 5 \cdot 17$," all of which are primes. How can we prove that this is always possible, no matter what the number?

Let P(n) be the proposition that the number n can be expressed as a product of prime numbers. Our proof goes like this:

1. **base case.** P(2) is true, since 2 can be written as "2," and 2 is a prime number. (Note we didn't use 0 or 1 as our base case here, since actually neither of those numbers is expressible as a product of primes. Fun fact.)

2. **inductive step.** We now must prove that $(\forall i \leq k \ P(i)) \Rightarrow P(k+1)$. Put another way, we *assume* that P(i) is true for every number up to k, and then use that assumption to prove that P($k+1$) is true as well.

    Regarding the number $k+1$, there are two possibilities: either it's prime, or it's not. If it is, then we're done, because it can obviously be written as just itself, which is the product of one prime. (23 can be written as "23.") But suppose it's not. Then, it can be broken down as the product of two numbers, each less than itself. (21 can be broken down as $7 \cdot 3$; 24 can be broken down as $6 \cdot 4$ or $12 \cdot 2$ or $8 \cdot 3$, take your pick.) Now we know nothing special about those two numbers... *except* the fact that the inductive hypothesis tells us that *all* numbers less than $k+1$ are expressible as the product of one or more primes! So these two numbers, whatever they may be, are expressible as the product of primes, and so when you multiply them together to get $k+1$, you will have a longer string of primes multiplied together. Therefore, $(\forall i \leq k \ P(k)) \Rightarrow P(k+1)$.

3. **conclusion.** Therefore, by the strong form of mathematical induction, $\forall n \geq 2 \ P(n)$.

You can see why we needed the strong form here. If we wanted to prove that 15 is expressible as the product of primes, knowing that 14 is expressible as the product of primes doesn't do us a lick of good. What we needed to know was that 5 and 3 were expressible in that way. In general, the strong form of induction is useful when you have to break something into smaller parts, but there's no guarantee that the parts will be "one less" than the original. You only know that they'll be *smaller* than the original. A similar example follows.

Example 2

Earlier (p.111) we stated that every free tree has one less edge than node. Prove it.

Let $P(n)$ be the proposition that a free tree with n nodes has $n-1$ edges.

1. **base case.** $P(1)$ is true, since a free tree with 1 node is just a single lonely node, and has no edges.

9.3. PROOF BY INDUCTION

2. **inductive step.** We now must prove that $(\forall i \leq k \ P(i)) \Rightarrow P(k+1)$. Put another way, we assume that all trees *smaller* than the one we're looking at have one more node than edge, and then use that assumption to prove that the tree we're looking at also has one more node than edge.

   We proceed as follows. Take any free tree with $k+1$ nodes. Removing any edge gives you *two* free trees, each with k nodes or less. (Why? Well, if you remove any edge from a free tree, the nodes will no longer be connected, since a free tree is "minimally connected" as it is. And we can't break it into *more* than two trees by removing a single edge, since the edge connects exactly two nodes and each group of nodes on the other side of the removed edge are still connected to each other.)

   Now the sum of the nodes in these two smaller trees is still $k+1$. (This is because we haven't removed any nodes from the original free tree — we've simply removed an edge.) If we let k_1 be the number of nodes in the first tree, and k_2 the number of nodes in the second, we have $k_1 + k_2 = k+1$.

   Okay, but how many *edges* does the first tree have? Answer: $k_1 - 1$. How do we know that? *By the inductive hypothesis.* We're assuming that any tree smaller than $k+1$ nodes has one less edge than node, and so we're taking advantage of that (legal) assumption here. Similarly, the second tree has $k_2 - 1$ edges.

   The total number of edges in these two trees is thus $k_1 - 1 + k_2 - 1$, or $k_1 + k_2 - 2$. Remember that $k+1 = k_1 + k_2$ (no nodes removed), and so this is a total of $k + 1 - 2 = k - 1$ edges.

   Bingo. *Removing* one edge from our original tree of $k+1$ nodes gave us a total of $k-1$ edges. Therefore, that original tree must have had k edges. We have now proven that a tree of $k+1$ nodes has k edges, assuming that all smaller trees also have one less edge than node.

3. **conclusion.** Therefore, by the strong form of mathematical induction, $\forall n \geq 1 \ P(n)$.

9.4 Final word

Finding proofs is an art. In some ways, it's like programming: you have a set of building blocks, each one defined very precisely, and your goal is to figure out how to assemble those blocks into a structure that starts with only axioms and ends with your conclusion. It takes skill, patience, practice, and sometimes a little bit of luck.

Many mathematicians spend years pursuing one doggedly difficult proof, like Appel and Haken who finally cracked the infamous four-color map problem in 1976, or Andrew Wiles who solved Fermat's Last Theorem in 1994. Some famous mathematical properties may never have proofs, such as Christian Goldbach's 1742 conjecture that every even integer is the sum of two primes, or the most elusive and important question in computing theory: does P=NP? (Put very simply: if you consider the class of problems where it's easy to verify a solution once you have it, but crazy hard to find it in the first place, is there actually an easy algorithm for finding the solution that we just haven't figured out yet?) Most computer scientists think "no," but despite a mind-boggling number of hours invested by the brightest minds in the world, no one has ever been able to prove it one way or the other.

Most practicing computer scientists spend time taking advantage of the known results about mathematical objects and structures, and rarely (if ever) have to construct a water-tight proof about them. For the more theoretically-minded student, however, who enjoys probing the basis behind the tools and speculating about additional properties that might exist, devising proofs is an essential skill that can also be very rewarding.

Index

n-choose-k notation, 154
n-to-the-k-falling operator, 150
a priori, 68
modus ponens, 199, 224
modus tollens, 224
quod erat demonstrandum (Q.E.D.), 224
reductio ad absurdum, 227

acyclic (graphs), 91
additivity property, 63
adjacent (vertices), 89
algorithm, 97, 126, 127, 131, 147, 148
Ali, Muhammad, 92
American Idol, 62, 68
ancestor (of a node), 115
and (logical operator), 18, 197, 201
antisymmetric (relation), 40, 43
Appel, Kenneth, 242
arrays, 13
artificial intelligence (AI), 195, 199, 223
associative, 20
asymmetric (relation), 41
ATM machines, 141

atomic (propositions), 196
AVL trees, 132
axioms, 224, 227

background knowledge, 68, 70
balancedness (of a tree), 131
base case (of a proof), 231, 238
bases (of number systems), 164, 167, 168
Bayes' Theorem, 75
Bayes, Thomas, 67
Bayesian, 66
BFT (breadth-first traversal), 95, 97
Big-O notation, 126
bijective (function), 49
binary numbers, 25, 175, 176, 178, 180
binary search trees, 123, 124
binary trees, 116
binomial coefficients, 154
bit, 175
Booth, John Wilkes, 86
BST property, 124, 130
byte, 178

Cantor, Georg, 7, 12, 17

capacity (of a byte), 180
cardinality (of sets), 16, 25, 28, 66
Carroll, Lewis, 225
carry-in, 187
carry-out, 187
Cartesian product (of sets), 19, 35
chess, 114
child (of a node), 114
closed interval, 61
codomain (of a function), 45
collectively exhaustive, 26
combinations, 152
combinatorics, 25, 139
commutative, 18, 20, 71
compilers, 114
complement laws (of sets), 21
complement, partial (of sets), 18
complement, total (of sets), 18, 65, 144, 160
complete binary tree, 121
conclusion (of implication), 198
conditional probability, 68, 72, 74, 78
congruent, 171
conjunction, 197, 206
connected (vertices/graphs), 89, 95
coordinates, 15
curly brace notation, 11
current node, 103
cycles, 90

DAGs (directed acyclic graphs), 90
data structures, 85

Davies family, 8, 19, 26, 145, 152
De Morgan's laws, 21, 22, 205, 206
decimal numbers, 163, 167, 171, 176
degree (of a vertex), 90
depth (of a node), 115
dequeueing, 96
descendant (of a node), 115
DFT (depth-first traversal), 99, 100
Dijkstra's algorithm, 101, 103
Dijkstra, Edsger, 101
direct proof, 225
directed graphs, 88, 91
disjunction, 197, 206, 224
disjunctive syllogism, 224
disk sectors, 154
distributive, 20, 206, 225
domain (of a function), 45
domain of discourse (Ω), 9, 19, 21, 24, 27, 60, 208
domination laws (of sets), 21
dominos, 232
drinking age, 230, 232
duplicates (in sets), 13

edges, 86, 87, 240
elements (of sets), 8, 15, 23
ellipsis, 12
empty graph, 87
empty set, 9, 16, 21, 24, 25, 36, 114
endorelations, 38, 93
enqueueing, 96
enumerating, 139, 147
equality (for sets), 11

equiv (logical operator), 200, 201
Euclid, 227
events, 60, 61
exclusive or, 63, 197
existential quantifier ($\exists$), 212
exponential growth, 123, 143
exponential notation, 167
extensional, 10, 11, 37, 48, 92, 201

Facebook, 87, 98
factorial, 145, 150
Federalist Papers, 77
FIFO, 96
filesystems, 113
Fisher, Ronald, 67
floor operator ($\lfloor \ \rfloor$), 172
Foreman, George, 92
France, 101
Frazier, Joe, 92
free trees, 111, 240
frequentist, 66
full binary tree, 121
function calls, 46
functions, 45, 61, 208
Fundamental Theorem of Counting, 140, 145

Gauss, Carl Friedrich, 234
Goldbach, Christian, 242
golf, 149, 152
graphs, 85, 86
greedy algorithm, 107

Haken, Wolfgang, 242
Hamilton, Alexander, 77
handedness, 79
Harry Potter, 35, 93

heap, 123
height (of a tree), 115
Here Before, 73
heterogeneous, 13, 15
hexadecimal numbers, 169, 171, 174, 178
homogeneous, 14
HTML, 114
human body, 113

identity laws (of sets), 21
image (of a function), 48
imaginary numbers, 17
implies (logical operator), 198, 201, 204, 211
in-order traversal, 119, 130
inclusive or, 63, 197
independence (of events), 78
indirect proof, 227
inductive hypothesis, 232, 238
inductive step, 231, 232, 238
infinite, countably, 17
infinite, uncountably, 17
infinity, 12, 16, 17
injective (function), 48
integers ($\mathbb{Z}$), 17, 24
intensional, 10, 11, 37, 48, 201
internal nodes, 115, 237
Internet, 87
intersection (of sets), 18, 197, 206, 225
interval, 61

Jarnik, Vojtech, 107
Jay, John, 77
Jumble®, 146

Kentucky Derby, 79
Knuth, Donald, 151

Laplace, Pierre-Simon, 67
Law of the Excluded Middle, 205
law of the excluded middle, 21
Law of Total Probability, 71, 76
least significant bit (LSB), 176
least significant digit, 167
leaves, 115, 128, 237
left child, 116
level (in a tree), 115
lg (logarithm base 2), 123
license plates, 142, 159
LIFO, 100
Lincoln, Abraham, 86
linked lists, 13
links (in a graph), 87
Liston, Sonny, 92
locker combinations, 141
logarithm, 123
logical operators, 196, 197
loops (in a graph), 87, 94
loosely-typed languages, 14

Madison, James, 77
MapQuest, 87, 92
marking (a node), 97, 103
mathematical induction, 229
medical test, 75
member (of set), 9
middle school, 151
minimal spanning tree, 112
modulo operator (mod), 171, 172
most significant bit (MSB), 176
most significant digit, 167
movie channel, 151, 154
movie theatre, 73

mutually exclusive, 26, 76, 80, 142

n-tuples, 15
NASCAR, 151
natural numbers ($\mathbb{N}$), 17, 24, 230
negation, 198, 206, 212
negative numbers (in binary), 181
New York City, 126
Newton, Isaac, 67
nibble, 179
nodes (of a graph), 87, 240
not (logical operator), 198, 201

O(lg n) algorithm, 127
O(n) algorithm, 126, 131
object-oriented design, 114
octal numbers, 169
odometer rollovers, 166
one-to-one (function), 49
onto (function), 49
or (logical operator), 18, 197, 201
order (in sets), 13
ordered pairs, 14, 19, 35, 45, 210
ordered triples, 15
org charts, 113
outcomes, 60, 62
overflow, 186

P=NP?, 242
parent (of a node), 114
partial orders, 43
partial permutations, 149, 152
partitions, 26, 71, 94
Pascal's triangle, 155

INDEX

passwords, 144
paths (in a graph), 87, 113
perfect binary tree, 122, 237
permutations, 145
PINs, 141
poker, 154
pop (off a stack), 99
posets, 43
post-order traversal, 118
postulates, 224
power sets, 24, 36
pre-order traversal, 116
predicate logic, 208
predicates, 208, 209, 230
premise (of implication), 198
Prim's algorithm, 107, 112
Prim, Robert, 107
prior probability, 68
probability measures, 61, 63, 65
product operator (Π), 140, 150
proof, 221
proof by contradiction, 227
propositional logic, 195, 223
propositions, 195, 208
psychology, 70, 86
push (on a stack), 99

quantifiers, 210, 213
queue, 96, 98
quotient, 171, 172

range (of a function), 48
rational numbers ($\mathbb{Q}$), 17, 24
reachable, 89
real numbers ($\mathbb{R}$), 17, 24
rebalancing (a tree), 131
recursion, 116, 120, 147, 229

red-black trees, 132
reflexive (relation), 40, 43
relations, 35, 210
relations, finite, 39
relations, infinite, 39
remainder, 171, 172
right child, 116
root (of a tree), 112, 114
rooted trees, 112, 114, 229
Russell's paradox, 15

sample space (Ω), 60
semantic network, 86
set operators, 18
set-builder notation, 11
sets, 8, 93
sets of sets, 15
sets, finite, 12
sets, fuzzy, 10
sets, infinite, 12, 13
sibling (of a node), 114
sign-magnitude binary numbers, 181, 187
Sonic the Hedgehog, 73
southern states, 72
spatial positioning, 92, 112
Spiderman: No Way Home, 73
stack, 99, 101
strong form of induction, 238
subsets, 23, 35
subsets, proper, 23
subtree (of a node), 116
summation operator (Σ), 73, 141
surjective (function), 49
symmetric (relation), 40, 93

tautologies, 205
tentative best distance, 103
text mining, 77
theorems, 225
top (of a stack), 99
total orders, 44
transitive (relation), 41, 43
traversal, 95, 116
trees, 85, 111, 112
truth tables, 201, 204, 207
truth value (of a proposition), 195
tuples, 15, 210
two's-complement binary numbers, 183, 187
typed, 13

unary operator, 198, 202
undirected graphs, 88, 93
union (of sets), 18, 197, 206, 225
universal quantifier ($\forall$), 210, 212
universal set, 9
unsigned binary numbers, 181, 187
untyped, 13

Venn diagrams, 63, 225
Venn, John, 67
vertex/vertices, 86, 87
visiting (a node), 97, 103
voting age, 230, 232

weak form of induction, 231
weight (of an edge), 88
weighted graphs, 88, 101
weightlifting, 157
Wiles, Andrew, 242

word ladders, 225
World War II, 101
World Wide Web, 87
WWE wrestling, 72

xor (logical operator), 197, 201

Printed in Great Britain
by Amazon